Transforming
Organizations

The PricewaterhouseCoopers Endowment for
The Business of Government

THE PRICEWATERHOUSECOOPERS ENDOWMENT SERIES ON THE BUSINESS OF GOVERNMENT

Series Editors: Mark A. Abramson and Paul R. Lawrence

The PricewaterhouseCoopers Endowment Series on The Business of Government explores new approaches to improving the effectiveness of government at the federal, state, and local levels. The Series is aimed at providing cutting-edge knowledge to government leaders, academics, and students about the management of government in the 21st century.

Publications in the series will include:

2001
E-Government, *edited by Mark A. Abramson and Grady E. Means*
Managing for Results, *edited by Mark Abramson and John M. Kamensky*

2002
Leadership
Financial Management
Human Capital
Innovation

Transforming Organizations

EDITED BY

MARK A. ABRAMSON
THE PRICEWATERHOUSECOOPERS ENDOWMENT
FOR THE BUSINESS OF GOVERNMENT
and
PAUL R. LAWRENCE
PRICEWATERHOUSECOOPERS

ROWMAN & LITTLEFIELD PUBLISHERS, INC.
Lanham • Boulder • New York • Oxford

ROWMAN & LITTLEFIELD PUBLISHERS, INC.

Published in the United States of America
by Rowman & Littlefield Publishers, Inc.
4720 Boston Way, Lanham, Maryland 20706
www.rowmanlittlefield.com

12 Hid's Copse Road
Cumnor Hill, Oxford OX2 9JJ, England

British Library Cataloguing in Publication Information Available

Library of Congress Cataloging-in-Publication Data Available

0-7425-1314-9 (alk. paper)
0-7425-1315-7 (pbk./alk. paper)

Printed in the United States of America

♾™The paper used in this publication meets the minimum requirements of American National Standard for Information Sciences—Permanence of Paper for Printed Library Materials, ANSI/NISO Z39.48-1992.

To

Leah B. Abramson
1924–1999

Paul B. Lawrence
1930–2000

TABLE OF CONTENTS

CHAPTER ONE

The Challenge of Transforming Organizations: Lessons Learned about Revitalizing Organizations

Mark A. Abramson
Executive Director
The PricewaterhouseCoopers Endowment for
The Business of Government

Paul R. Lawrence
Partner
PricewaterhouseCoopers

1

Introduction

Transforming organizations is hard work. It is not for the fainthearted or thin-skinned. A leader is not going to win many new friends or popularity contests by undertaking major transformation initiatives. In spite of its difficulty, we expect transformation to continue as 20th century bureaucracies are streamlined into high performing 21st century organizations. For executives at the helm of these changes, there is much to learn from the experience of others.

The key question is: How do leaders successfully transform organizations? To better understand the transformation challenge, The Pricewaterhouse-Coopers Endowment for The Business Government supported a series of case studies of the most successful transformation initiatives of the 1990s in the federal government. The goal was to document these initiatives and identify lessons learned that could be shared with other executives seeking to change their organization. Organizations selected for case studies were:

- Department of Defense (DoD) under Deputy Secretary (and then Secretary) William Perry. The DoD case study focuses on procurement reform within the Department of Defense, including key roles placed by Under Secretary of Defense for Acquisition and Technology Paul Kaminski, Deputy Under Secretary for Acquisition Reform Colleen Preston, and Administrator of the Office of Federal Procurement Policy Steve Kelman
- Federal Emergency Management Agency (FEMA) under Director James Lee Witt
- National Aeronautics and Space Administration (NASA) under Administrator Daniel S. Goldin
- Veterans Health Administration (VHA), Department of Veterans Affairs under Under Secretary for Health Dr. Kenneth Kizer

From these case studies of the four organizations, eight common lessons emerged about how leaders successfully undertake large-scale transformation initiatives.

Lessons Learned

Lesson One: Select the right person

The four transformation initiatives all began with the appointment of the right person to the right job in the right organization at the right time. In chapter three, R. Steven Daniels and Carolyn L. Clark-Daniels write,

"Recruitment ... may be one of the president's ... most critical decisions at the start of an administration." In selecting James Lee Witt to head FEMA, President Clinton selected an individual with extensive experience in emergency management, a sharp departure from past appointments to the agency. Director Witt then used his influence in the appointment process to select a team of political executives who were all experienced and highly qualified in emergency management. Daniels and Clark-Daniels conclude that the cumulative experience of the senior political appointees vastly improved the organization's capability and made its transformation possible.

The selection of highly qualified, experienced individuals was also key to the success of transformation at DoD. In chapter two, Kimberly A. Harokopus writes, "The leaders of defense procurement reform were remarkably well suited for the tough job at hand. They all had experience with the acquisition process—some as practitioners, others as researchers, still others as members of the defense industry seeking to comply with the sometimes byzantine set of procurement rules. With the exception of Kelman, each had previously worked inside the Pentagon as a military or civilian leader. Each had recognized the failings of the defense acquisition system and each had struggled to remedy it—through advisory boards, informal correspondence to defense leaders, and published scholarly works. It was as if they had been preparing for years to meet this challenge."

From his analysis of the VHA transformation, Gary J. Young writes in chapter five, "VHA's transformation highlights the importance of having leaders whose backgrounds and experiences fit the needs of the transformation." Young dates the start of the VHA transformation initiative with the appointment of Dr. Ken Kizer. Young concludes that Dr. Kizer proved to be a highly effective leader for the VHA transformation. His effectiveness, writes Young, was largely the result of the match between his professional experience and the needs of the transformation. "... [A]lthough Dr. Kizer

---

Lessons Learned about Transforming Organizations

- Lesson One: Select the right person
- Lesson Two: Clarify the mission
- Lesson Three: Get the structure right
- Lesson Four: Seize the moment
- Lesson Five: Communicate, communicate, and communicate
- Lesson Six: Involve key players
- Lesson Seven: Engage employees
- Lesson Eight: Persevere

was new to VHA, he did have substantial leadership experience in the public sector.... Dr. Kizer was an astute student of innovations in the financing and delivery of health care services. He had witnessed many innovations firsthand through his professional experiences in California...."

The appointment of Dan Goldin at NASA also demonstrates the importance of making the right match to the right job. In chapter four, W. Henry Lambright writes, "The choice of Dan Goldin was fortuitous given the need. He was a good match for the organization and times. He replaced a man who was forced to leave because he was not viewed as the right person for the challenges facing the agency.... On the whole, ... his original appointment and retention by Clinton were good for NASA and the country."

Lesson Two: Clarify the mission

Witt, Dr. Kizer, and Goldin followed similar paths during the early days of their tenure. James Lee Witt spent his initial days refocusing FEMA's mission on emergency management rather than national preparedness. This change in focus redefined the agency's primary client to be disaster victims and served as the central tenet of all the management reforms that followed.

At VHA, Dr. Ken Kizer spent his early days spearheading the creation of a vision for the transformation of the organization. In describing the blueprint report, *Vision for Change*, Young writes, "The document articulated the basic philosophy, principles, and organizational framework to which a transformed VHA would adhere."

At NASA, Dan Goldin went through a similar process. Lambright writes, "Given the budget constraint Goldin faced when he first was appointed, he was forced to deal with the question, 'What do I do to bring NASA's expectations into line with likely funding?' His answer was not to eliminate programs. Rather, he intended to promote technological and managerial reforms that would allow the agency to carry out all of its existing programs and even provide funds to make new starts."

Lesson Three: Get the structure right

While leaders frequently shy away from structural reorganizations because of the difficulty in doing so, Dr. Kizer, Witt, and Goldin all decided reorganizations were crucial to their ability to transform their organization. Within the first year of the transformation, Dr. Kizer proposed and enacted a sweeping change in the agency's organizational structure. The new structure entailed the reorganization of all VHA operating units into 22 networks. In chapter six, Marilyn A. DeLuca concludes that large-scale change frequently necessitates organizational redesign. DeLuca writes, "The agency's structure should facilitate reform, and consideration should be given to the function, size, and organizational placement of various managerial and advisory units within the organization. The distance between the agency 'center' and 'field' is important to ensure sound communication and exchange of information. As too much change can create chaos, thoughtfully planned and executed redesign is key. Such redesign should consider the reform objectives as well as organizational culture and the existing productive linkages."

To better structure the agency to pursue its newly refocused mission on disaster management, FEMA created new agency directorates organized around the basic functions of emergency management. Director Witt separated the operational components of the State and Local Programs and Support Directorate into separate Preparedness, Mitigation, and Response and Recovery Directorates. In a finding similar to that of DeLuca, Daniels and Clark-Daniels describe the reorganization process: "Most public officials recognize the importance of matching agency structure to agency policy goals. Implementing a program using existing agency structures and procedures invites policy conflict and the inefficient use of personnel and resources. One of the leading causes of the proliferation of government agencies is the recognition that matching agency structure to agency mission is easier in a new agency than an ongoing one."

Like Dr. Kizer and Witt, Goldin also concluded that organizational realignment was necessary. Six months after his arrival, Goldin reorganized the Office of Space Science and Applications (OSSA). In reorganizing OSSA, Lambright writes that Goldin wanted more visibility for the earth observation and life science elements of the enterprise. By splitting OSSA into three offices, earth observations and life sciences would each have its own director.

Lesson Four: Seize the moment

The key to the success of any executive is finding precisely the right time in the organization's history to undertake large-scale transformation. The DoD team, Dr. Kizer, and Goldin all used the changing external environment to bring about internal transformation of their organizations. Regarding the DoD team, Harokopus writes, "The era of defense procurement reform was also an era of political, technological, and national security changes.... While these conditions created a climate for reform, it was key individuals, taking advantage of those circumstances, which made the crucial difference. Opportunity is worthless unless it is seized. These leaders recognized the opportunity for tremendous change in public management and they acted on it."

The situation at the Veterans Health Administration was similar. By the early 1990s, Young reports that VHA had become out of sync with the prevailing trends in the delivery of health services. The advent of health maintenance organizations and developments in medical technology had begun the shift away from inpatient-based medicine to outpatient-based primary care medicine. Dr. Kizer himself concluded that change within VHA must move in harmony with environmental or externally focused change. Dr. Kizer writes, "Top managers, particularly those in the public sector, cannot hope to stand against the 'forces of nature'.... In the case of the VHA, that means being in sync with broad trends, such as the national revolution in health care, the explosion of biomedical research and knowledge, the shift to 'an information society,' and the aging of the eligible VHA population."

In examining reform within both the United States Veterans Health Administration and the United Kingdom's National Health Service, DeLuca observed the importance of finding a "window of opportunity." She concludes that environmental factors, including socioeconomic and political conditions and pressure from the public or interests groups, can often prompt the need for organizational change.

When he was appointed in 1992, Goldin was given the task "to reinvent NASA in the post-Cold War era and take it into the 21st century." Lambright writes, "When Goldin became administrator, many observers saw NASA as a bloated bureaucracy pursuing missions that took too long, cost too much, and used technology that was old by the time it was put into space." In addition, the changing environment also included new foreign policy objectives. The new NASA administrator, reports Lambright, "would have to deal with the foreign policy need of the United States to forge a new relationship with the Russians and the world. Goldin, through the Space Station, made NASA a positive instrument of this policy need, elevating NASA to a component of presidential foreign policy and making it more relevant to the times."

All the leaders profiled used real and perceived crises to support and speed up their transformation initiatives. Lambright writes, "A crisis situation creates an organizational need for leadership and willingness of the organization to go along, at least for a while. Goldin proved an effective crisis manager. He seized command of Space Station decision making from those formally in charge and created what was, in effect, a parallel unit under his direction, which redesigned the Space Station."

James Lee Witt effectively used the historically poor reputation of FEMA in 1993 to stimulate change within his organization. The DoD procurement reform team successfully capitalized on the procurement "scandals" of the 1980s to successfully implement procurement changes in the 1990s.

The importance of a perceived crisis cannot be underestimated. Lambright writes, "The lesson is that a crisis can help the leader in forwarding major change. Crisis allows the leader to pull power to himself. Because he spans the boundary across organizational programs and negotiates the space between organization and environment, he is in a strategic position to seize the initiative. He can use a crisis to go beyond incremental to radical change. A leader who successfully leads his organization through a crisis can secure his position, neutralize rivals, and enlarge the change coalition within the organization through his appointees and insiders, who become believers."

Lesson Five: Communicate, communicate, and communicate

All the case studies conclude that effective communication is crucial to the success of any transformation initiative. In the case of procurement reform, Harokopus writes, "… each leader sustained a remarkable communications strategy with constant but varied platforms for publicizing their message. From public speeches at symposia, conferences, and industrial gatherings, to brown bag lunches, town-hall-style meetings, and electronic chat sessions, there was always a variety of styles, media, and audience. The end result was an environment charged with enthusiasm over the new possibilities for acquisition."

At FEMA, James Lee Witt concluded that external communication was crucial to reshaping the agency. Daniels and Clark-Daniels report that when Witt arrived, he found that "FEMA was used to operating in anonymity, and had no effective plan for involving the media and, by extension, the public in FEMA operations." Under Witt, the agency reshaped FEMA's communications to actively engage the media throughout the response and recovery period. "By making the agency more accessible and by providing the media with prompt answers and information, FEMA disarmed much of the inevitable criticism that arose in the immediate aftermath of a disaster. More significantly, the agency opened a two-way channel for information between itself and the disaster victims it was serving," write Daniels and Clark-Daniels.

DeLuca also found the importance of communication in her cross-national study of health care reform. DeLuca concludes, "Transformation of large systems is best accomplished by setting goals and communicating those objectives both within the organization and to interest groups." Both DeLuca and Young give the Veterans Health Administration a mixed report on communicating to those both inside and outside of VHA. DeLuca writes, "While the goals were clearly communicated to the VISN (Veterans Integrated Service Networks) and medical center executives, communication varied across other levels of staff and was often lacking to interest groups."

Young concludes that failure to effectively communicate was a major weakness of the VHA transformation initiative. Young writes, "VHA's transformation offers another of many examples where conventional communication strategies did not work to keep frontline employees informed during a large-scale change effort. To inform employees about the transformation, the senior leadership team distributed written notices and videotapes, held town meetings, and conducted video conferences. However, the survey data collected as part of this study indicate that these methods of communication were not reaching frontline employees."

Communication was sometimes a problem at the National Aeronautics and Space Administration under Dan Goldin. Lambright concludes that a hard-driving administrator with a confrontational style can sometimes shut off the flow of communication. "Communication, communication, and more communication in an organization is the answer to heading off disaster. The communication has to flow freely and candidly from the bottom to the top and vice versa. A leader has to work overtime to assure he gets such communication and feedback. This is especially the case where the change process is so strongly pushed from the top. If a leader is perceived as closed-minded by his officials and staff, he will be a barrier to his own reforms," writes Lambright.

Lesson Six: Involve key players

In all the case studies, a key to the organization's successful transformation was the realization that there were nongovernmental entities deeply interested and involved in the organization's business. The challenge was then to find innovative ways in which to engage them in support of the organization's mission. In the case of FEMA, Director Witt consistently emphasized the importance of partnerships with state and local governments, nonprofit organizations, and the private sector.

At the Department of Defense, Secretary William Perry clearly recognized the importance of involving the defense contractor industry in the dialogue over procurement reform. Harokopus writes, "Perry's team was convinced that the acquisition community should be the primary source for reform initiatives." Perry, reports Harokopus, made the entire acquisition community—both those inside and outside of government—party to the problem as well as part of the solution. The Department's Process Action Teams (PATs) were charged to seek defense industry involvement in the development of all procurement reforms.

Based on both the experience of the National Health Service and the Veterans Health Administration, DeLuca concludes that it is essential to involve interest groups and pertinent community members in reform discussions and debates around workable strategies. "While interest-group participation may be perceived as slowing the change process or, more commonly, be restricted due to concern that these groups may derail or undermine change, exclusion of interest groups limits the effectiveness of the reforms in the long run. Cooperative partnerships that permit participation in change, an emphasis on communication, and avoidance of perverse incentives minimize dissatisfaction and tension among staff as well as interest groups," writes DeLuca.

Lesson Seven: Engage employees

While undertaking organizational transformation, agency leadership must pay special attention to employees. Young reports that while VHA had planned several educational and training initiatives as part of their transformation, most of the initiatives were not in place at the time the agency was undergoing its sweeping change in structure. Looking back, Young concludes that "VHA's senior leadership placed too little emphasis on training and education." As a consequence, Young recommends, "... in situations where swift change is deemed necessary, senior managers should not overlook the importance of training and education to support employees in developing needed skills in a timely manner."

DeLuca also emphasizes the need for staff engagement. She writes, "The manner in which reform is introduced, particularly regarding staff involvement and communication, affects the response of staff to the reform process. Leaders should be knowledgeable and sensitive to the process of change, as well as the desired objectives. Employees who are more empowered and engaged in the change are more involved in the reform process."

At the Department of Defense, recognition, awards, and training were integral to the defense reform initiative. Harokopus writes, "Defense procurement could not change without acceptance by the practitioners.... The leadership understood that for practitioners to become reform enthusiasts, they would need incentives for accepting change and reinforcement from top leaders. Acquisition practitioners needed to know that their opinions were valued and their participation was essential. As a result, the leaders focused on a strategy that included recognition, awards, and training."

But not all efforts to engage employees succeed. At NASA, Goldin's efforts to encourage a bottom-up strategy were not totally successful. Lambright reports that Goldin "wanted the organization to reach a consensus and then interact with the public in creating an even larger consensus for change. Unfortunately, this participative strategy was coupled with financial costs. He ordered 'red and blue' teams to counter one another in downsizing various programs, even as they sought a vision statement and engaged in strategy planning. Cutback planning was a threat to many inside officials."

Lesson Eight: Persevere

The final lesson is that it isn't going to be easy. The challenge is described well by Gary Young: "All transformations generate controversy and criticism. Such criticism and controversy often distract leaders of transformations from focusing on the central goals of the change effort. In the case of VHA, the senior leadership kept its sights fixed on key transformation goals while making mid-course correction to address technical problems as they were recognized."

"No transformation will be perfect," writes Young, "and those who oppose the changes will seek to exploit flaws or limitations to derail the effort. Leaders of transformation need to be responsive to legitimate criticisms, but they also must avoid being swallowed up in technical details."

Transforming and revitalizing government organizations is difficult, time-consuming, but is possible. The leaders profiled in these case studies demonstrate that transformation can be done. Executives in both the public and private sector can learn much from the experiences of the leaders profiled in this volume.

CHAPTER TWO

Transforming the Department of Defense: Creating the New Defense Procurement System

Kimberly A. Harokopus
Visiting Scholar
Political Science Department
Boston College

Introduction

This report examines a cadre of dedicated and innovative public executives, leaders who attacked the historic deficiencies and systemic conditions surrounding the defense procurement system. Their goal was laudable and extremely difficult: fundamentally restructure the way in which the Pentagon designs and purchases its weapons and support systems. Historically, the weapons acquisition process has never been efficient. Under the pre-reform system, it took longer and cost more to design, produce, and field weapons than the military, the Congress, or the public would have liked. It was not uncommon for the acquisition of a sophisticated weapon system to take 10 to 15 years to reach the final development stage while encountering cost increases of 20 to 40 percent.[1]

The problems of defense procurement were well known and, surprisingly, so were some of the solutions. But rarely had implementation of those solutions been achieved. While there are many government leaders to be commended for their commitment to the current reform effort, focus is given to four individuals—William Perry, Paul Kaminski, Colleen Preston, and Steven Kelman. These leaders had to defy long-standing trends and successfully introduce revolutionary methods into a seemingly intransigent bureaucratic system.

How did these leaders transform the largest federal bureaucracy from a rule-bound, inflexible system to one defined by more innovation and case-specific application? How does one remove the safety net of bureaucratic rules and demand adherence to a fundamentally different method of operation? How do you change a public procurement system that has resisted wide-scale change for over 40 years?

Clearly, Perry, Kaminski, Preston, and Kelman were leading a challenging enterprise, one with an energetic schedule of opportunities. Every essential element of the procurement system had to be revised to fit a new approach to public procurement. How does one begin such an endeavor? The leaders had no precise roadmap for successful implementation. But they did have personal passion, historical lessons, and some interesting ideas about achieving organizational change. An investigation of their efforts has revealed six key factors for implementing change.

This report begins with a brief discussion of roles and objectives, specifically the executive positions each leader held and the reforms they intended to implement. Following that are personal profiles of Perry, Kaminski, Preston, and Kelman, illustrating their unique yet synergistically well-meshed professional histories. Attention then turns to each of the six key factors that the leaders used to implement acquisition reform. Each of the factors reveals a strategy for fostering acceptance of procurement reform. Taken together the factors offer an impressive set of tools for achieving widespread organizational change. The report concludes by offering concise recommendations and synopses of the management techniques that helped reverse years of failed procurement reform attempts.

Background

Only a month after his first inauguration, Bill Clinton, the candidate who had campaigned on the need to make government work more efficiently, with less waste, and with more appreciation for the citizen, was quoted as saying, "...[the federal procurement system] would have broken Einstein's brain."[2] Here was the nation's chief executive, a man committed to the ability and power of government, a man who had spent years studying the country's greatest inspirational leaders, commenting on the frustration of federal acquisition, the apparent intransigence of the system, and leaders' seeming inability to effect change. Clinton and his team had miles to go on a path littered with the failed attempts of previous leaders.

Since the nation's founding there has been a public debate regarding the efficient design, production, and delivery of weapons. In March 1794, Congress authorized the building of six large frigates, intending that these ships would be the basic components of an emerging U.S. Navy. But by August 1795, the War Department had run into delays, and cost overruns resulted. Congress eventually cut production by half, acquiring just three frigates. Two hundred years later, the Department of Defense (DoD) was still facing cost overruns, schedule slips, and technical performance problems in acquiring its weapons. From $500 hammers and ashtrays to design and performance problems with the B2, it seemed that defense acquisition was destined for ridicule and perpetual cost and schedule troubles.

That is not to say that there have not been several attempts at reform of the acquisition process. In fact, during the last four decades there have been more than a dozen review panels and commissions chartered to examine the perpetual problems of procurement. Yet none of the reform efforts have been particularly broad or effective. Instead, there has been a continual tinkering with the procurement system, as if a few singularly placed administrative changes could achieve wholesale reform. The problems persisted.

Now, however, through a confluence of international and national events, timely advances in information technology, bipartisan political support, and—perhaps most importantly—skillful efforts by government leaders, an extraordinary, broad-based effort to reform the defense procurement system is underway. In fact, it is this unique set of operating parameters, political conditions, and outstanding leadership that has made the procurement reform initiatives of the mid-1990s more successful than any other previous attempt.

At bottom, the reforms seek to introduce market-centered approaches to public procurement. It is an effort to replace unique and onerous military acquisition processes with industrial practices and commercial managerial techniques. It loosens the restrictions of bureaucratic rules set forth in the Federal Acquisition Regulations, invoking greater use of subjective, case-specific, and participatory decision-making. It trades a rule-bound system for devolution of power to front-line bureaucrats with the ability to use personal discretion and best judgment.

Remarkably, the time-honored but previously ill-fated defense reform effort has finally met with success. In large measure, a cadre of top leaders is responsible for that success. Their feats are remarkable, in part, for the sheer scope of the reform. The changes involve almost every aspect of defense procurement:

- Replacement of overly prescriptive military specifications and standards with commercial or performance specifications;
- Widespread applications of process-speeding information technologies and the introduction of electronic commerce;
- Loosening of the restrictions on communications between government personnel and industry;
- Increased use of corporate past performance as a factor in subsequent contract awards;
- Greater use of commercial products; and
- Use of functionally integrated government acquisition teams, also called Integrated Product Teams (IPT).

Any of these changes would have been viewed as a positive and necessary improvement to the defense acquisition system. Applied in the aggregate, they are astounding. Indeed, these initiatives represent an incredible change for any organization—public or private. As defense acquisition reform seems to be making so much progress relative to past efforts, one can be sure that government leaders have been a major influence on the effort. Never has the impact of and necessity for strong, innovative leadership been more apparent.

Publicly, leaders within the Defense Department credit much of the success of the procurement reforms to the acquisition workforce, but the reforms initiated under the Les Aspin/William Perry Defense Department began very much as a top-down initiative. Therefore, it is imperative that one considers the political leaders involved in the procurement reform enterprise.

Aspin and Perry began the defense procurement reform initiative immediately upon Aspin's 1993 confirmation as secretary of defense. As deputy

Reform Success Stories

Using milspec reform initiatives and better communication with industry, the acquisition office for the Joint Direct Attack Munitions program eliminated all but one of the milspecs on the project. The data requirements were reduced from 243 to 29 items. And the Statement of Work (formerly a 137-page document) was whittled down to a two page Statement of Objective. The result: The unit cost shrunk from $42,000 to $14,000; development costs were reduced by $70 million; and production costs were reduced by an estimated $1.5 billion.[3]

It used to take the Office of Naval Research (ONR) 57 days to pay vouchers under the previous paper system. Today, with electronic funds transfer and other automation, the Navy pays vouchers in five days.[4]

An acquisition office at the Army's Fort Sam Houston implemented a new approach in selecting contractors. With greater reliance on oral presentations, rather than the traditional paper proposals, they cut their source selection schedule from 15 to five months.[5]

It used to take the Defense Personnel Support Center in Philadelphia 60 days to deliver supplies to DoD mess halls, commissaries, and hospitals. The introduction of new technologies has lowered operating costs, boosted productivity, and, remarkably, turned a 60-day delivery schedule into one of less than 72 hours.[6]

The Armed Forces used to have a library of military specifications and standards containing over 30,000 documents. Within two years of the July 1994 start of Milspec Reform, over 4,400 military specifications and standards had been canceled, over 2,600 documents had been inactivated for use in new weapon system designs, over 1,700 non-governmental standards had been adopted, and over 360 simplified, performance-oriented commercial item descriptions had been added.[7]

Using Electronic Data Interchange, Walter Reed Army Medical Center (the Army hospital outside of Washington, D.C.) was able to reduce its pharmaceutical inventories by 89 percent and eliminate six warehouses. The result: a savings of more than $6 million a year.[8]

secretary of defense, Perry was the "point man" on this effort. Together they initiated an effort to attack the perpetual problems of weapons acquisition. With Aspin's untimely death and Perry's subsequent nomination as secretary of defense, as well as the introduction of Paul Kaminski into the reform movement and the ongoing efforts of Colleen Preston, the endeavor was changed but not stalled. As this report explains, these individuals became critical actors in this policy drama. As under secretary of defense for acquisition and technology and deputy under secretary of defense for acquisition reform respectively, Kaminski and Preston formed, with Perry, a cadre of top-echelon Pentagon leaders who were instrumental in achieving procurement reform.

Outside the Pentagon, perhaps the most influential leader in the procurement reform effort was the administrator of the Office of Federal Procurement Policy (OFPP)—Dr. Steven Kelman. Like his DoD counterparts, Kelman would be a critical actor in this drama. Much of the legislative changes to defense acquisition reform were actually government-wide initiatives, changes in the overall federal statute. Kelman would be the crucial link, widening the defense procurement effort to an initiative that would serve the entire federal government.

These leaders were not the first to uncover the problems of defense acquisition. A number of chronic technical problems plagued the pre-reform system, and these problems were well documented. But the leaders astutely recognized that *none* of these issues could be ignored if the team hoped to defy the odds and institute real reform. This was because the problems were interrelated. Attacking one without the others would inevitably lead to half-measures and unfulfilled opportunities.

True reform required a kind of chain reaction. Perry, Kaminski, Preston, and Kelman had to shed the peculiarities of military procurement. Consequently, they had to dismantle the safety net of milspecs—a library of standards and regulations that have been used by the military to prescribe every facet of a weapon's development and production. But in its place there needed to be alternatives—commercial approaches. But for commercial approaches to be successful there needed to be good and continuous communication with industry, both at the design alternative phase, through the contractor selection process, and throughout product development and production. Similarly this joint approach needed to extend inward as well, creating integrated government acquisition teams infused with a devolution of authority so that flexible development approaches were possible.

The leadership team also needed to provide the defense bureaucracy access to and training with the latest information technology, providing government practitioners with the tools to improve the speed and clarity of their acquisition decisions. But these efforts would be most effective if they were accomplished with (1) a degree of uniformity that allowed commonality and synergy, and (2) a level of autonomy that allowed the acquisition process to be customized to service-specific missions and agency-unique requirements.

The problems were widespread. The solutions would have to be equally as encompassing. That in turn meant a massive shift in organizational policies and practices. It meant big changes ahead.

The Leaders

The department, bureaus, and agencies of the federal government all need good leaders to be effective. But a select few are especially critical in the political and administrative battles to enact public policy. William Perry, Paul Kaminski, Colleen Preston, and Steven Kelman came from various professional backgrounds, yet they shared a remarkable passion. This fortunate if rare occurrence was one reason that the leadership team was so successful. Although each held a number of different positions before coming to their roles in the Clinton administration, they were never far removed from their common policy theme of procurement reform.

Each had been fighting for a decade or more to move policy solutions to the problem of inefficient procurement into political focus—Preston on Capitol Hill; Kaminski and Perry through appointed government service in the Pentagon and membership on presidential and defense review panels and committees; and Kelman in his academic research, published books, and lectures to senior Pentagon officials through his affiliation with the Kennedy School of Government. In short, there was never a time in the last decade when these individuals were not prepared for procurement reform to move onto the political agenda.

And while their professional paths to the Pentagon and OFPP may have differed, while their personal preferences, politics, and expertise may have varied, they were stalwart and uncompromising in their insistence that defense procurement needed to be repaired. Furthermore, they were equally convinced that the repairs the system needed were not a new application of regulations but rather a *deregulation* of the system. Below is a brief account of the professionals who led acquisition reform. The number of parallels between these impressive leaders is intriguing.

William Perry

In 1993, the White House selected Dr. William J. Perry as deputy secretary of defense. Serving under Secretary Les Aspin, Perry came to the position thoroughly prepared for the rigors of the job. In fact, Perry, like his reform-minded boss, already was convinced of the need for reform of the defense acquisition system. He was committed to the notion of revamping defense procurement. His professional background had demonstrated first-hand the need for such a reform.

Perry had a long history of work with DoD along with experience in academia and commerce. He has an academic background in the sciences, having earned a Ph.D. in mathematics. Perry also served in the military both as an enlisted person and as an officer. He has been a business entrepreneur, a leader in the defense industry, and a senior executive in an investment banking and consulting firm specializing in high-technology companies. In addition, he spent four years in the Pentagon as under secretary of defense for research and engineering, a position in which he was responsible for all weapon systems procurement and all research and development. In short, Perry was probably the best-prepared public servant for the job of acquisition reform.

Perry struggled as a member of the defense industry in trying to comply with the special requirements of government procurement. Although he appreciated the drive for technology and the strategy that the United States had chosen in its quest to provide security for the country, he also knew the rigors of executive leadership in the Pentagon. In fact, his position as under secretary from 1977 until 1981 demonstrated a commitment to the job and the acquisition system that was extraordinary for the field.

In addition, Perry had served on a number of U.S. government advisory boards including the Technical Review Panel of the Senate Select Committee on Intelligence. He was also a member of the Carnegie Commission on Science, Technology, and Government. In these roles Perry was party to reviews and assessments of the technical standards of the national industrial base and the overhead costs associated with the U.S. weapons procurement process. No doubt these affiliations, as well as Perry's personal, first-hand dealings with the Pentagon procurement system, prompted his passionate stand on the issue of procurement reform.

During 1993 Perry led the daily operations of acquisition reform as Les Aspin's second-in-command. With his assumption of duties as secretary in

February 1994, Perry still maintained a strong leadership role in the reforms, even as his responsibilities multiplied. Like Kelman, Perry was interested in making reform a reality. To that end, he stayed active within the effort throughout his four-year tenure at the Pentagon. He was also concerned with enlisting a cadre of leaders within the Pentagon who shared his passion for procurement reform. His selection of Paul Kaminski and Colleen Preston as members of the acquisition reform leadership team were two of his most critical decisions.

Paul Kaminski

Dr. Paul Kaminski was an extremely influential figure in defense procurement reform. He came to the position of under secretary of defense for acquisition and technology in October 1994 with a 20-year career in the Air Force, a 10-year career as a founding partner for a high-technology consulting and investment banking firm, and a commendable academic career. He combined a strong appreciation for the role of defense procurement with an intolerance for its problems and an unyielding advocacy for repairing those deficiencies.

Kaminski had been a program manager during his Air Force career for what was then a highly classified program for a stealth technology aircraft. Because it was in the so-called "black world" of super top-secret acquisitions, many of the traditional regulations and military specifications did not apply. The funding was relatively secure for the program, and it did not meet the same public scrutiny requirements that many unclassified programs faced. As such, the advocacy, protectionism, and parochialism that usually surround high-value programs were less invasive. Similarly, the oversight requirements that typically bog down weapon systems development were not present. The result, according to Kaminski, was that the acquisition staff developed some rather innovative and creative contracting procedures. They worked intimately with the contractor and included an integrated team approach to the system's technical development. In short, they were using streamlined reform techniques a generation before today's current effort. And they worked!

That experience left a lasting impression on Kaminski. His appreciation for the business side of acquisition was further confirmed during his tenure as a banking and investment partner. Throughout his "civilian" period,

Kaminski maintained links to the military. He served as chairman of the Defense Science Board and was also a member of the Defense Policy Board. Defense procurement reform was not a new wave or a trendy topic onto which Kaminski just happened to stumble. He had been advocating such policy initiatives for years. When the timing was right, he was ready. With Perry at the helm of the Pentagon and all the other factors in place, Kaminski was the perfect choice for leading acquisition reform. He was ready to go when Perry gave him the opportunity.

Colleen Preston

Another instrumental leader was Colleen Preston. The deputy under secretary of defense for acquisition reform was sworn into her position in June 1993. For almost four years she was relentless in her efforts to revamp the defense procurement process. Perry created Preston's position in his effort to focus leadership attention and department resources on the need for reform. Preston was a key and founding member of the reform leadership team that helped propagate acquisition reform initiatives within the Pentagon. And she readily admits that her background as a policy advocate for reforming the public procurement system, including her time as an officer in the Air Force and a staffer on Capitol Hill, was crucial in preparing her for the extraordinary opportunities that were present in the Perry Pentagon.

Like many of the other leaders of this effort, Preston is a former military officer who dealt first-hand with the failings of the acquisition system. As a member of the Air Force General Counsel's Office, she witnessed the problems that allocation of defense resources and contract management present. After her departure from the military, Preston worked for over 10 years on Capitol Hill as a staffer for the House Armed Services Committee and was later named the committee's general counsel. Her position enabled her to be involved in writing much of the acquisition legislation that preceded the 1994 Federal Acquisition Streamlining Act, including the Defense Acquisition Workforce Improvement Act. Regardless of the workload she took on in those positions, she never strayed too far from her involvement in procurement reform. These experiences proved valuable for Preston, who, after a move from Capitol Hill to the Pentagon as special assistant to the secretary of defense for legal matters, was chosen later for the deputy under secretary position. With her move to the Pentagon, but before the creation of the deputy under secretary position, Perry and Preston were talking and writing to each other regarding the unique opportunity they might have to implement acquisition reform. Preston recounts:

> In talking to Dr. Perry ... as we went through the confirmation process, and based on some dealings with Dr. Perry previously, it was obvious to me that they [the leadership team] were so committed to acquisition reform that if there was ever a chance for it to succeed, this was it.[9]

Preston's assessment would prove to be prophetic.

Steven Kelman

One of the most influential "civilian" leaders in the defense acquisition reform effort has been Dr. Steven Kelman. Indeed, the selection and November 1993 Senate confirmation of Kelman as administrator of the Office of Federal Procurement Policy (OFPP) was a crucial step. Dr. Kelman is a vigorous and vibrant advocate for his cause. Although the OFPP is only 20 people strong, Kelman gave it a vitality and reach well beyond its size.

Kelman characterizes himself as an outsider, an amateur in the sea of professional politicians and Washington beltway regulars. But Kelman, like his similarly reform-minded cohorts at the Pentagon, had been thinking and writing about federal procurement reform for over a decade. Indeed his 1990 book, *Procurement and Public Management: The Fear of Discretion and the Quality of Government Performance*, is a thoroughly researched and respected case-study approach to the problems of over-regulation in the federal procurement of computer systems. It forms, along with his other academic work, a theoretical underpinning for the value and need for deregulating the federal procurement system. In fact, Kelman's ideas about the devolution of power to front-line civil servants, the use of past-performance information as a critical component in selecting contractors, and the need to establish longer-term relationships with suppliers are key concepts of the current reform effort.

Before his move to OFPP, Kelman was a professor at Harvard's Kennedy School of Government. From that venue he was not shy about his political and public policy convictions. Kelman is a self-professed liberal. He celebrates the power of government for accomplishing noble goals, and he accepts that civil servants can and should be given freer rein to accomplish the objectives set forth for them. According to Kelman, enactment of good government ideas is not possible without the trust of public servants and the empowerment of that group to accomplish the requirements of governing. Although the federal bureaucracy faced downsizing, restructuring, and reorganization, members of the civil service had no stauncher supporter than Kelman, a man who believes forcefully in the power of government and its ability to do extraordinary things.

Kelman's ideas about procurement reform gained not only acceptance but acclaim. In fact, this policy-minded academic became the darling of Republicans, Democrats, and industry alike. In an uncharacteristic intermingling of policy ideas, the bipartisan appeal of acquisition reform made sense for the liberal left and the conservative right. For the political left, reforms to government operations that included downsizing and deregulation were the first step in freeing government to accomplish greater goals of public service. The political right was equally concerned with trimming government. However, conservatives saw a trimmed-down, smaller-scale federal government as an end in itself, a condition that freed the citizenry from meddlesome, inefficient government-managed programs.

As an astute and thoughtful leader, Kelman capitalized fully on this unconventional condition. He emphasized that there could be a "confluence of agendas" that was appealing to both industry and government.[10] Kelman stepped into his leadership role, bridging many sides effectively. He demonstrated the bipartisan appeal of procurement reform and also forged a respected, amiable, and effective relationship between DoD, OFPP, and industry.

The success of the reforms is due in large measure to leaders like Kelman, Perry, Kaminski, and Preston. They were each extremely well suited for their roles. They had a depth of experience that made them experts on the subject and sympathetic to all parties involved. They were proactive to the point of being passionate, both within their appointed positions and on the policy matter overall. And they were diligent in their personal attempts to institute acquisition reform, continually advocating their cause but also waiting for the perfect confluence of events to help bring about their shared vision of reform. As that time came, these four leaders devised an effective implementation strategy, one that depended upon the skillful application of six key factors.

Key Factors for Success

A Cohesive Leadership Team

Procurement reform demanded concerted and uninterrupted leadership attention. It demanded an experienced leadership team that knew intimately the problems, peculiarities, and strengths of the public procurement process. Indeed, a key factor to successful implementation of acquisition reform was creating a cohesive leadership team, a team that shared a common vision of reform and a shared implementation strategy. Appointed leaders represent forces for change and inspiration, a conduit for bringing innovation and invigoration into the machinations of federal bureaucracy. Often they are sources of great leadership. And yet, historically, there are patterns associated with appointed leadership that inhibit organizational change. Chief among them is the issue of tenure and experience.

Generally, political appointees serve only briefly in their positions—an average of 18 months.[11] What does this mean for the bureaucracy, for presidential policies, for implementing change within an organization? With such a short tenure, a newly appointed leader barely has time to establish goals before he leaves the organization. Most appointees come to the position, take several months to learn the job, and invest energy into specific initiatives. The bureaucracy then finds that upon the leader's departure, the organizational goal or project must be turned over to yet another appointee, who may or may not share the first leader's enthusiasm, appreciation, or orientation of the project. As a result, it is tempting for appointed leaders to initiate projects that are short range.[12] While those projects may be well-intentioned efforts, significant achievements in public policy or organizational change require emphasis on the long range. Institutionalizing bureaucratic operations means long-term commitment to the effort—a feat that is hard to accomplish when the top leaders of the organization are changing every year and a half.

Similarly, a lack of experience with the agency and unfamiliarity with its processes and systems can have serious repercussions. While arborists do not run the National Institutes of Health and physicians do not lead the Park Service, professional expertise and background are not always well matched. This means leaders have to take so much time trying to "learn the ropes" that they waste precious time at the outset of their tenure trying to become knowledgeable about the very processes they need to change. Rarely does starting with a "fizzle" rather than a "bang" provide the organizational momentum needed to jump-start an initiative.

The habitual weaknesses within appointed leadership—lack of experience and familiarity, short tenure and rapid turnover, and orientation toward short-range projects—have made sustained, cultural, and widespread change difficult to achieve within the defense bureaucracy. These systemic shortcomings have made previous attempts at acquisition reform difficult, even impossible. As this section reveals, the procurement reform leaders highlighted here have overcome these weaknesses.

The leaders of defense procurement reform were remarkably well suited for the tough job at hand. They all had past experience with the acquisition process—some as practitioners, others as researchers, still others as members of the defense industry seeking to comply with the sometimes byzantine set of procurement rules. With the exception of Kelman, each had previously worked inside the Pentagon as a military or civilian leader. Each had recognized the failings of the defense acquisition system and each had struggled to remedy it—through advisory boards, informal correspondence to defense leaders, and published scholarly works. It was as if they had been preparing for years to meet this challenge. Moreover, Perry, Kaminski, and Preston had worked together previously. They had shared their frustrations with the pre-reform system, corresponded on the subject, and had come to appreciate their common desire to change the status quo.

Leaders without the authority or passion to promote reform could easily have become dissuaded from this issue. But this was a group of committed advocates. In fact, it was this shared commitment to reform that cemented their team. And as the account below reveals, this cohesiveness of vision and shared commitment was a prerequisite for admission to the team. It was a vital selection criterion.

By 1993, the stirrings of a revolution in acquisition had begun within the Pentagon. Then Secretary of Defense Les Aspin knew defense procurement needed an overhaul. He came to the job with the political backing of the President but the skepticism of the DoD workforce. (Trimming an organization rarely breeds goodwill.) Perhaps one of his most important and useful decisions was the selection of William Perry as deputy secretary of defense.

It would be Perry's job to overhaul and streamline the acquisition system. Like Aspin, Perry recognized the importance of having the right leaders in the correct positions. If acquisition reform was going to work this time, then key appointments of personnel central to the reform effort would be a crucial first step. The individuals in these positions would not have the luxury of on-the-job-training. They needed to come to the job knowing well the difficulties and problems of the Pentagon's acquisition system. The Aspin/Perry strategy: act quickly and decisively. Perry and Aspin went to Vice President Gore with their recommendation for establishing a leadership team for changing defense acquisition. The vice president agreed with their plan and understood the need for a coordinated team. He allowed Aspin and Perry to recommend a complete slate of candidates for these positions. While Gore did not give Perry and Aspin carte blanche (after all, the nominations would have to fall or stand on the merits of the individual appointees), the opportunity to nominate an entire slate of key appointment positions was instrumental—and rare.

Perry did most of the leadership search, creating a team of candidates who had worked together previously, who had long-term experience in the acquisition field, and who had agreed that defense acquisition was in great need of change. Commitment to reforming defense acquisition had been a litmus test for nomination. As the members were confirmed in their positions, they clearly understood that acquisition reform was a personal priority for Aspin and Perry and that their placement and selection was dependent upon a shared vision of implementing procurement reform.[13]

Even with an experienced group that was committed to procurement reform, could the effort be accomplished before the attrition of leaders began? Regardless of the initial enthusiasm a proposed organizational change might enjoy, substantial, institutional change requires sustained effort. There could be no quick fix solution to the problems procurement reform sought to address. In an environment where leaders depart routinely after only 18 months on the job, this team showed remarkable stability. Not only had they worked together previously, Perry's leadership team stayed on the job for almost *four* years.

This was crucial for several reasons. First, while the leaders wanted to work quickly to initiate reforms, it would still take time to filter the message throughout the workforce and industry. Even the most efficient reforms take time to disseminate and adopt. Second, there were sure to be doubters within the organization, those who were willing to "wait out" the appointees. Ordinarily, it would be a good strategy: If you do not like the message, wait for a new messenger. Only this time the strategy failed. The fortitude of this group of policy advocates was remarkable, sending a signal to even the most hardened of acquisition specialists that this time was different.

Kelman too did not take a quick strike at this effort and then retreat to a less publicly scrutinized position, leaving the initiative to dangle without a committed leader at the helm. He was in his position at OFPP for over four years, leaving at the end of 1997. During that tenure, Kelman was an important bridge between the Clinton administration and the Pentagon.

For many years, federal procurement was defense procurement. The Pentagon led the way from a policy standpoint when it came to federal acquisitions. If Kelman and Clinton wanted to reform federal procurement, DoD was going to have to play a vital role. Yet historically, the relationship between OFPP and DoD had not been particularly amicable. To DoD, OFPP appeared as a meddlesome staff agency that was unfamiliar with DoD's needs and bent on intrusive oversight of its procurement operations. To OFPP, the DoD was the elephant of federal procurement that deserved watchfulness and containment.

Kelman, appreciating the magnitude of the effort, did not try to bulldoze or sidestep the elephant in his path, but worked in unison with Pentagon leaders to make reform successful. In fact, he and his colleague at the Pentagon, Colleen Preston, devised a respectful, effective working relationship. Clearly the two offices had different constituents, but as Kelman explained, the OFPP-DoD relationship was "superb…it was effective and highly complementary."[14] This newly forged relationship can be attributed to the personal efforts of Preston and Kelman. Neither claimed singular expertise on the subject of procurement reform. They were eager to develop the ideas of practitioners and to involve industry as well. This willingness to change the parameters broke the traditional roles of the two offices, allowing a fresh start and cooperative approach.

The alliance of Pentagon leaders and White House officials produced a strong team. The combination of mutual goals and experience allowed the team to initiate reform quickly and to sustain the effort. As Kaminski commented, "We had a common vision… It was clear to everyone that no one would be able to penetrate this team. From the Vice President on down, we had a very proactive policy."[15]

Preston also confirms that the relationship among the key acquisition reform leaders at the Pentagon was unique and very close-knit. "We [the leadership team] established relationships that normally would never have occurred. The leadership team was small, focused, a tight nucleus. It made a huge difference. We were very committed, and really believed we could make some revolutionary changes."[16] Creating a team that had the experience, constitution, and managerial abilities to achieve department-wide reform was not easy, but it did pay off.

Competing organizational goals are constantly vying for leaders' attention. The fact that the team did not allow any of these competing objectives to derail their procurement reform effort is testimony to the fortitude of the individual leaders and the criticality with which they *all* viewed acquisition reform. Certainly it would have been easier to target a simpler, more short-term project. It would have been financially more rewarding to leave after a year or two on the job. But it would not have produced the same successes. With a collective objective, a shared passion, and a common strategy, this group of leaders dismantled a pre-reform system that had gone unrepaired for 40 years; and, in its place, they helped erect new and fundamentally different practices.

Inclusion of Industry and Acquisition Practitioners

A key and sustaining factor in the leaders' implementation strategy was the inclusion of the acquisition workforce and the defense industry. From the beginning, Perry's vision of defense procurement focused on the need for cross-service, cross-functional, even cross-agency advice and coordination regarding reform issues. His message was clear: Defense procurement reform was to be a system-wide effort demanding widespread participation. Indeed, Perry was forceful in securing the inclusion of all branches of the military, all levels of the acquisition bureaucracy, and even the defense industry. That involvement was not just cursory. Perry's team was convinced that the acquisition community should be the primary source for reform initiatives.

Given Perry's vision and demand for inclusion of acquisition practitioners, the creation of Process Action Teams, or PATs, proved to be an especially useful approach. Process Action Teams provided a forum for developing solutions to the problems of defense procurement. In fact, PATs became the preferred method for kicking off the various reform initiatives. A PAT's mission was demanding. The team was required to analyze a current acquisition practice; identify the failures and benefits of the existing approach; identify alternatives that would streamline and improve the practice; develop incentives for implementing that new approach; draft any statutory or regulatory changes necessary to implement the new process; consider training requirements for that new effort; and, finally, develop measures for gaining feedback on the new approach. These PATs, and the working groups they formed, sought out and included the opinions of the acquisition workforce, supervisors, *and* the defense industry. In effect, it made the entire acquisition community party to the problem as well as part of the solution.

The PATs and working groups were the direct link to the workforce and industry. Perry and the other defense reform leaders did not dictate daily operations from above; rather, they allowed the operators to develop their own solutions. This would ensure that the reform initiatives would be truly compatible with day-to-day procurement needs. Unattainable, highly theoretical, or overly complicated approaches would not work. PATs were a way to ground the reform efforts and ensure their survivability. Perry's team realized that real empowerment of the PAT demanded strong advocacy and a consistent reliance on the approach by top-echelon leaders. This, in turn, would provide legitimacy to the PAT's role and acceptance by the working-level bureaucracy.

To appreciate the importance of this approach, consider the implementation of the milspec reform initiative. This effort required exceptional leadership skills and produced dramatic change. In August 1993, Deputy Under Secretary Preston directed that a Process Action Team be established to investigate milspec reform. Based upon that charter, the PAT developed a strategy for changing the Pentagon's reliance on milspecs (*Blueprint for Change: Report of the Process Action Team on Military Specifications and Standards*, April 1994). On June 23, 1994, the DoD published an implementation plan for the PAT's reform program. Six days later, Secretary of Defense Perry issued a memorandum accepting the PAT recommendations, outlining his milspec reform initiatives, and directing all the military services and DoD agencies to take *immediate* action to implement his policy changes. The PAT's report and plan, together with the Perry memorandum, formed the basis of DoD's efforts to reform milspecs.

Milspec reform was not a minor undertaking. Perry directed that all traditional milspecs be replaced with performance specifications. He further clarified that military specifications and standards could be used only as a "last resort" and only with an approved waiver. The scope of this directive was astounding. Any procurement of financial consequence (above the $100,000 threshold) was subject to Perry's policy change. Secretary Perry turned the traditional weapons requirement process on its head. His direction to use performance specifications almost without exception and to require waivers for use of any milspec ran squarely against customary practice.

Although Perry's directive was traditional in one sense—a direct order sent down by the top boss—it was also quite unorthodox in the making. First, the milspec initiative had been crafted according to recommendations from the Process Action Team. Although Perry was very anxious to move forward on the reform effort, particularly with respect to milspec reform, he refrained from issuing an immediate decree. He waited for the recommendations of the Milspec Process Action Team. His delay demonstrated a personal resolve to include the thoughts, perspectives, and recommendations of the front-line acquisition community in his first major reform initiative. Second, Perry depended quite heavily on industry, relying on their technical ingenuity and their willingness and desire to see the milspec requirement and design system replaced with a more flexible, commercial-like purchasing system. Further evidence of that reliance came in Perry's directive that industry-government partnerships be formed for the purpose of establishing non-government standards to replace existing military standards. In fact, Perry specifically identified the defense and high technology industries as participants in this initiative. He asked Paul Kaminski to draft and pass language for the Defense Federal Acquisition Regulation Supplement (DFARS) that encouraged contractors to propose non-government standards and industry-wide practices that met the intent of military specifications and standards.[17]

Perry understood that milspec reform was designed to change a closed, prescribed system into an open, more flexible one—a major transformation. The secretary also recognized that clear direction, publicity for the effort, and training would be needed to implement reform. But perhaps most importantly, Perry was intent on crafting the new approach to weapons design according to the recommendations of industry and the acquisition workforce. Indeed it was a careful combination of top-down direction (with the June 1994 memorandum) and bottom-up implementation (with the PAT's recommendation and the inclusion of industry and the workforce). This combination approach signaled the leaders' desires to focus on practitioners as the source for building the new acquisition system.

All the reform leaders used this atypical approach to policy change. Although Kelman had researched and written about the procurement process, he took a valuable step in not claiming singular expertise on the subject. Upon his arrival in Washington, he solicited comments and opinions from both government agency leaders and the acquisition workforce. He met as well with industry association representatives and other "civilians" who could provide perspective on the system. His appreciation for the insights of these groups was only heightened during his tenure at OFPP. He consistently looked to the bureaucracy and industry as a source for new ideas and system improvements.

In fact, all the leaders recognized that reform could be structured so that industry and government could *both* benefit from procurement reform. As Kelman explained, there was a "confluence of agendas between government and industry...there was an alliance on particular reform efforts."[18] This did not mean there was industry-wide, or even consistent, support for *all* of the reform initiatives. But on the vital and initial efforts such as reducing government oversight and streamlining the audit and paperwork processes, there was widespread appeal and terrific cooperation.

Inclusion of the government workforce and industry was also a major component of Kelman's effort to rewrite Part 15 of the Federal Acquisition Regulations (FAR). This section of FAR details how contractors are selected for award of government contracts. Rewriting this section was critical work. It would determine how government contracting personnel considered past performance information, what methods they used for gaining information (such as use of oral presentations and other forms of communication with industry), and how much discretion was acceptable for determining overall best value to the government.

In keeping with his open-door policy, Kelman accepted any and all suggestions about the rewrite. It took two years, three drafts, and over 2,000 comments, but the end product was better—a well-conceived, operator-approved regulation that would better suit the needs of the acquisition community. That is not to say that it is without flaws. There was no way to make every participant happy. But when registering a complaint or suggestion was as easy as logging on to a website, no one could say they did not have a chance to add their two cents.

Similarly, Kelman and his colleague from DoD, Colleen Preston, initiated the "Front-Line Procurement Professionals Forum in 1996." Preston and Kelman solicited nominations of nonsupervisory contracting professionals from each cabinet department and each of the military services. Eventually, they selected 30 individuals (about half of whom worked outside of Washington). The group began meeting approximately once every six weeks in the White House Conference Center. The objective was a front-line discussion of procurement practices—processes that worked, failures of the system, ideas for improvement, successful and unsuccessful attempts at change. The group brought these ideas back to their own offices, to their bosses, and to their peers. Ultimately, it helped spread the reform notions faster by including field operators in the latest efforts to support change.

Under Secretary Kaminski was also a strong proponent of front-line involvement. There would be no ivory towers here. The practitioners needed to be fully engaged in reform. When Kaminski set out to implement the initiative on Integrated Product Teams, he filled an auditorium at Defense Systems Management College with the program managers of major weapons systems and the principal members of the Defense Acquisition Board to introduce the initiative. (Recall that IPT is an effort that established a cross-functional, interrelated team approach to the development of weapons systems).

His action brought together two important groups—the overseers of the defense acquisition system and the program managers themselves anything else would have been a failure of the IPT enterprise. Yet, it was the first time both groups had been brought together at the same place with time to listen and discuss the initiatives that concerned them both. According to Kaminski, this forum was critical: "It was clear at that point that everyone was beginning to understand. I could see the switch begin to click—they were willing to give this a try."[19]

Recall that these leaders had been preaching about their cause for years. One might think that the long-waged battle to bring about reform might have soured them on the abilities or commitment of the acquisition workforce. And yet ironically, Kelman, Preston, Perry and Kaminski were firmly committed to the competency and dedication of the acquisition workforce. In fact, while they saw themselves as catalysts for change, they were convinced that the acquisition practitioners themselves would design lasting and worthwhile reforms. As Colleen Preston recalls:

> The real key was the focus on the front-line practitioners.
> It was fundamental. We got people who were involved in

the day-to-day basis of procurement, we got bureaucracy
out of the way and let them come up with the solutions.[20]

Indeed, one of the leaders' most far-reaching implementation strategies
was the inclusion of practitioners in the design and implementation of the
reforms. They believed forcefully and acted diligently to include the workforce and industry in their plans. It would not be an exaggeration to say that
Kelman had made himself and OFPP a conduit through which front-line
practitioners could create and shape the policies that would eventually
become the new acquisition system. Similarly, Perry, Preston, and Kaminski
focused on energizing lower-level acquisition leaders to take on the reform
notions for themselves, enabling them to personalize the opportunity for
change. They were not abdicating their responsibility for creating change.
Rather, they were inspiring creative workplace environments and fostering
an organizational climate that treated reform as an invitation for personal
participation and improvement, not as a directive levied upon employees.

Continuous Communication

Policies tend to fade from the limelight absent some pressure or event
to draw attention to them. The leaders were determined that would not happen to defense procurement reform. And yet, getting the message out is
tough within a bureaucracy as large as DoD. The effort can be truncated,
misstated, or reinterpreted at any one of hundreds of bureaucratic levels.
Diligent and consistent communication would be necessary. Moreover, the
leaders' insistence that practitioners be the source for reform ideas added to
that burden. To get those front-line solutions, to foster an environment conducive to change, the leaders needed to listen. There needed to be continuous communication.

All the reformers worked hard to ensure that there was a dialogue
between government leaders and operators. Their open door and open
e-mail policies were instrumental in instituting changes to the procurement
system. They worked tirelessly to communicate their efforts on reform to the
acquisition workforce. They spoke freely and whenever possible to industry
and government groups, urging them to examine the changes and to communicate their thoughts on proposed policy changes. Perry and his team
insisted that the message on acquisition reform be constant.

Preston especially was a vocal and prolific advocate for the cause,
appearing in numerous panel discussions, conferences, and symposia. In
coordination with OFPP, she was responsible for the implementation of a
monthly column featured in the National Contract Management Association

"Taking the Pledge"

Soon after Steven Kelman was confirmed as head of OFPP, he initiated a series of five very successful "pledge programs." Kelman's pledge notion involved getting a number of agencies to voluntarily agree to undertake a particular reform action—not a report or recommendation but a tangible accomplishment, a specific action.

One major pledge program was the use of past performance data in the selection of contractors. Kelman spent weeks telephoning procurement executives to line up support for this multiple-agency effort. At first the "marketing" of the past performance pledge program was slow going. Kelman relied on his personal contacts within agencies and on the combined efforts of a small cadre of procurement executives whom he had come to know as true "reformers." But as Kelman recounts, by the time he had convinced eight agencies to sign up, "the number of participants started snowballing," and by the week before the public announcement of the pledge, OFPP staffers were like "salespeople receiving orders over the telephone as agencies called in to announce two or three or four more contracts."

In all, 20 agencies (including DoD) pledged to make the past performance of bidders a major factor in selecting the winner on a total of 60 contracts. A public signing of the pledge contract was held in the Indian Treaty Room of the Old Executive Office Building. The event even received coverage in the *Washington Post* and *Washington Times*.

Ultimately, the pledge helped get procurement reform rolling. It created a fervor over reform, generating publicity for the cause. And as Kelman anticipated, the media coverage and departmental attention levied on the pledges provided much needed recognition—of the individuals involved, of the particular initiative, and of reform overall.

trade publication. She held her own town meetings, roundtable discussions, and brown bag lunch sessions. Anywhere an audience could be found, Preston was spreading the word.

Kaminski too was well traveled on the reform speaking tour, providing what at times seemed like nonstop, play-by-play action calls regarding Perry's reform program. He found that relating success stories and actual accounts of acquisition dilemmas and concerns provided his audiences with real insight into the need for reform. And Kaminski did not simply target government personnel in his endless effort to publicize reform. He filled conference centers across the country with industry's aerospace, electronics, and manufacturing professionals and captured the attention of industry in a way that signaled the critical need for industry's involvement in procurement reform.

Kelman was another consistent and vocal advocate for reform. Consider that his first year on the job was very successful: Major legislation was passed with the signing of the 1994 Federal Acquisition Streamlining Act, and several pilot programs were introduced as a way to initiate trial solutions to various procurement ailments. But in 1995 Kelman focused intently on "marketing" the procurement reform effort. In fact, he designated 1995 as the "Year of Implementation." To that end, Kelman set off on a nonstop whirlwind of appearances, speeches, and town-hall-type discussions. Approximately once every two weeks, Kelman visited a buying office. He would give a talk and then meet with local contracting officials to share ideas and discuss operational frustrations. During 1995 and 1996, Kelman estimates he spent about 15 to 20 percent of his time visiting and speaking with procurement practitioners. And like Kaminski, Kelman recounted a procurement reform success story in almost every communication effort he made.

Whether it was through the front-line forum, in articles written for trade publications, in congressional testimony, during town hall meetings, or in published interviews, all the leaders could be heard using the same rhetoric: "DoD would become the smartest, most efficient, most effective buyer of goods and services to meet warfighter needs." The unofficial marketing slogan for acquisition reform was simpler; it was pared down to a mantra of three words, "better, faster, cheaper." That phrase was soon adopted by the military services as the informal credo for describing the objectives of acquisition reform.

Perry, Preston, Kaminski, and Kelman all subscribed to the theory of continuous communication. The strategy was targeted to many audiences— the workforce, industry, the legislature, even the general public. Their outlets were as diverse as their audiences, from national symposia and major media sources to brown bag lunches at local buying offices. Where they delivered their message was not as important as the need to continuously speak of the effort. Without this constant reminder from the top leadership that procurement reform was a "hot" topic for the administration and the Perry Pentagon, the initiative would naturally atrophy. With each member of the leadership team making a continued effort to showcase procurement reform, the initiative maintained (and even improved) its organizational precedence.

Recognition, Awards, and Training

Another key element for reform success was convincing the acquisition workforce and industry of their vital roles. Defense procurement could not change without acceptance by the practitioners. Yet simply sending forth a policy memo declaring full workforce involvement would hardly meet that objective. The leadership understood that for practitioners to become reform enthusiasts, they would need incentives for accepting change and reinforcement from top leaders. Acquisition practitioners needed to know that their opinions were valued and their participation was essential. As a result, the leaders focused on a strategy that included recognition, awards, and training.

The first crucial element was a sustained campaign of recognition. Keeping the spotlight on reform was critical. Moreover, it was the work the practitioners themselves were doing that had to take center stage. Recall that the leaders' communication strategies often involved the recital of an anecdote from the "field." In relating these procurement success stories, the leaders accomplished two objectives: First, they propagated a particularly effective acquisition practice. But they also sent a signal regarding the source of that practice—acquisition practitioners. Recognition of theses "front-line reformers" created incentive for others to follow suit. To that end, the leaders took great strides to recognize workforce contributors in their public speeches, in organizational newsletters, during Congressional testimony, and in submissions to trade publications. By spotlighting the contribution of the workforce to the reform effort, the leaders hoped to extend the reach of the initiatives and accelerate implementation.

Even in the early days of the reform effort, the leaders described the efforts underway on the pilot programs. They highlighted the new methods taken by these test-case offices and motivated their audiences with the possibilities that these new approaches offered for the entire department. As reform progressed, there were even more opportunities for the leaders to highlight field accomplishments.

Consider, for example, the National Contract Management Association and the efforts of Preston and Kelman. These leaders initiated a column, "Reinventing Acquisition," in the association's monthly magazine. But rather than Preston or Kelman authoring top-down, policy-style pieces, they selected a member of the acquisition workforce to be a featured author. In this monthly forum, the practitioner would relate a particularly innovative or new approach to procurement. The column became a chronicle of workforce experiences and a way to recognize acquisition reformers. Real-life stories from the field held more sway with the workforce, and they reinforced the notion that leaders truly wanted a grass-roots approach to reform.

Yet another unconventional approach for recognizing workplace initiatives came through Kelman's nationwide procurement office visits. This series of visits made to various field offices presented Kelman an opportunity to reinforce the crucial role of the procurement workforce. At each stop Kelman would ask pointedly, "What are you most proud of as an acquisition professional?" This tactic accomplished two objectives: It offered an opportunity to spread the word on good acquisition reform ideas, and, even more importantly, it confirmed that the leaders thought highly of the work the acquisition community accomplished.

Similarly, when Preston and Kelman started the front line forum, they had several objectives in mind. Of course they wanted an outlet to disseminate new acquisition practices. But they also intended to showcase the source of those bright ideas. Reform initiatives were not to be solely the brainchild of thoughtful but once-removed academics, or foreign companies, or even domestic business executives. Kelman and Preston expected great ideas and new approaches from the real front-line acquisition practitioners. And just as importantly, they wanted the government workforce to recognize that the inspiration for those great ideas was the colleague next to them.

A staple of managerial techniques—awards and commendations—continued to be a major part of the leaders' efforts to encourage acceptance of the new system. But there was also a new twist. In keeping with the premise of acquisition reform (and the IPT initiative in particular), it was *team recognition* that was especially valued. Kaminski was able to introduce the Packard Awards. These commendations were given not to individuals but to teams of people who had worked successfully in an integrated approach to make an acquisition program successful.

In fact, many organizational awards were changed either to reward the *group* rather than the individual or the *results* rather than the process. Awards have always been a method for reinforcing desired workforce behavior. But by changing the criteria upon which award selection was based, leaders focused the workforce on the basis for procurement reform—integrated product development and results-based management.

A third incentive used by the reform leaders was training. It would be useless to devise new approaches to acquisition if the workforce was unable to put them into practice. While good ideas might stem from individual offices and agencies, the entire workforce as well as industry would have to be given the tools to succeed. In short, they needed training. Whether it was conducting market research via the Internet, accomplishing "best-value" source selections, or learning new cost-benefit analysis techniques, there were many skills the workforce needed to make their acceptance of reform possible.

One effort on this front included the creation of the Acquisition Reform Communications Center (ARCC). This is a central coordinating office whose mission is to be a focal point and clearinghouse for reform training efforts. The ARCC organizes satellite broadcasts on different reform topics with guest "experts" as well as panelists from industry and the acquisition workforce allowing viewers to call in with questions or concerns. The ARCC also produces videotapes of these sessions. And in true reform fashion, these training modules are made available to the defense industry as well as to the government workforce.

In addition, OFPP began publishing "Best Practices Guides," which presented nonregulatory suggestions and ideas for implementing new acquisition policies. The handbooks offered straightforward advice on putting reform ideas into practice. OFPP published four guides. But other agencies including the Defense Department followed suit with guides on topics from software acquisition to civil engineering. Based upon feedback from the workforce, Kelman believes that these guides were a well-accepted and crucial component of the reformers, incentive plans.

The guides were a good reference for practitioners, but the leadership also responded with more traditional training courses. This approach included seminars and symposia on reform; coordinated efforts with agencies like the Small Business Administration (with particular focus on reform implications for small businesses); and even "Acquisition Stand Down Days," in which normal business operations are suspended and all-day focus is given to reform initiatives and methods for improving an agency's acquisition approaches. Of course there were also more informal approaches to training—brown bag discussions, town hall meetings, and newsletters. In fact, Preston and Kelman were strong proponents of this informal training approach, arguing that it not only provided a forum for training, but offered an opportunity to exchange good ideas.

In a somewhat unconventional approach to training, Kelman worked directly with commercial training firms. He sent letters to various private sector training vendors, urging them to add certain materials to their courses. Kelman's direct mail approach was beneficial to everyone: Industry was made aware of a new area for business development, and the government workforce got training experts to focus on a new and much-needed curriculum.

In fact, what made the overall training effort so successful was the scope of the approach. From handbooks to seminars to town hall meetings, the leaders were careful to create a program that encompassed a wide range of topics and varied forms of presentation.

Kelman, Preston, Kaminski, and Perry were not so naïve as to believe that procurement reform would be accepted simply on its good merits alone.

They recognized early on that a set of incentives would be needed to create a workforce conducive to change and capable of implementation. Their three-part system of recognition, awards, and training proved to be responsive and practical. With it they created an environment that sought out the good ideas of practitioners and then recognized and praised that valued source. From their use of team awards for innovations in process, to programmatic anecdotes that found their way into their public speeches, reform success stories and the contributions of the workforce were part and parcel of the leaders' plan to create incentives for change. They capitalized on an internal, if latent, source of reform creativity, moving front-line reformers to a position of prominence through awards and frequent recognition. Then they followed with a varied and constant source of education and training. In total it was a considered and effective implementation strategy.

Autonomy vs. Uniformity

Related to the three-part system of recognition, awards, and training was the leaders' remarkable ability to "read" their agencies. Although they were convinced that the bulk of the procurement changes needed to be conceived and implemented by the workforce itself, they also were aware that organizational change as encompassing and ground-breaking as procurement reform demanded clear and forceful direction. Consequently, the leadership effort revolved around a delicate balance of top-down direction with fist-pounding orders on one hand and a more delicate, once-removed appreciation for the ideas and actions of the individual services and the acquisition workforce on the other. It was a balancing act between uniformity and autonomy, between discretion to create the new system and imperatives that the old ways be eliminated.

The reform leaders possessed a rare ability to assess the climate of the department. And, once capturing that essence, they either promoted reform with a top-down push (when initiatives were introduced or demanded greater standardization) or inspired continued front-line involvement (when the workforce responded to freer rein and the initiative lent itself to customization). The leaders could not be in the thick of it, but they needed to be in constant touch. It was a remarkable blend of management strategies in which the dominant strategy was dependent upon the type of reform effort and the willingness of the workforce to accept it.

This feat of leadership is even more impressive when one considers the historic and often unreconcilable problems of factionalization between the Office of the Secretary of Defense (OSD) and the military branches. James Forrestal, the first secretary of defense, once said, "The peacetime mission of the Armed Services is to destroy the secretary of defense."[21] Forrestal's remark underlines a difficulty that all his successors have had to face. Specifically, if a secretary of defense hopes to succeed in revamping the acquisition process, or even submitting a well-rounded, prudent budget proposal, he must gain and maintain the support of the military commanders; yet, his hands are tied to a remarkable degree. These are strong, established organizations that fiercely protect their autonomy and honor their historical legacies. And the military services rightly believe that they know and appreciate better than outsiders what their service members need to do the mission. How then can a department secretary hope to bring about substantive, widespread change?

Certainly, these historic tensions and the factionalization that often arose between the military services and OSD could have had a deleterious effect upon reform success. A potentially serious management predicament needed attention: The leadership team was anxious for individual buying offices to take the initiative, to develop new procurement approaches, and to implement reform, but they did not want to unleash a free-wheeling and uncoordinated effort. Nor did they want competing approaches to reform, leaving some military branches stuck in a pre-reform system and others immersed in a new, streamlined approach. In short, they were unwilling to let the traditional friction between OSD and the services become an insurmountable obstacle to implementation.

Customization of particular reform initiatives to suit the needs of an individual procuring agency would promote greater organizational acceptance. Moreover, best judgment and devolution of authority were tenets of procurement reform. One could not simply disregard them when it came to implementation strategy. Still, in some cases, the services needed to follow the explicit directions of OSD in order for an initiative to be useful and successful department-wide. And a level of uniformity was needed to ensure compatibility between acquisition offices; a shared vision would end the myopic focus that also had plagued the pre-reform system. How did the leadership team handle this dilemma?

In an effort to allay this friction, Kaminski began holding biweekly working lunches with each of the Service Acquisition Executives (SAE). This time-consuming and very visible schedule date on his calendar made it clear that procurement reform could be customized to best fit the mission needs of an organization, but the basic principles of the effort still had to be supported by all the military services. According to Kaminski, "There would be no wedge between OSD and the services on this [acquisition reform]."[22] Indeed, the technique worked well. Each SAE led reform within his own service, but did so in a manner that supported the overall thrust of the administration's reform concepts.

The leaders also employed another tactic. They adapted their implementation plans according to the particular reform initiative. In general, the leadership wanted to give as much discretion and autonomy to the government procuring agencies as possible. Consequently, for the bulk of the initiatives—the Integrated Product Teams, commercial item purchases, and improved communication strategies—the agencies developed initiatives and practices that best suited their organization. According to Kaminski, speed of implementation and a desire for acceptance overrode the strict need for uniformity among these reform efforts. Indeed, the opportunity to customize the initiatives created incentive within the workforce to accept reform.

While this approach was appropriate for the bulk of the reform efforts, at other times uniformity of operation was more crucial. Generally a more top-down approach was needed when (1) introducing a major initiative or (2) when a more consistent department-wide application was necessary. Consider, for example, the milspec reform initiative. Although Perry's intent was to have the individual procuring agencies devise performance specifications that met programmatic needs, the initial effort to eliminate the long-standing, much embedded milspec design system demanded that a forceful, top-down directive be announced. Later, as the reform progressed, individual offices could customize the approach, using more commercial specifications or relying upon performance specifications alone, or even utilizing new contractor-conceived standards.

In other cases the leaders demanded continued compliance with definite guidelines. Perry opted for a more rigorous adherence to uniform standards for the past performance initiative. Past performance data needed to be collected in a systematic and consistent way in order to provide useful information to all the military services during source selection processes. To ensure integrity of the data and an equitable use of information across the entire department, a consistent approach was required. This consistency of effort and standardized collection system was fostered by an educational campaign. One of the crucial elements was OFPP's publication of the "Best Practices Guide to Past Performance." But as Under Secretary Kaminski pointed out, this uniform approach, while necessary, also slowed implementation of the initiative.

The leaders' efforts to demand uniformity were not always as successful as they had been with the past performance initiative. The effort to introduce greater use of electronic commerce (EC) as a move toward "paperless" acquisition was hailed as a productivity enhancement of tremendous proportion. In fact, the Federal Acquisition Streamlining Act of 1994 specifically called for the creation of a government-wide EC/EDI initiative known as FACNET—the Federal Acquisition Computer Network. FACNET required the establishment of an electronic architecture and infrastructure that would enable *all* federal agencies and vendors to do business electronically and in a standard way. Lawmakers envisioned a network that was identical for any user regardless of what was being bought, which agency was conducting the purchase, where the seller was located, or whether the seller was a large conglomerate or a small business. Through FACNET, industry would have the ability to access information on almost any federal contracting opportunity.

These requirements meant that FACNET needed to serve *any* company with only a minimum of technical requirements. And, it needed to be suited for *any* federal solicitation, from purchases of ammunition at DoD to photocopying services for the Government Printing Office. This was a broad and definitive set of requirements for a government-wide acquisition network. Unfortunately, the uniformity that leaders sought to bring with FACNET turned out to be too restrictive. The system was plagued by a variety of operational troubles. Moreover, for many businesses, the costs of becoming FACNET-compliant were simply too high. The start-up and recurring costs could not be offset by the limited number and value of procurement actions that the FACNET system handled. The result: This government-wide acquisition computer network was never adopted with the speed and dedication that leaders envisioned. At bottom, the leaders had tilted too heavily on the side of uniformity. As they discovered, unless the electronic commerce initiative was tailored to the organization and matched the resources of the procuring organization and the resources of its customary vendors, then it would not be supported by that acquisition community. In this case, a directive to apply strictly uniform standards was inappropriate and ultimately unfulfilled.

Although the promise of FACNET was never realized, the leaders discovered that the workforce was not averse to utilizing new electronic technologies. In fact, the workforce moved swiftly and with great vigor in adopting the Internet as a tool for market research, for communications with industry, and even for purchasing small dollar items. Acquisition practitioners showed, with great determination and drive, a desire to use the new technology tools to improve their procurement process.

With the exception of FACNET, Perry, Preston, Kaminski, and Kelman were very much on target in assessing how best to navigate between uniformity and adherence to common standards on one side, and flexibility of approach and customized application on the other. Generally, they showed a tremendous deference to the desires of the workforce and industry. And for the majority of the reform initiatives, they allowed these practitioners to design implementation processes that worked best for the buying offices. But as with the past performance effort—and sometimes when introducing a reform effort—it was necessary to push down direct and unwaiverable demands for implementing reform. Of course knowing when to ease the directives and relinquish control was a key factor in their successful implementation strategy.

Capitalizing on Climate

Using history as a guide, one might assume that any attempt at defense procurement reform would be nothing extraordinary, just one more in a string of reports. In fact, the odds would have favored a short burst of effort followed by a stack of paper and not much action. However, this time there were other history-making events to consider. Indeed, the political, technological, and national security environments fundamentally altered the situation. And while the leaders of acquisition reform cannot take credit for these important, world-altering circumstances, they must be commended for recognizing the unique opportunities presented and for moving swiftly and surely.

In the early 1990s, the country was basking in its victories in the Cold War and Desert Storm. There was a public sentiment that it was time to scale back; the nation was looking for the so-termed "peace dividend." Many leaders in government wanted to reduce the size of the armed forces, to reallocate funds to other national priorities, to reconfigure the defense industrial base, and to reconsider the nation's "stockpile strategy" for weapons and armaments. It was appropriate that the Pentagon leadership reevaluate the traditional procurement system—a process that touched on all those elements. It was time for review and revision.

Defense leaders could now devote more resources to reinventing their procurement operations. It was not that the notion of acquisition reform had never been developed or even appreciated. But in the prioritization of efforts, fighting the Cold War was an appropriate reason for leaders to push acquisition reform to the background. And when the issue did bubble up to the top for consideration, it was not an impassioned desire for efficient government but a response to scandal. To clamp down on the indiscretions and crimes of a few, another layer of rules would be applied across the entire bureaucracy. Previous efforts were never integrated efforts to repair the inefficiencies of the entire system. That piecemeal effort was about to change.

The new international conditions enabled innovative thinking. But so too did the technological realities of the times. The United States was witnessing an unprecedented advance in information technology. Design-to-market timetables had accelerated sharply. New applications in telecommunications and advances in software and hardware development were happening with great speed.

Commercial advances in these sciences were outpacing DoD's traditional role as a trailblazer in high-tech R&D. Defense leaders knew the horror stories of the Pentagon's inability to buy the latest technologies even as commercial firms sold state-of-the-art products to private customers. They knew the price tags on their custom-made weapons and support systems were eating up funds, causing a reduction in force modernization. The leaders worked from the DoD's historical legacy that held continual technology advances in high regard. But they were also realistic about the source of the new breakthroughs. The commercial firms were developing the breakthroughs faster than the Pentagon. Leaders reasoned that it was better to capitalize on this trend than to buck a wave they had no hope of fighting. The answer was to move toward integration of more commercial firms as DoD product sources, a condition that could only be achieved through reform of milspecs and traditional source selection processes.

Still defense procurement was only partly about the technology needed to create the weapons. Defense acquisition had been operating in much the same way for four decades; changing it would mean significant cultural changes. Some of those changes would require statutory modifications. Others were regulatory but would still require the visible support of the nation's highest leaders. That meant political assistance.

A leadership team with a combination of experience and empowerment could do remarkable things. The reform leaders had the group commitment and experience to move rapidly to introduce their initiatives. What they also needed was the political support of the White House and Congress. Both were present.

Clinton had made his reinvention goals public and a priority. Recall that presidential candidate Clinton had campaigned on a promise to create a federal government that was leaner and more responsive to its taxpayer customers. Accordingly, President Clinton initiated an effort to reform government operations. Under Vice President Gore's leadership, the administration launched a national agenda for reinventing government—the National Performance Review (NPR). The six-month effort to review all systems within the government was a measure to create change within all facets of government operations, including defense procurement. Perhaps it was the president's reputation as a "policy wonk"; maybe it was Vice President Gore's commitment to his first major public policy initiative. Whatever it was, strong leadership for procurement reform at the top of government was critical in the reform effort. It allowed Aspin and Perry to nominate an entire slate of candidates for appointed positions within the Pentagon. The common theme among these candidates was procurement reform. Indeed, White House support of the effort inspired a team of dedicated leaders who made changing acquisition a top priority. In addition, the publicity surrounding the president's NPR advanced the defense procurement reform effort. The political commitment to reinvention fueled the defense reform rhetoric and showed Defense Department personnel that they were part of an important presidential effort.

Congress for its part was also supportive—a position that had not historically been its role. But Congress was responding to the public demand for a peace dividend and was not about to be seen as an obstacle for fixing a system most Americans believed needed improvement. A rather unglamorous but very important part of the puzzle was Section 800 of the Fiscal Year 1991 National Defense Authorization Act. That section of the act created the Acquisition Law Advisory Panel, which came to be known as the "Section 800 Panel." Like many study groups before it, the Section 800 Panel was to investigate the inefficiencies of the defense procurement system and to suggest remedies for the problems it uncovered. Given the climate of reduction, Congress requested that the Section 800 Panel actually rewrite statutory code based upon their findings. The panel's report provided Congress with a vehicle to respond to public opinion, as it became the foundation for the Federal Acquisition Streamlining Act (FASA) of 1994.

Even the partisan divisions that might normally derail congressional objectives were not present. Republicans are loath to oppose any initiative that deregulates a system swarming in restrictions, governmental control, and oversight. Although reducing DoD funding to the levels desired by Democrats was not their intent, conservatives were not opposed to an overhaul of the acquisition system that untied the hands of defense contractors. Democrats, for their part, were siding with their new president, the Democratic initiative to reinvent government, and a chance to reduce defense spending in favor of other allocations. The result was a winning combination of policy outcomes.

Inspired by world events, technological advances, commercial trends toward industrial streamlining, and personal appreciation for reform of government operations, the president and congressional leaders had set the stage for defense procurement reform. Indeed, the Perry Pentagon had tremendous backing from the Clinton administration and the Congress: They had the benefit of acquisition reform legislation, a public campaign to support reinvention of government, and the ability to choose their own reform-minded appointees. Moreover, the reform leaders moved quickly to take advantage of the political opportunities—a condition that would not last forever. This political support, in combination with the leaders' own personal commitment to reform, allowed them to move further and faster than ever before.

The climate of the era—political, technological, and national security—facilitated reform efforts. This cannot be overlooked as a critical

---

"Too Many Good Intentions: Making FASA"

Only days after Steve Kelman's confirmation, the OFPP administrator began an effort to save the stalled and potentially fatal legislative process surrounding the Federal Acquisition Streamlining Act of 1994 (FASA). Friction between the Defense Department, the Office of the Vice President, and the Senate threatened to derail the effort to gain statutory changes in procurement law. The Pentagon wanted an aggressive bill that would take a firm stand in deregulating the procurement system. The Senate bill was less hard-hitting and assertive than expected, given the "Section 800 Panel" recommendations. As a result, a long list of recommended changes to strengthen the bill came from the Pentagon. This in turn upset the Senators who claimed that such a major overhaul could not be passed as quickly as the administration would like. Indeed, the Office of the Vice President was anxious to see reform legislation passed quickly, seeking to create momentum for the reinvention effort.

Kelman sided in part with the Defense Department, agreeing that more substantive and NPR-related provisions should be added to the bill. But he also understood the administration's perspective and appreciated how failure to pass any reform legislation would be a detriment to the reinvention and procurement reform efforts. In the end, Kelman's negotiation skills resulted in seven substantive changes to the bill. The changes brought the bill closer to the Section 800 Panel recommendations, removed provisions that had decreased rather than increased the bill's streamlining effects, and added some specific NPR recommendations.[23] Although the vice president, the Defense Department, and the Senate all appreciated and desired procurement reform, creating a law that satisfied all the good intentions had begun to look treacherous. Reform leaders on all sides could not "have it all." But thanks to skillful brokering, everyone ended up with a winning outcome.

---

element for reform success. It was great leaders taking advantage of those conditions that enabled the widespread and swift adoption of procurement changes. At bottom, the leaders acted with a clarity of vision that allowed them to capitalize on the climate.

Conclusions and Recommendations

The Defense Department has been led by many dedicated public leaders, but their efforts never brought about substantial and widespread changes to the procurement system. The Perry Pentagon was different. Broadly speaking, six factors distinguish this effort from previous initiatives.

1. A Cohesive Leadership Team

One of the most uncommon but essential features about the leaders of defense acquisition reform is the set of unifying characteristics they shared, characteristics not usually found within a cadre of appointed leaders. This report has pointed out that the government's appointed leadership, while well qualified in many ways, often has shortcomings that inhibit the attainment of strategic and cultural change. Limited tenure leads to shortsighted, near-term goals, a lack of strategic planning, a failure to follow through, and the interruption of long-term projects. In addition, a lack of relevant experience often means a sharp learning curve and a delayed start to agency initiatives. The acquisition reform leaders did not have those shortcomings. They had previous government experience, had a strategic outlook for reengineering the procurement system, held their positions for over four years, and had first-hand experience with the acquisition system.

Moreover, most of the people selected for the key acquisition positions had worked together before, either in government or industry. This familiarity allowed the leaders to gain synergy and strength as a team. They all held the same vision for the acquisition system. In fact, Perry had the rare opportunity to nominate a self-chosen slate of key appointments within DoD. He created a complementary leadership team with members who recognized that their selection was based upon a shared commitment to reform. Not only did DoD leaders share a desire to reform the system, but they were prepared to begin the transformation immediately because they were all long-time reform enthusiasts.

This preparation and commitment did not occur by happenstance. Rather, it was a considered strategy initiated by Perry, agreed to by Aspin, authorized by Vice President Gore, sustained by Kaminski and Preston, and expanded by Kelman. Their efforts demonstrate a successful approach to initiating organizational change.

Recommendations:
- *Prioritize organizational goals.* Missteps at the outset can doom an initiative. Decide up front what the key agency objective will be. Then get moving.
- *Choose colleagues and subordinates wisely.* The campaign to institute change begins with the selection of leaders. Membership in the leadership team should be based on shared convictions and personal commitment to the top goal. Be sure all included know the price of admission.
- *Be realistic about timing.* Cultural change is not quick and requires sustained attention.
- *Forge effective relationships with coordinating and staff agencies by starting at the top.* New leaders offer a chance for new interagency cooperation. A clear signal from the top leaders can revitalize stalled or ineffective relationships.

2. Inclusion of Industry and the Acquisition Workforce

Perry, Kelman, Preston, and Kaminski did not simply "order" reform; they brought the bureaucracy into their implementation plan. By using Process Action Teams, by soliciting comments from the "field," by disregarding organizational hierarchy and soliciting recommendations on a nonattribution basis, by including operators in roundtable reform discussions, and by involving industry in a complete and untraditional way, they brought the entire workforce into the reform effort in a way that earlier reform efforts had failed to do.

In part the bureaucracy wanted to be involved, recognizing for themselves that budget figures and manpower numbers meant changes for their organization, whether they participated personally or not. But the leaders' willingness to establish an environment that allowed the workforce to announce their ideas on reform was a creative and successful strategy for instituting the organizational changes.

Although the leaders of reform at the Pentagon were well prepared for their role, they did not attempt a unilateral decree of reform upon the workforce or industry. Striking a complementary balance between advocate and initiator on one side, and facilitator and coordinator on the other, truly allowed the devolution of power to begin immediately. If the leadership team had not had the depth of experience in the acquisition process, had not understood the magnitude of the changes they were seeking, or if they had felt compelled to corral their power and demand change (without recommendation or comment from the workforce), it is doubtful that the reforms would have been as successful.

Recommendations:

- *Include the front-line practitioners in developing any major organizational change.* Often they are the ones who know best what the problems are; and, given the opportunity, they are the best ones to design a solution.
- *Be willing to form untraditional alliances.* Consider *all* the actors. Ultimately, an internal reform will not be successful unless the external actors—industry, legislators, other agencies—are considered. Neglecting their insights only proves problematic in the long run.
- *Be aware that not everyone in the organization will be amenable or even interested in change.* Begin the change process by unleashing what Kelman terms "the internal constituency for change" to get the ball rolling.
- *Create an environment accepting of ideas and conducive to untraditional approaches.* This will move others to join with the initial enthusiasts.
- *Foster a creative workplace environment.* Use a variety of forums, including open dialogue between leaders and practitioners via e-mail, an open door policy, internal conferences, town hall meetings, and brown bag lunch discussions.

3. Continuous Communication

The incorporation of industry and the acquisition workforce was accomplished in concert with another tactic—consistent and continuous communication of the reform effort. The key leaders of acquisition reform were vocal and persistent. Their vision for DoD acquisition system was constantly reiterated. In speech after speech, in testimony, on websites, in memoranda, and in policy letters, the idea that DoD would become "the smartest, most efficient, most effective buyer of goods and services to meet warfighter needs" could be heard over and over. There was persistent and uninterrupted advertising.

A critical component of the communication strategy was the inclusion of reform success stories. Reiterating success stories provided not only a model of desired behavior and incentives for future performance, but as Kelman has pointed out, they were an effective antidote for warding off a reversion to pre-reform ways. What better way to promote reform ideas and to encourage acceptance than through public recognition of new approaches.

Recommendations:

- *Keep communication consistent to avoid atrophy of the issue.* Even a good idea will fade from the limelight absent a concerted effort to maintain its distinction and prominence.

- *Vary the venue.* A full spectrum approach is needed for a successful communications campaign. From brown bag lunches and town hall meetings to national symposia and congressional testimony, use every audience and medium as a pulpit for encouraging change.
- *Market the message.* The three-word slogan "better, faster, cheaper" did not begin to capture the reasons why procurement reform was needed or what it entailed, but it did keep the initiative in the forefront. The workforce could easily latch on to this short, catchy reminder about a huge organizational movement.

4. Recognition, Awards, and Training

Kelman, Preston, Kaminski, and Perry focused on three incentives for achieving acceptance of the various reform initiatives: recognition, awards, and training. It was important that the acquisition workforce acknowledge their critical role in reform: Leaders expected front-line practitioners to be not only the *implementers* but also the *source* of reform initiatives. The leaders focused on this role by publicly recognizing the contributions of the workforce—in speeches, during congressional testimony, in trade publications, and in visits to local buying offices. The accomplishments of the workforce and their innovative ideas for changing defense procurement were an ever-present part of the leaders' management strategies. Still, they did not abandon the tried and true of organizational incentives—awards.

However, Under Secretary Kaminski felt strongly that procurement awards should focus on the same criteria as the reform initiatives themselves. To that end, organizational rather than individual awards became the standard. One could hardly promote the Integrated Product Team reform initiative and then focus solely on individual contributors, failing to recognize the accomplishments of the acquisition program office. The leaders were practicing what they had taught.

Of course, the workforce, even with bright ideas and great individual inspiration could not be expected to implement the reform ideas without training. They needed the knowledge and the practical tools to make the new practices a reality. From the creation of the Acquisition Reform Communication Center, to the Best Practices Guides published by OFPP, to Acquisition Stand-Down days and brown bag tutorial lunches, a full spectrum of training opportunities was prepared.

Recommendations:
- *Push even the best ideas.* Do not expect an organization to accept the changes simply on good merit alone.

- *Focus on the carrots, and use very few sticks.* Procurement reform was about devolution of authority, innovation, and best judgment. Leaders cannot lecture on these values and then crack down with harsh repercussions for setbacks or failures.
- *Spotlight the source of reform.* It creates incentive for repetition.
- *Give the workforce the tools to do the new job.* Training is essential, but it is better applied using a variety of media, from the informal and free-of-charge to the structured and more costly.

5. Autonomy vs. Uniformity

The leaders appreciated the magnitude of the changes they expected. Clearly there was much to be accomplished. And for many of the reforms, it was beneficial to allow the services as much autonomy as possible in defining and implementing the reform notions. Customized approaches were likely to be more easily accepted since they were tailored to the particular needs of a specific buying agency. And yet, to get the ball rolling, to provide for some level of consistency, the top reform leaders needed to provide specific and unwaivering direction. The solution to this dilemma came first from recognition of the potentially serious management problem, and second from a careful determination about which reforms demanded uniformity and which could more easily accommodate variation. The leaders believed that the past performance initiative (and, for a time, the milspec reform) needed specific and unwaivering direction. This slowed the speed of implementation but was necessary for overall success. With the bulk of the other initiatives (IPT, communications, commercial items, and eventually electronic commerce), more autonomy was given to the individual services and buying organizations. As a result, these initiatives gained a momentum and organizational acceptance that would not otherwise have been possible.

Recommendations:
- *Provide as much discretion and autonomy as possible.* Ownership begets responsibility. It also makes implementation faster.
- *Offer clear, top-down direction.* Workforce participation and autonomy can only be achieved *after* the leadership has established the framework. Do not expect practitioners to develop innovations without being given the signal from above.
- *Decide up front when uniformity is crucial.* The workforce will be unwilling to trust top leadership if they are given the autonomy to proceed with a new idea and are later reined in by a leader who changes his mind.

6. Capitalizing on Climate

Perry's team had incredible backing from outside the department in the persons of President Clinton, Vice President Gore, and OFPP Administrator Kelman. The highest leaders within government were ready to enact change. The leaders outside of government were similarly inclined; the defense industry and the public interest groups were ready to implement acquisition reform, at least in the main. Dissension would grow as splinter groups within industry found reason to oppose specific changes. But, overall, during the initiation period when momentum and buy-in are crucial, Perry had them all. It was an enviable situation for a leader.

Ironically, the procurement reform initiatives were not trailblazing management ideas. What distinguished this effort were the leaders. They were combining their shared historical experiences, the practical experience of industry leaders and the acquisition workforce, and the public sentiment and bipartisan commitment to reduce government and increase efficiency. The geopolitical situation moved procurement reform to a more prominent position. The technological exploits of the commercial world accelerated the need for reform. And the intellectual novelty surrounding business reorganization and industrial reengineering fed the government's move toward acquisition reform.

Parts of the acquisition reform effort were innovative, and the application of technology was new, but most of the reforms were recycled editions of past concepts never applied. However, this time they were working. Why? Defense and White House leaders had seized an opportunity. They had capitalized on a unique period of national security, a technological revolution, and bipartisan political support. They had capitalized on climate.

Recommendations:
- *Do not work in a vacuum.* Appreciate the conditions that surround you and work quickly to take advantage of them. They will not last forever.
- *Seek common ground and shared objectives.* Changing conditions— political, technological, national security, even environmental—create new constituencies and the possibility for new partnerships. With a confluence of agendas, progress becomes easier.
- *Technological advances will make the time tested ways of the past obsolete.* Rather than buck a trend one cannot stop, focus on the opportunities it presents. Initiate change quickly, but be ready for the long haul. The big changes take time.

Summary

Perry, Kaminski, Preston, and Kelman were truly skilled leaders. Here was a team of executives committed to defense procurement reform. They capitalized on the political environment of the time and were ready to move when the conditions were right. There was no fumbling over objectives. There were no initial missteps to derail the critical initiation stage. Moreover, as the initiatives progressed, they were capable of enlisting and maintaining the support of political leaders, industry, and the acquisition workforce. They wisely interpreted and marketed their initiative as a "common sense" approach. As such, they did not alienate the defense industry or the acquisition workforce but rather elevated the role of these groups, continuously soliciting their comments and suggestions. And they never let the spotlight fall from the reform effort. They adapted their implementation strategy to fit the type of initiative and the climate of the department, thoughtfully moving between autonomy and uniformity as the situation demanded. In total, it was a successful strategy. And in the end, their diligence and considerate approach prevailed.

Endnotes

1. U.S. General Accounting Office, *Weapons Acquisition: A Rare Opportunity for Lasting Change* (Washington, D.C.: Government Printing Office, 1992) 20.

2. Joseph A. Pegnato, "Procureosclerosis," *National Contract Management Journal*, January 1995, 65.

3. Paul G. Kaminski, *Institutionalizing Standards Reform*, Speech by Under Secretary of Defense (Acquisition and Technology) to 1996 Joint Conference on Standards Reform, Arlington, Virginia, November 13, 1996.

4. Lisa Corbin, *Los Angeles Times*, "Electronic Commerce Strategies," December 1996 (electronic version http://www.govexec.com/tech/articles/1296info.htm) 2.

5. Brian Friel, "Acquisition Regulations Rewritten," *Government Executive*, October 1997, 2.

6. Lisa Corbin, *Los Angeles Times*, "Electronic Commerce Strategies," December 1996 (electronic version http://www.govexec.com/tech/articles/1296info.htm) 2.

7. Office of the Under Secretary of Defense (Acquisition and Technology), *Milspec Reform: Results of the First Two Years* (Washington, D.C.: Department of Defense, June 1996) 2.

8. Lisa Corbin, *Los Angeles Times*, "Electronic Commerce Strategies," December 1996 (electronic version http://www.govexec.com/tech/articles/1296info.htm) 2.

9. As quoted in "Colleen Preston on Acquisition Reform: The Most Critical Factor That Faces Us — Completing That Process of Cultural Change," *Program Manager*, January-February 1997, 24.

10. Steven Kelman, interview with the author, December 1999.

11. Statement of Louis J. Rodrigues, Director, Defense Acquisitions Issues, General Accounting Office before Subcommittees on Military Procurement and Military Readiness, Committee on National Security, House of Representatives, *Linking Workforce Reductions With Better Program Outcomes* (Washington, D.C.: General Accounting Office, April 7, 1997), 6.

12. James W. Fesler and Donald F. Kettl, *The Politics of the Administrative Process* (Chatham, New Jersey: Chatham House Publishers, 1991), 153.

13. Charles L. Beck, Nina Lynn Brokaw, and Brian Kelmar, "A Model for Leading Change: Making Acquisition Reform Work," *Report of the Military Research Fellows of the Defense Systems Management College 1996-1997* (DSMC Press: Fort Belvoir, Virginia, 1997), 5-2.

14. Interview with the author, December 1999.

15. Interview with author, August 25, 1999.

16. Interview with the author, March 14, 2000.

17. William J. Perry, *Specifications and Standards: A New Way of Doing Business* (Washington, D.C.: Secretary of Defense Policy Memorandum, 29 June 1994).

18. Interview with the author, December 1999.

19. Interview with the author, August 25, 1999.

20. Interview with the author, March 14, 2000.

21. J. Ronald Fox, *The Defense Management Challenge: Weapons Acquisition* (Boston: Harvard Business School Press, 1988) 114.

22. Interview with the author, August 25, 1999.

23. Steven Kelman, "White House-Initiated Management Change," in James P. Pfiffner, ed. *The Managerial Presidency* (Texas A&M University Press: College Station, 1999) 239-264.

Appendix:
Major Defense Procurement Reforms

Milspec Reform

A library of standards and regulations known as "milspecs" has been used by the military to prescribe every facet of a weapon's development and production—its technical design, operation, environmental constraints, transportation requirements, maintenance requirements, etc. These legally binding and overly detailed specifications ensured uniformity and precise operating conditions, but at a very high cost. Reformers are replacing this system of unique specifications with commercial and industrial standards, including performance specifications that tell industry "what" needs to be built, but not "how" to make it.

Integrated Product Teams

Traditionally, design approval, operational endorsement, maintenance considerations, and funding authority are not situated in the same individual or even the same office. The fragmentation of decision-making lengthens the acquisition process because there must be a series of reviews and approvals for each corresponding change in design or funding profiles. If these technical-logistical-financial tradeoffs could be made quickly, ideally with both the financial and engineering offices working in tandem, the development process would move more quickly. Reformers recognized that DoD needed flexible, integrated teams with the authority to make far-reaching and timely choices.

Use of Past Performance

Although DoD had long recognized that past performance offered an indication of future capabilities, a systematic and reliable method for collecting and using such data was never fully developed. In many ways, every source selection was a "new ball game." While it offered redemption from programmatic ailments that were beyond a contractor's control (Congressional program budget cuts, for instance), it did nothing to reward valued companies. It provided no incentive for firms to perform above and beyond minimum contract requirements. Now an evaluation of a company's past work is mandatory for all new contract awards, and a systematic collection method is being implemented. Eventually reformers hope that a national, service-wide collection and retrieval system will help incentivize industry and offer insight to government contracting officers who are awarding new contracts.

Improved Communication between Industry and Government

The Pentagon has never fully capitalized on the defense industry as a source of creativity and inspiration for design ideas. A fear of favoritism and corruption in the award of contracts led DoD to construct a wall between itself and industry, prohibiting the free exchange of ideas, needs, and design concepts. What began as a rational approach for ensuring equity and fair opportunity among contractors deteriorated to a point where industry and government personnel did not communicate freely for fear of wrongdoing and reprimand. In the end, the lack of communication resulted in improper specification of weapons, misunderstanding of program requirements, and ultimately a more expensive weapon. Now reformers are including industry as a vital component in weapon designs, involving them earlier in the acquisition process, and even offering financial incentives for their creative approaches to design. A strong reliance on written correspondence (especially during the contract award phase) has given way to oral presentations and greater use of industry-government conferences.

Electronic Commerce and Applied Information Technologies

Beginning in 1993, reformers made a concerted effort to bring Uncle Sam "online." The increased efficiencies made possible by the introduction of information technologies were not lost on the federal government. The acquisition workforce readily accepted the new approach. They have latched onto the Internet as a source for market research on products and suppliers. Contracting officers are now posting contract solicitations on the Internet, buying smaller-priced items with government purchase debit cards, and soon will be making all payments to vendors electronically. However, a provision in the 1994 Federal Acquisition Streamlining Act requiring the creation of a Federal Acquisition Computer Network (or FACNET) has not met with the success legislators and leaders anticipated. Technical architecture problems and third-party network requirements plagued the system, making it less effective than expected.

Greater Use of Commercial Items

Historically the peculiarities of the government marketplace created a wide gulf between commercial and defense contractors. Specialized management and design responsibilities distinguished these two groups. The dichotomy was so great that it prevented the Pentagon from purchasing items from commercial companies even when their costs were cheaper. Reformers sought to change that predicament by eliminating the specialized management and accounting requirements demanded of contractors and by increasing the threshold for so-called "small purchases." This eliminates the need for a time-consuming and rigorous contractor selection process.

CHAPTER THREE

Transforming the Federal Emergency Management Agency: The Renewal and Revitalization of FEMA

R. Steven Daniels
Professor and Chair
Department of Public Policy and Administration
California Sate University, Bakersfield

Carolyn L. Clark-Daniels
Bakersfield, California

Lessons Learned From the Transformation of the Federal Emergency Management Agency (FEMA)

Introduction

An excellent example of a best practice in agency transformation is the revitalization of the Federal Emergency Management Agency (FEMA) under the leadership of Director James Lee Witt. FEMA serves as an instructive case study of how to transform a troubled organization. Many public administration academics and practitioners have studied the changes in FEMA under Director Witt to understand how organizations can be renewed and revitalized.

Lesson 1: Experience Counts—Recruit the Best

Recruitment leadership may be one of the president's and the agency director's most critical decisions at the start of an administration. The appointment of competent and experienced senior agency officials with a strong interest in the agency's policies can overcome even intermittent attention by the president. As long as the senior officials have the direct and constant support of the president, experience, competence, and interest can produce successful policy implementation.

Much of the success of the Federal Emergency Management Agency under James Lee Witt came from President Clinton's confidence in his leadership and competence, a fact that was evident to the president's staff and members of Congress. A senior White House official argued that future presidents should "pick as close as possible to the James Lee Witt model" in selecting agency heads, emphasizing "professionalism, empathy, articulateness with the media and disaster victims, non-political management, and a strong relationship with the President." Unfortunately, consistent recruitment is often the poor stepchild of presidential and agency management. Weak appointees can undermine implementation of the president's program and damage the public image of the administration.

Many of the problems in disaster management under the administration of President George H. W. Bush can be traced to its failure to appoint competent, experienced individuals to the senior positions in FEMA. Under President George H. W. Bush, congressional investigators concluded that FEMA was a "dumping ground" for political appointees.

Many of FEMA's senior officials were transfers from other agencies, often as punishment for political infractions. Bush's only permanent FEMA director was an associate of Chief of Staff John Sununu who served as New Hampshire's transportation director. Conversely, President Clinton's FEMA appointments were all officials with considerable experience in emergency management. Two served as state emergency management directors. Two served as FEMA regional directors. One served as Governor Clinton's liaison with the Arkansas emergency management agency. Their background in emergency management allowed FEMA officials to restructure the agency's mission and organization within a year of the appointment of the new director. The cumulative experience of the senior political employees improved the integration of the agency's various directorates, a critical component of response and recovery to catastrophic disasters.

Lesson 2: Clarify Your Mission

Agencies need a clear mission and well-defined target population. One of the key weaknesses of the "reinventing government" movement's attention to customer service and agency performance is the often unspoken assumption that public agencies, like businesses, have a single, well-defined goal, such as profit, and clearly identified customers. Most public agencies, especially social service agencies, have multiple purposes and clients. Not all of these goals and clients are compatible. Most agencies resolve these conflicts by emphasizing one goal or population more than others. The choice of goals and populations is critical. To perform effectively and efficiently, the agency must define its mission and target population to make the most consistent use of its personnel and resources. This choice cannot be unilateral; it requires the support of both the administration and the agency's authorization and appropriations subcommittees and committees in Congress.

During most of President George H. W. Bush's administration, FEMA was a schizophrenic agency forced to respond to catastrophic disasters with two incompatible missions—preserving the government during nuclear attack and providing support to state and local governments following natural disasters. The lack of cooperation among FEMA's key directorates made effective response and recovery difficult.

James Lee Witt and his senior staff refocused FEMA's mission on emergency management rather than national preparedness. The national preparedness functions were not abandoned, but were integrated with the more basic emergency management functions. The change in focus redefined the agency's primary target population as disaster victims, rather than executive branch officials central to the survivability of national decision-making capacity following a nuclear war.

Lesson 3: Structure Your Agency to Reflect the Agency's Mission

Most public officials recognize the importance of matching agency structure to agency policy goals. Implementing a program using existing agency structures and procedures invites policy conflict and the inefficient use of personnel and resources. One of the leading causes of the proliferation of government agencies is the recognition that matching agency structure to agency mission is easier in a new agency than an ongoing one. Ongoing agencies usually are expected to provide at least some of the new program functions from existing resources. Nevertheless, an ongoing agency with political support, strong presidential and agency leadership, a clear mission, and a well-defined clientele generally can find the wherewithal to implement a new program.

FEMA's structure under President George H. W. Bush reflected its divided mission. The agency's prime missions were divided between the National Preparedness Directorate and the State and Local Programs and Support Directorate. Under Director Witt, FEMA resolved the conflict between national preparedness and disaster assistance by redesigning the agency structure to emphasize the latter. Director Witt separated the operational components of the State and Local Programs and Support Directorate into separate Preparedness, Mitigation, and Response and Recovery Directorates. The functions of the National Preparedness Directorate were spread throughout the agency. In addition, Witt assigned every employee of the agency critical roles during response and recovery operations, regardless of their normal agency functions.

Lesson 4: Leverage the Presidency

Effective policy implementation requires presidential support. Unfortunately, such support is a limited commodity. The demands of the office often focus the attention of the president on crisis decisions, symbolic leadership, and priority setting at the expense of routine decisions, coalition building, and implementation. Presidents frequently shift their attention from one policy priority to another once legislation has been signed into law. The absence of presidential support allows other forces to shape the implementation of presidential policy, frequently with contradictory results. Presidents need not follow administrative performance in detail. Nevertheless, failure to provide consistent policy leadership and appoint sympathetic administrators can lead to policy implementation that undermines the original intent of the statute.

One of the major differences between the George H. W. Bush and Clinton administrations was the level of support provided by the president to disaster management. Bush's disaster response was largely reactive and bypassed the existing disaster management structure. Clinton's disaster management policy was more proactive and politically sensitive. Clinton also improved FEMA's political stature by emphasizing the lead disaster role of the agency and its director, and by raising the FEMA director to cabinet status. One former state emergency management official argued, "Witt's greatest impact was the fact that he linked FEMA to the executive branch, the Executive Office of the President, and the president. Witt had access." Given the increasing vulnerability of the United States population to natural and man-made disasters and the rudimentary steps taken toward sustainable development, access to the president and the elevation of FEMA to cabinet level seem to be critical first steps in ensuring presidential support into the future.

Lesson 5: Use Your Career Staff

None of the changes outlined above will be successful unless the political and career staffs of the agency are well integrated. Effective recruitment of experienced and competent agency leaders and program directors provides a basis for this integration. Of equal importance, however, is the degree to which the policy goals of the administration and the career staff mesh. The more common the policy ideas that are shared between an agency's political and career staff, the greater will be the likelihood of cooperation.

Most of the burden of pursuing cooperation between political and career staff will rest with the agency director. Successful directors achieve policy unity through one of two methods: political management or shared experience. The political managers enforce administration policy directives by issuing clear, consistent, and precise instructions. The more coherent, the more congruous, and the more exact the message, the more difficult it becomes for career staff to ignore or distort the intent of the policy. The Reagan administration changed the direction of federal government policy in many agencies by appointing secretaries or directors with clearly defined conservative philosophies promoting smaller government.

Managers who rely on shared experience most often lead by example. Cooperation between political and career staff arises from shared professional standards and general agreement on policy goals arising from those standards. Successful managers often know as much or more about the current policy functions of the agency as the career staff. Experienced managers also act as effective two-way communication conduits between the president and the career staff. The Clinton administration clearly chose the shared experience strategy in appointing James Lee Witt as FEMA director.

Lesson 6: Don't Be Afraid of the Press

For a modern government agency, the public affairs director plays a critical role in defining successful agency performance. Although most modern journalists are not investigative reporters, the standards of investigative journalism have permeated media coverage of government. A substantial proportion of Pulitzer Prizes for journalism have gone to news organizations that have exposed government malfeasance, misfeasance, and nonfeasance. Therefore, agencies that can enlist the media in the pursuit of agency goals will better manage the flow of information concerning agency success.

Many of FEMA's difficulties under the George H. W. Bush administration arose from its already negative public image in the media. Congressional reports charged that the agency was a "political dumping ground" for unqualified and marginal appointees. News stories highlighted tensions between political and career employees, prompting the creation of a FEMA chapter of the American Federation of Government Employees. FEMA officials aggravated the agency's media problems by trying to force a gay employee to identify other gay employees before releasing his travel funds for an overseas trip. These administrative failings prepared the Washington and national media to look for examples of FEMA incompetence.

Director Witt and Public Affairs Director Morrie Goodman quickly recognized that FEMA under President George H. W. Bush had failed a critical political test. Even though FEMA performed well in some areas during Hurricane Hugo, the Loma Prieta Earthquake, and Hurricane Andrew, the firestorm of media criticism drowned much of this positive information. FEMA was used to operating in anonymity, and had no effective plan for involving the media and, by extension, the public in FEMA operations. As a result, many initial reports of FEMA response were based on inaccurate and incomplete information. Under Witt, Public Affairs Director Goodman and subsequent public affairs directors reshaped FEMA's communications to actively engage the media throughout the response and recovery period. By making the agency more accessible and by providing the media with prompt answers and information, FEMA disarmed much of the inevitable criticism that arose in the immediate aftermath of a disaster. More significantly, the agency opened a two-way channel for information between itself and the disaster victims it was serving.

Lesson 7: Provide Governmental and Nongovernmental Partners a Stake in the Outcome

State and local governments, nonprofit agencies, and private organizations implement most federal domestic policy. The relationship between the federal government and the other organizations is usually as principal and agent. The federal government provides incentives to the implementing organization to induce them to provide federal goods and services; and imposes penalties (usually the reduction or elimination of federal funds) for cooperating organizations that fail to follow federal guidelines.

The absence of direct authority between the federal government and its governmental and nongovernmental partners increases the likelihood that the policy goals of principal and agent will be incompatible. The nature and effectiveness of the federal incentives and penalties becomes critical to the overall success of the policy. The funding penalties are largely blunt instruments whose overuse undermines their effectiveness. The most effective incentives are those that recognize the differing goals of the federal agency's partners and actively enlist the state, local, nonprofit, or private organizations in the development, planning, and implementation of federal response.

Although the federal role has been increasing steadily, the intergovernmental context of disaster management is easy to forget. Only the affected local jurisdictions can provide the kind of direct assistance that most disaster victims require immediately after a disaster. State and federal efforts remain largely supportive and financial. Mitigation and preparedness policies are only as effective as the local economic development policies make them. Under both George H. W. Bush and Clinton, the political realities of disaster assistance steadily increased the scope of federal intervention. Over the long run, however, such federalization does not guarantee the kind of prompt response that comes from adequately prepared state and local jurisdictions. Director Witt has attempted to buck the trend toward federalization by emphasizing the importance of government, nonprofit, and private partnerships.

The FEMA Case Study

Taking Over: FEMA Under President George H. W. Bush

At the start of the George H. W. Bush administration, FEMA was an agency with serious organizational problems that functioned adequately through the Carter and Reagan administrations only because the disasters between 1979 and 1988 were not catastrophic enough to exceed the agency's limited capacity. Unfortunately, the historical experience of the agency under the previous administrations provided President George H. W. Bush with little incentive to overcome FEMA's organizational weaknesses. President Bush did not appoint a permanent agency director until August 1990, 19 months after his inauguration. Presidential attention to disaster management issues largely was reactive, responding to a series of catastrophic disasters throughout the administration.

The disaster agency that President George H. W. Bush inherited was under-funded, loosely structured, poorly integrated, overly specialized in national security preparedness, and weakly led by a succession of political appointees with little emergency management experience. FEMA was adequate for the typical disasters confronted during the Reagan and George H. W. Bush administrations where state and local governments provided significant resources. However, the agency proved entirely unprepared for catastrophic disasters like Hurricanes Hugo and Andrew and the Loma Prieta Earthquake, which shattered state and local capabilities.

Problems to be Fixed: The FEMA Legacy

In the wake of Hurricane Andrew, public and congressional response to FEMA's performance was extremely critical. In 1993, several organizations conducted formal evaluations of FEMA's performance during Hurricane Andrew including the FEMA Inspector General's Office ([FEMA-IG] 1993), the United States General Accounting Office ([USGAO] 1993), and the National Academy of Public Administration ([NAPA] 1993). Both the informal and formal criticisms of FEMA highlighted four critical organizational problems.

Problem 1: The Inconsistency of Presidential Support

During much of the history of federal intervention, emergency management coexisted uneasily with the institutionalized presidency. During the

Cold War, the national security concerns of emergency management (civil defense and continuity of government) seemed more critical and consistently important to presidents than response and recovery to natural disasters. The more formally organized and well-defined functions of commander-in-chief reinforced this focus. On the other hand, effective management of the domestic elements of emergency management (disaster preparedness, mitigation, response, and recovery) suffered from the high impact and low probability of most disaster events, the resulting fluctuation of presidential attention between crisis and indifference, and the need of the president to provide psychological support to the public but maintain administrative distance from the disaster agency's decisions (NAPA 1993: 21-23).

The consolidation of numerous federal emergency management programs into FEMA in 1979 offered the promise of enhanced authority. "The agency thus created came closer to having the size and substance needed to successfully stand outside the institutional presidency and to be of sufficient importance to warrant the attention and support of the presidency when needed (NAPA 1993: 23)." Despite the consolidation, however, a relatively small agency like FEMA found it difficult to command and coordinate much larger agencies without the Cold War connection. The President's executive power proved less useful than his commander-in-chief power in the development of emergency management authority in the institutionalized presidency. In foreign policy crises, FEMA could draw on the president's military authority to assure compliance by other agencies. In disasters, FEMA had less reliable access to the president's executive authority to guarantee performance. The end of the Cold War in 1989 further complicated FEMA's authority problem. One former FEMA and state emergency management official noted to the authors that "the George H. W. Bush administration brought an end to the Cold War, but FEMA was slow to respond."

Problem 2: The "Stovepiping" of FEMA

The unprecedented scope of the disasters (Hurricanes Hugo and Andrew and the Loma Prieta Earthquake) confronting the George H. W. Bush administration overwhelmed both the limited resources and the disjointed organizational structure of FEMA. The various functions and organizations within FEMA never fully integrated after the creation of the agency in 1979. One former senior official at FEMA noted that the agency was in "total organizational chaos. The director was isolated from the directorates and he was isolated from the regions."

NAPA concluded that FEMA lacked a coherent set of governing ideas. The absence of vision and mission prevented the development of core organizational values, which in turn precluded the agency's constituent parts from consolidating into a workable organization (NAPA 1993: 42-43). The lack of core values only reinforced the "stovepiping" of agency functions, the division of the agency into independent and poorly synchronized directorates (FEMA, 1993-1994). Several current and former FEMA officials, some of whom served in FEMA under the Carter, Reagan, George H. W. Bush, and Clinton administrations, specifically identified the key agency problem as stovepiping.

The worst organizational separation and the worst tensions arose between the National Preparedness Directorate and the State and Local Programs and Support Directorate. These directorates performed the primary preparedness and disaster assistance functions of the agency and were continuations of the Federal Preparedness Agency and the Federal Disaster Assistance Administration, respectively. The two directorates were intended to be the core of the dual use strategy envisioned by the President's Reorganization Project in 1978 (McIntyre, May 25, 1978). However, the high level of secrecy associated with the preparedness function made the transfer of information and technology across directorates nearly impossible. As a result, even 10 years after the creation of FEMA, dual use was honored more in the breach than in practice.

Problem 3: The Circumvention of FEMA

The organizational instability and limited resources of the disaster assistance agency often prompted earlier presidents to bypass the agency altogether during catastrophic disasters. Following the Alaskan Earthquake in 1964, the Johnson administration and Congress created the Alaskan Reconstruction Commission (ARC) to fund the rebuilding of the Alaskan cities and towns destroyed by the earthquake and subsequent tsunami. Although the director of the Office of Emergency Planning (OEP) was on the commission, OEP had little responsibility for the recovery operation. After the collapse of the Teton Dam in 1976, the Ford administration quickly concluded that the federal government had political, if not legal, responsibility and used Interior Department authority to compensate for private damages (Lynn, June 5, 1976). The funding was provided by a supplemental appropriation and administered by the Department of the Interior rather than the Federal Disaster Assistance Administration (FDAA).

The George H. W. Bush administration continued this tradition of bypassing FEMA during particularly devastating disasters. After Hurricane Hugo's landfall in South Carolina, President Bush sent Secretary of the Interior Manuel Lujan to assess damages in the Virgin Islands and Puerto Rico (Bates, September 27, 1989). In the aftermath of the Loma Prieta Earthquake on October 17, 1989, the president appointed Secretary of Transportation Samuel Skinner to oversee the recovery operation in California (Skinner, November 16, 1989). In the wake of Hurricane Andrew, President George H. W. Bush went a step further and appointed a task force headed by Secretary of Transportation Andrew

Card to coordinate federal efforts (Bush, August 26, 1992).

The bypassing of the official disaster agency by various presidents had a number of serious consequences. The first was the inevitable duplication of effort. Despite presidential intervention, FEMA and its predecessors nevertheless retained both the inclination and the statutory requirement to intercede on behalf of disaster victims. The separate presidential and agency response efforts unavoidably wasted resources. The second consequence was the management of disaster response and recovery by less qualified personnel. The

President George H. W. Bush at site of the Loma Prieta Earthquake, San Francisco Marina District.

White House staff invariably had much less emergency management experience than permanent agency employees. As a result, each administration that relied heavily on presidential preemption of disaster recovery had a much longer learning curve than administrations that relied on a permanent disaster agency, such as FDAA or FEMA.

The third serious side effect of presidential preemption of disaster relief was politicization. White House interventions generally had more direct and short-term political goals than relief efforts mounted by FEMA and other disaster relief agencies. The final serious side effect of presidential intervention in disaster management was federalization. The centralization of disaster management in the White House usually emphasized response and recovery over mitigation and preparedness. Combined with the short-term, political focus of most White House disaster efforts, the outcome of the federal disaster program has been the gradual shift of responsibility from the state and local governments to the national government.

Problem 4: Reactive versus Proactive Response

During the George H. W. Bush administration, federal law, FEMA regulations, and FEMA policy limited the agency's ability to anticipate disasters for which there was adequate warning. Although FEMA officials were in place 24 hours prior to landfall of both Hurricanes Hugo and Andrew, resources took much longer to deploy. Sufficient quantities of food and clothing did not arrive in Charleston until six days after Hugo's landfall ("Charleston Begs Government for Help," September 28, 1989). Following Hurricane Andrew, FEMA found itself unable to respond quickly despite administrative changes. The bulk of the federal aid effort did not arrive until August 29, again six days after the disaster (Clary, August 29, 1992).

These delays seriously damaged FEMA's political reputation and its support base in Congress. Part of the difficulty rested with FEMA's coordinating function. The Stafford Act required FEMA to coordinate the activities of 26 federal agencies (including FEMA) and the American Red Cross. Most organizations resisted such outside direction. Without top-level presidential support, FEMA found it difficult to achieve rapid response. Coupled with the level of damage in South Carolina in 1989 and South Florida in 1992, FEMA's ability to act was strictly limited. Nevertheless, to most political and media observers, FEMA's performance was unnecessarily bureaucratic and dilatory (Andrews, August 27, 1992; Lippman, August 28, 1992).

FEMA Under James Lee Witt: The Phoenix Rises

The criticism directed at FEMA's response to Hugo, Loma Prieta, and Andrew demoralized agency staff and seriously compromised public confidence in federal response to disasters. Nevertheless, the controversy provided a new president and a new FEMA director a unique opportunity to redefine agency performance.

The Appointment of James Lee Witt

Reflecting President Clinton's commitment to emergency management, in April 1993 James Lee Witt became the first director of FEMA who had extensive emergency management experience. Director Witt brought a different focus to the agency. Several FEMA and White House staffers interviewed by the researchers indicated that he arrived at the agency with a greater knowledge of agency functions, limitations, and possibilities than even long-term employees of the agency.

Witt took over FEMA with several organizational changes in mind:
- The reestablishment of FEMA's authority in disaster management
- The appointment of senior executives with extensive emergency management experience
- The redefinition of FEMA's missions and goals
- The restructuring of the agency along functional lines

- The redesign and reinterpretation of the Stafford Act and supporting legislation
- The creation of effective media and political linkages
- The development of a proactive strategy for disaster response

The Reestablishment of FEMA's Disaster Authority

Critical to FEMA's transformation was presidential confidence in FEMA's ability to perform its statutory functions. President George H. W. Bush bypassed the agency and established independent task forces for the Loma Prieta Earthquake and Hurricanes Hugo and Andrew, relying on his Secretaries of Transportation (Samuel Skinner and Andrew Card) for leadership. By contrast, President Clinton placed primary responsibility for response and recovery with FEMA Director James Lee Witt. President Clinton raised the FEMA directorship to cabinet-level status in February 1996. Interviews with White House personnel conducted by the researchers suggested that the Office of the Secretary of the Cabinet placed a priority status on communications from Director Witt. The Office had more contacts with FEMA's director than with any other cabinet post.

James Lee Witt

James Lee Witt was appointed by President Clinton and confirmed by the U.S. Senate as director of the Federal Emergency Management Agency in 1993. He was the first agency head who came to the position with experience in emergency management, having previously served as the director of the Arkansas Office of Emergency Services for four years.

Mr. Witt's professional career includes the formation of Witt Construction, a commercial and residential building company. After 12 years as a successful businessman and community leader, he was elected county judge for Yell County, serving as the chief elected official of the county, with judicial responsibilities for county and juvenile court. After being re-elected six times to that position, Mr. Witt was tapped by then-Governor Bill Clinton to assume leadership of the Arkansas Office of Emergency Services.

The Appointment of Experienced Emergency Management Executives

Unlike President George H. W. Bush, President Clinton had a strong interest in disaster management. On Witt's recommendation, the President filled the many politically appointed positions in FEMA with individuals with extensive experience in emergency management. Deputy Director Robert M. "Mike" Walker served previously as under secretary of the Army, where, in addition to his general management responsibilities, he supervised the Defense Department's response to domestic disasters. Executive Associate Director for Response and Recovery Lacy E. Suiter worked in the Tennessee Emergency Management Agency for 30 years, the last 12 as its director. Associate Director for Mitigation Michael J. Armstrong worked as Regional Director of Region VIII, after working for more than 10 years in Colorado state and local government specializing in conservation, land use, and personnel matters. Kay Goss, the associate director for preparedness, worked for 12 years as then-Governor Bill Clinton's senior assistant for intergovernmental relations, often acting as liaison with the State Office of Emergency Services.

The Redefinition of FEMA's Mission and Goals

Director Witt's experience and the ongoing criticism of FEMA performance led him to strategies to make FEMA function more productively. Relying on input from FEMA employees, emergency management partners, and an internal reassessment of priorities, the agency developed its first new mission statement in 10 years: "The mission of the Federal Emergency Management Agency is to provide the leadership and support to reduce the loss of life and property and protect our institutions from all types of hazards through a comprehensive, risk-based, all-hazards management program of mitigation, preparedness, response, and recovery" (FEMA 1994).

Under Witt's direction, the agency based future management decisions and programs on six goals related to the new mission:

- Create an emergency management partnership with other federal agencies, state and local governments, volunteer organizations, and the private sector.
- Establish, in concert with FEMA's partners, a national emergency management system that is comprehensive, risk-based, and all-hazards in approach.
- Make hazard mitigation the foundation of the national emergency management system.
- Provide a rapid and effective response to any disaster.
- Strengthen state and local emergency management.
- Revitalize the agency and develop a more effective and involved cadre of FEMA managers, permanent employees, and disaster reservists (FEMA 1994: 2).

The goals reflected a shift in agency focus from national preparedness to disaster assistance. The dominant philosophy became one of customer service. All senior managers in the agency participated in a retreat to outline the customer service strategy. The managers then had to sell the philosophy to FEMA employees and implement training programs.

The Reorganization of FEMA

To better structure the agency to pursue its mission, FEMA undertook an extensive reorganization. Maximizing input from all levels of the agency, FEMA restructured itself over a six-month period in 1993. The new structure reflected the changes in the mission statement and highlighted the agency's commitment to a comprehensive, all-hazards approach to disaster management. The new agency directorates were organized around the basic functions of emergency management: mitigation, preparedness, response, and recovery.

The reorganization ensured rapid and effective response to any disaster. FEMA also overhauled the Disaster Assistance program to take advantage of developing technology (National Performance Review, 1996). It streamlined the disaster application process through teleregistration, computerized application forms, computerized inspection through the use of palm-pad computers, and centralized processing at two locations.

Part of the process of reorganization was Director Witt's commitment to improving agency morale. He actively sought employee input on the reorganization. He made all agency personnel critical elements in the disaster assistance effort. In addition, Witt instituted extensive cross training of FEMA personnel. Under his authority FEMA conducted numerous workshops, retreats, and conferences to educate FEMA staff in the revised mission and

President Clinton talking to California disaster survivors.

President Clinton in Davenport, Iowa, at site of Great Midwestern Floods.

goals of the agency. He empowered employees with more responsibilities and obligations (Schneider 1998), and sought to improve labor-management relations by creating the Labor-Management Partnership Council to maintain strong relationships between senior officials and FEMA staff.

The Redesign and Reinterpretation of the Stafford Act

Before James Lee Witt became director, FEMA had already begun the process of improving coordination among the various elements of disaster response and recovery. In April 1992, FEMA negotiated the Federal Response Plan with other federal agencies and the American Red Cross. The firestorm of criticism that followed Hurricane Andrew revealed serious weaknesses in the Plan. The most serious were FEMA's belief that the Stafford Act (for more information about the Stafford Act, see Appendix II) prevented federal intervention until after the disaster, and FEMA's assumption that federal, state, and local agencies would cooperate without prior planning (Schneider 1998).

One of Director Witt's first actions in cooperation with his senior staff was to broaden the agency's interpretation of the Stafford Act to allow for the prepositioning of personnel and resources when adequate warning existed. The director's plan also included the development of multi-agency Emergency Response Teams, Emergency Support Teams, and Field Assessment Teams with the ability to respond to disasters within four hours of occurrence (FEMA 1996; Schneider 1998). The director worked closely with the interagency Catastrophic Disaster Response Group that served as the focal point for the Federal Response Plan. He also promoted a risk-based, all-hazards emergency management system with state and local governments and directed regional offices to work more closely with their state and local counterparts on a regular basis (FEMA 1994).

The Establishment of an Effective FEMA Media and Political Presence

One of FEMA's most critical failings under President George H. W. Bush, however, was its lack of public visibility and support. In the period following Hurricane Hugo and Loma Prieta, several FEMA officials cited the agency's relative obscurity as an indication that the agency functioned smoothly under most circumstances because it did not receive either much attention or criticism (McAllister, Oct. 6, 1989). By comparison, Witt aggressively increased the agency's attention on its public education function. He continued the *Recovery Times*, a newsletter first developed during Hurricane Andrew that provided direct information on FEMA disaster relief efforts. Under his leadership, FEMA introduced *The Recovery Channel*, a satellite-delivered television production that broadcasts over public television stations and cable networks in areas where disasters are declared.

Unlike many earlier directors of FEMA, Witt was especially sensitive to media and political implications of the agency's decisions. Senior FEMA staff credited FEMA's public affairs director at the start of Witt's tenure, Morrie Goodman, with a significant role in changing the agency's public image. Under Witt and Goodman, FEMA sought to make the media an active partner in the dissemination of disaster information. Given FEMA's poor history with Congress, Witt also aggressively pursued connections with Congress. He testified numerous times before congressional committees, doing so 15 times in his first year alone (FEMA 1994). The Office of Congressional and Governmental Affairs served as a two-way conduit of information between the agency and congressional offices. FEMA used information from these exchanges to improve disaster response in the field.

The Development of a Proactive Strategy

The long-term goal of all of the changes was to decrease disaster costs by refocusing the disaster management system on mitigation, defined as minimizing the probability and scope of future disasters. Witt pursued the mitigation strategy on several fronts. The creation of the Mitigation Directorate combined for the first time the Floodplain Management, Earthquake Hazards Reduction, National Hurricane, National Dam Safety, and post-disaster mitigation programs. In response to Witt's urging following the Great Midwestern Floods, Congress expanded the Hazard Mitigation Grant Program from 15 percent of public assistance funds to 15 percent of all disaster funds, increasing mitigation resources fivefold.

Following the Northridge Earthquake, FEMA reinforced the role of the Federal Coordinating Officer (FCO) in future disasters by introducing a deputy FCO for mitigation.

The most significant mitigation activity that FEMA and Director Witt initiated, however, was Project Impact. Project Impact attempted to build disaster-resistant communities by developing public-private-nonprofit partnerships in local communities, by examining the community's risk of and vulnerability to natural and man-made disasters, by identifying and ranking risk-reduction actions in the community, and by communicating the benefits and responsibilities of mitigation to the disaster resistant community (FEMA, July 1998).

Challenges Ahead for the Next Administrator

Despite the laudable changes in FEMA's mission, operations, and public image, the agency is still not free of problems. President Clinton's decision to increase the political profile of disaster management probably contributed to the increase in requests and declarations during his administration (see Figure 3.1). More seriously, FEMA was slow to develop explicit or more stringent criteria for providing major disaster assistance (FEMA-IG, March 1999; USGAO, March 26, 1998). Both GAO and the FEMA-IG criticized state governors, the president, and FEMA for failing to match requests and findings to factual data or published criteria. In fairness, much of this difficulty rested with the reluctance of members of Congress to abandon their roles as disaster ombudsmen for their districts and states.

Figure 3.1: Number of Major Disaster Declarations and Turndowns, 1953-1998

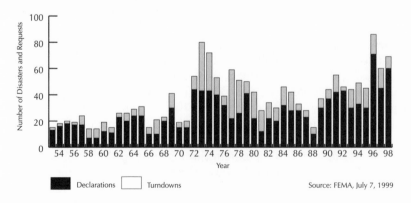

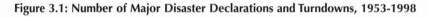

Beyond ambiguity in the declaration process, FEMA's financial system was not operating up to federal standards until 1995. An audit by the FEMA-IG of the Disaster Relief Fund in July 1995 revealed unreliable fund financial data, unclear standards of appropriateness for expenditures, inadequate grants management, irregular and incomplete loan data, and, in several instances, inefficient and uneconomical field operations (FEMA-IG, July 1995).

FEMA did not use appropriate cost-effectiveness criteria to evaluate Project Impact programs. State and local governments did not always submit evaluation data when applying for hazard mitigation grants. Although FEMA reported cost-benefit analysis as the basis for grant recommendations, fully one-third of all hazard mitigation projects were exempted from cost-benefit analysis by FEMA policy. The criteria for these exemptions were rarely clear.

Overall, most of FEMA's current problems arose from Director Witt's decision to balance the dilemma of "works better" and "costs less" in favor of productivity. In practice, pursuing both goals proved unworkable. "Working better" suggested eliminating structures and procedures that inhibited the creative use of resources by FEMA officials. "Costing less" implied constraining those same officials with strategic plans and demanding the achievement of measurable outcomes. Witt clearly chose to "work better." The benefits of this approach were short term and were evident in FEMA's more rapid response and improved public image. The costs were longer term and resulted in poorer evaluation procedures and weaker financial management. A senior congressional staff member investigating Project Impact found it "difficult to measure before and after. Some people consider it [Project Impact] to be a political slush fund."

Director Witt's stature within the Clinton administration deflected much of the criticism that might otherwise result from these financial and evaluation concerns. The director has proven to be adept at anticipating and minimizing dissatisfaction with FEMA policy and operations. He has also undertaken substantial financial reforms since the publication of the 1995 FEMA-IG report. A future director with weaker connections to the White House may find these concerns to be more critical. Pressures from Congress, the Office of Management and Budget, and the General Accounting Office may force the agency to shift the balance back from productivity ("works better") to cost-effectiveness ("costs less").

Bibliography

Andrews, Edmund L. August 27, 1992. "Hurricane Andrew; Storm Poses Test for a Much-Blamed Agency." *New York Times*, Section B, p. 8, Col. 3, National Desk. Accessible by *Lexis-Nexis Academic Universe* Document.

Bates, David Q. September 27, 1989. "Interior Department Report on Hurricane Hugo." Memorandum for the President. White House Office of Records Management (WHORM), DI-002, 082106SS, George Bush Presidential Library.

Bush, George. August 26, 1992. "Remarks on Hurricane Andrew and the Situation in Iraq and an Exchange with Reporters." *Weekly Compilation of Presidential Documents* 28: 1512.

"Charleston Begs Government for Help." September 28, 1989. *St. Louis Post-Dispatch*, p. 10A. Accessible by *Lexis-Nexis Academic Universe* - Document.

Clary, Mike. August 29, 1992. "Federal Disaster Relief Buoys Battered Florida; Hurricane: Local Officials' Animosity Fades as Troops and Supplies Arrive. The Toll of Homeless Rises to 250,000." *Los Angeles Times*, Part A, p. 1, Column 2, National Desk. Accessible by *Lexis-Nexis Academic Universe* - Document.

Federal Emergency Management Agency [FEMA]. 1994. *Reinventing Disaster Response 1994: Northridge Earthquake – The First Five Weeks*. Washington, D.C.: U.S. Government Printing Office.

_____. April 1994. *Renewal of Emergency Management: The FEMA One-Year Report, April 1993-April 1994*. Washington, D.C.: FEMA.

_____. January 24, 1997. "Midwest Floods 1993 (Web site)." Virtual Library and Electronic Reading Room. Accessible on the World Wide Web at http://www.fema.gov/library/mw.htm.

_____. September 30, 1997. *Strategic Plan FY 1998 through FY 2007 with Operational Objectives through FY 2003: Partnership for a Safer Future* (Web site). (http://www.fema.gov/library/splan.pdf). Washington, D.C.: FEMA.

_____. July 1998. *Project Impact: Building a Disaster Resistant Community*. Washington, D.C.: FEMA.

_____. April 1999. *Federal Emergency Response Plan*. Washington, D.C.: FEMA. Accessible on the World Wide Web at http://www.fema.gov/r-n-r/fed1.htm.

_____. July 7, 1999. "Declarations and Turndowns (Detail)." DARIS Run. Washington, D.C.: FEMA.

_____. December 23, 1999. "FEMA Organization." Washington, D.C.: FEMA. Accessible on the World Wide Web at http://www.fema.gov/about/femaorg.htm.

Federal Emergency Management Agency, Office of the Inspector General, Audit Division. January 1993. *FEMA's Disaster Management Program: A Performance Audit after Hurricane Andrew* (H-01-93). Washington, D.C.: FEMA-IG.

_____. July 1995. *Audit of FEMA's Disaster Relief Fund* (H-16-95). Washington, D.C.: FEMA-IG.

Federal Emergency Management Agency, Office of the Inspector General, Inspections Division. March 1999. *Review of Governor's Disaster Requests.* Washington, D.C.: FEMA-IG.

Kettl, Donald F. September 1998. *Reinventing Government: A Fifth-Year Report Card* (CPM 98-1). Washington, D.C.: Brookings Institution. Accessible on the World Wide Web at http://www.brook.edu/gs/cpm/government.pdf.

Lippman, Thomas W. August 28, 1992. "Wounded Agency Hopes to Heal Itself by Helping Hurricane Victims." *Washington Post,* 1st Section, p. A21, The Federal Page. Accessible by *Lexis-Nexis Academic Universe* - Document.

Lott, Neal. September 1993. "The Summer of 1993: Flooding in the Midwest and Drought in the Southeast (TR 93-04)." Washington, D.C.: National Oceanographic and Atmospheric Administration. Accessible on the World Wide Web at the National Virtual Data System http://nndc.noaa.gov/?http://ols.nndc.noaa.gov:7777/plolstore/plsql/olstore.prodspecific?prodnum=C00487-PUB-A0001.

Lynn, James T. June 5, 1976. "Handling of Damages for Teton Dam." Memorandum for the President. Domestic Council. F. Lynn May. Box 9. Folder: FDAA Teton Dam Disaster June 5, 1976 (1). Gerald R. Ford Presidential Library.

McAllister, Bill. October 6, 1989. "FEMA Officials Admit Response to Hugo Was Slow." *Washington Post,* 1st Section, p. A29, The Federal Page. Accessible by *Lexis-Nexis Academic Universe.*

_____. July 31, 1992. "Appropriations Report Calls FEMA 'a Political Dumping Ground.'" *Washington Post,* 1st section, p. A21, The Federal Page. Accessible by *Lexis-Nexis Academic Universe.*

McIntyre, James T. May 25, 1978. "Reorganization of Emergency Preparedness and Response Programs." Memorandum for the President. Staff Offices. Office of the Staff Secretary. Handwriting File. Box 89. Folder 6/2/78. Jimmy Carter Presidential Library.

McLoughlin, David. 1985. "A Framework for Integrated Emergency Management." *Public Administration Review* 45 (January, Special Issue): 165-172.

Mileti, Dennis S. 1999. *Disasters by Design: A Reassessment of Natural Hazards in the United States.* Washington, D.C.: Joseph Henry Press.

National Academy of Public Administration. *Coping with Catastrophe: Building an Emergency Management System to Meet People's Needs in Natural and Manmade Disasters.* Washington, D.C.: NAPA.

National Archives and Records Administration [NARA]. December 2, 1999. *Guide to Federal Records in the National Archives of the United States. Records of the Federal Emergency Management Agency [FEMA]* (Web Site). Washington, D.C.: NARA. Accessible on the World Wide Web at http://www.nara.gov/guide/rg311.htm.

National Partnership for Reinventing Government [NPR]. 1996. Washington, D.C.: NPR. Accessible on the World Wide Web at http://www.npr.gov/cgi-bin/print_hit_bold.pl/library/nprrpt/annrpt/vp-rpt96/appendix/fema.html?federal+emergency+management+agency.

Osborne, David, and Ted Gaebler. 1992. *Reinventing Government: How the Entrepreneurial Spirit Is Transforming the Public Sector.* Reading, MA: Addison-Wesley.

President's Council on Sustainable Development (PCSD). February 1996. *Sustainable America: A New Consensus for Prosperity, Opportunity, and a Healthy Environment for the Future.* Washington, D.C.: PCSD. Accessible on the World Wide Web at http://www2.whitehouse.gov/ PCSD/Publications/Progress_Report.html.

_____. January 1997. *Building on Consensus: A Progress Report on Sustainable America.* Washington, D.C.: PCSD. Accessible on the World Wide Web at http://www2.whitehouse.gov/PCSD/ Publications/TF_Reports/amer-top.htm.

_____. May 1999. *Towards a Sustainable America: Advancing Prosperity, Opportunity, and a Healthy Environment for the 21st Century.* Washington, D.C.: PCSD. Accessible on the World Wide Web at http://www2.whitehouse.gov/PCSD/ Publications/tsa.pdf.

Ryan, Richard A. "Politics of Disaster Relief: Reformed Agency Improves Assistance as It Reaps Benefits of 'Buying Votes.'" *The Detroit News,* July 13, 1997, Outlook, p. B5. Accessible by *Lexis-Nexis Academic Universe.*

Schneider, Saundra K. 1995. *Flirting with Disaster: Public Management in Crisis Situations.* Armonk, NY: M. E. Sharpe.

_____. 1998. "Reinventing Public Administration: A Case Study of the Federal Emergency Management Agency." *Public Administration Quarterly* 22 (Spring): 36-57.

Skinner, Samuel K. November 16, 1989. "Northern California Earthquake Recovery Update." Memorandum for the President. Thru: The Honorable John H. Sununu, Chief of Staff. WHORM, DI002, 098764SS. George Bush Presidential Library.

Sylves, Richard T. 1996. "Redesigning and Administering Federal Emergency Management." Chapter 1 in Richard T. Sylves and William L. Waugh, Jr., eds., *Disaster Management in the U.S. and Canada: The Politics, Policymaking, Administration and Analysis of Emergency Management* (pp. 5-25). Springfield, IL: Charles C. Thomas, Publisher, Ltd.

United States General Accounting Office. July 1993. *Disaster Management: Improving the Nation's Response to Catastrophic Disasters* (GAO/RCED-93-186). Washington, D.C.: USGAO.

United States House of Representatives. Committee on Public Works and Transportation. Subcommittee on Investigations and Oversight. 1994. *Federal Response to Midwest Flooding* (H.Doc. 103-42). 103rd Cong., 1st Sess. October 28, 1993. Washington, D.C.: U.S.G.P.O.

Wines, Michael. September 29, 1989. "Congress Votes Sharp Increase in Storm Relief." *The New York Times*, Section A, p. 1, Col. 5, National Desk. Accessible by *Lexis-Nexis Academic Universe.*

Appendix I:
An Interview with James Lee Witt, Director, Federal Emergency Management Agency

(The interview below is excerpted from May/June 1998 issue of *The Business of Government*, published by The PricewaterhouseCoopers Endowment for The Business of Government.)

In your role as chief executive officer of the Federal Emergency Management Agency (FEMA), how do you define your job?

I found that the job came with a lot of responsibility, and I have taken the job very seriously. Shortly after assuming office, I undertook two major initiatives. First, I worked within the agency to strengthen it. I wanted to involve employees in the future of the agency. Second, I refocused the organization on the customer by placing emphasis on those we were serving externally.

As a new agency head, it was my job to describe where FEMA needed to go. After describing where we wanted to go, it was my job to involve the entire organization. I wanted employee input into how we could best meet our goals because I strongly believe in involving our people. I met with FEMA's senior managers during a three-day retreat in which I described where I thought the agency was heading.

Can you tell us more about your efforts to involve your employees?

I made a special effort to visit with employees, both at headquarters and in the regions. I am constantly asking them what they think we should be doing. I also developed an open-door policy: Any employee can make an appointment to see me on Tuesdays to discuss any matter. For those in the regions, they can call and make telephone appointments to speak with me on Tuesdays. The open-door policy has been very effective. I also started lunch sessions with employees from all over the organization.

I have worked closely with members of the Senior Executive Service (SES) in FEMA. When I came in, I told them that I thought the agency needed new ideas and new faces. I thought that they could all benefit from a rotation system for SES members. All but two of the SES members were enthusiastic about assuming a new job and new challenges. The two who were reluctant turned out to be happy with their new assignments, and they are now two of my most effective senior managers.

How do you spend your time externally?

I spend a lot of time with Congress. Since President Clinton elevated the position of FEMA director to cabinet status, I've spent more time with other cabinet members and on special assignments from the White House. For instance, FEMA was placed in charge of the Church Arson Program. Being in the cabinet has also allowed me to share my experiences at FEMA with other cabinet departments. FEMA is responsible for coordinating 27 federal agencies. This takes time.

What is the best preparation for the position of director of FEMA?

There is no shortcut for experience in emergency management. As a local elected official in Arkansas, I had the opportunity to work with FEMA at the local level. As state director of the Arkansas Office of Emergency Services, I saw how FEMA programs could be run more efficiently and effectively.

In the future, I think it is likely that Congress will require that all FEMA directors have some experience in emergency management. I think state and local experience provides an essential background for this job.

How did you go about selecting your team at FEMA?

When President Clinton appointed me, I asked him for the opportunity to interview all the political appointees who might serve with me in FEMA. The president agreed, and it has made a huge difference. I was able to put together a top-notch team. It has worked out very well.

Another factor that has made a big difference is the "crash" training program that we provide to all new political appointees. The training course discusses all issues, programs, and problems they will be dealing with. It has made a difference. We try to train them during the time period prior to their confirmation. We have also found that our effort in preparing appointees for their confirmation hearings is a tremendous learning experience by itself.

FEMA has dramatically improved its image and performance under your leadership. How did you do it?

As I mentioned before, a major part of the transformation was getting all employees involved. We worked hard at creating a more customer-focused agency. A major initiative was to provide customer service training to all FEMA employees, including senior management. This was a huge undertaking.

Our goal was to make FEMA a better agency, a better place to work, and an agency that provided better service to its customers. We were very pleased that our latest customer survey found that over 85 percent of our clients approved of our programs.

Another aspect of managing change is constant communication to employees. You have to keep employees informed. I have a director's report that goes out weekly. I have received a very positive response to it. The report, two to three pages in length, describes what is going on in the agency and how we are doing in meeting our goals for the agency.

At the same time that we were involving employees, we were also improving the operations of the agency. We decreased the number of our financial accounts from 45 to 14. We simply had too many accounts. We have also moved to quarterly spending plans, which was a major change from the past when we never quite knew how much money we had remaining. I am now holding our senior managers responsible for their spending. In addition, I'm working closely with our chief financial officer in overseeing the agency's financial management systems.

All of our changes at FEMA were based on my trusting my managers. I trusted my people to make the agency work. I gave them authority to do their jobs and I resisted the temptation to micro-manage.

We also found that we could improve the delivery of our services. After the Northridge earthquake, we found ourselves facing long lines of people waiting to apply for loans. Based on that experience, we revamped our 800-telephone system. We also worked with other agencies, such as the Small Business Administration, in improving the loan process. We have dramatically speeded up the process and made it more user friendly. We also gave our field investigators the latest technology to do their jobs. They now all have Palm Pilot computers to take their claims that can then be downloaded and transmitted. The system used to be paper based, with the forms being sent via Federal Express. All these efforts have reduced the cost of an application from $100 to $46. This has resulted in $35 million in savings, as well as improved customer service.

Another major innovation was our initiative to close out as many previous disasters as we could. I found that we were still working on Hurricane

Hugo. We created special closeout task forces across the nation. This was a huge problem in that we were still holding money for those disasters. As a result of this initiative, we have found $485 million that can now be transferred to our emergency disaster account. We anticipate that we will find over $800 million after we close out many of our open accounts. I found that we had over 476 open disasters that needed to be closed out.

We have also worked hard to cut out as much red tape as possible and make the agency more responsive to its customers. We are now operating in a much more business-like environment; we are serving customers and taking responsibility for how our business is run.

What have you learned about public private-sector partnerships from your experience at FEMA?

Our newest project is Project Impact. It is based on creating more public-private partnerships. We have found that while we can't prevent disasters, we can do a much better job at prevention. Investing in prevention can improve the economic impact of disasters, which now cause so much pain, anguish, and suffering by disaster victims.

We have selected seven pilot communities for Project Impact. In these communities, business CEOs and elected local officials, as well as FEMA staff, are working together to undertake prevention initiatives. Our goal is to build disaster-resistant communities. We have learned from our experiences, such as the 1993 Des Moines floods. While we could rebuild the water treatment facility in Iowa at a cost of about $14 million, the local economy lost over $300 million. We now need to take more preventive measures in advance of disasters. Another example is Seattle, which has an important project to retrofit homes to make them more disaster-resistant.

Are you enjoying your second term? You now have the longest tenure of any FEMA director. What are the advantages of a second term?

After the 1996 election, I thought long and hard about returning to Arkansas. But I talked to the President about this and he asked me to stay and finish the job. I am now looking forward to working with Congress in a bipartisan initiative to get FEMA ready for the 21st century. We have made much progress and now have the opportunity to really put FEMA on solid footing for the future. I'm also enjoying our new initiatives, such as Project Impact, which I think can really make a difference.

Appendix II:
History of Federal Emergency Management

Legislative History

The formal history of federal disaster management policy dates from the passage of the Disaster Relief Act of 1950. Prior to 1950, federal response to natural and man-made disaster was largely ad hoc. Between 1803 and 1950, the U.S. Congress enacted 128 separate laws to deal with individual disasters (Sylves 1996). After 1950 the federal government committed itself to supplementing state and local disaster relief on a more systematic basis. At the time, no one realized the precedent-setting nature of the policy change.

The Disaster Relief Act of 1950 for the first time provided a general, federal-level framework for the provision of emergency relief. The initial law provided only "public assistance" to restore public facilities and buildings to pre-disaster standards. Once the precedent of federal intervention had been established, however, considerable pressure developed in the system to expand the federal role (Schneider 1995).

The Disaster Relief Act of 1970 introduced temporary housing, legal services, unemployment insurance, and other individual assistance programs. The Disaster Relief Act of 1974 introduced the distinction between emergency and major disaster assistance and the Individual and Family Grant program. What is most important, the 1974 act broadened federal emergency management policy from the reactive policies of response and recovery to the more proactive policies of mitigation and preparedness. The act also introduced the concept of "multi-hazard" or integrated emergency management: National, state, and local policies should uniformly handle all types of hazards rather than deal with each disaster as a unique event.

Discontent with the continuing ambiguities of federal disaster policies prompted the passage of the Robert T. Stafford Disaster Relief and Emergency Assistance Act of 1988. The act clarified emergency declarations, delineated the relief responsibilities of public institutions, reiterated the importance of mitigation and preparedness functions, and outlined the intergovernmental process for relief. No major legislative changes have occurred since 1988.

The net effect of these legal changes has been a gradual increase in the federal role in disaster assistance. Under the Disaster Relief Act of 1950, the federal government was primarily responsible for the restoration of public facilities. With the passage of the Stafford Act, federal aid expanded to include various kinds of individual, nonprofit, and private assistance. One long-term consequence (as indicated in Figure 3.1) has been an uneven but steady increase in the number of federal disaster requests and declarations (Federal Emergency Management Agency [FEMA], July 7, 1999).

Organizational and Administrative Change in Federal Disaster Management

The gradual expansion of the federal role in disaster assistance was accompanied by considerable organizational instability. The functions of federal disaster management had no long-term organizational home for much of the 1950s, 1960s, and 1970s. Many of the organizational changes that occurred during this period reflected the uneasy coexistence of the disaster assistance, national preparedness, and civil defense functions. The requirement that the statutory disaster agency coordinate the activities of 26 federal agencies (including itself) and the American Red Cross further complicated the organizational ambiguity of emergency management.

Excluding name changes, five different agencies coordinated disaster assistance between 1950 and 1979: the Housing and Home Finance Administration (HHFA), the Office of Defense Mobilization (ODM), the Office of Civil and Defense Mobilization (OCDM), the Office of Emergency Preparedness (OEP), and the Federal Disaster Assistance Administration ([FDAA] National Archives and Records Administration [NARA] 1999, McLoughlin 1985, Schneider 1995). At various times, these agencies were organized as independent agencies, departments within the Executive Office of the President, and sub-cabinet agencies. Whereas FDAA and HHFA exercised only the disaster assistance functions, ODM and OEP performed both disaster and preparedness assignments, and OCDM executed all three primary functions.

Disaster assistance was also seriously understaffed and underfunded for much of its history. One senior FEMA official who worked under OEP, FDAA, and FEMA noted that during Hurricane Camille in 1969, only 15 people staffed the OEP response effort. Disaster relief traditionally was funded with emergency, off-budget appropriations. In some cases, the funding occurred completely independently of existing organizational and financial structures. Following the Alaskan Earthquake in 1964, the U.S. Congress was forced to set up a separate government commission to oversee the recovery effort. The Ford administration found itself confronted with a similar necessity after the collapse of the Teton Dam in 1975.

The Early Years of FEMA

By 1978, the president, Congress, and state and local officials all expressed concern over the state of disaster relief. The sub-cabinet status of the key operational agencies for disaster assistance, preparedness, and civil defense (FDAA, the Federal Preparedness Agency [FPA], and the Defense Civil Preparedness Agency [DCPA] respectively) made it difficult for them to direct the activities of other higher-level agencies. The separation of disaster assistance, preparedness, and civil defense functions under the Disaster Relief Act of 1974 divided responsibility and generated conflict over appropriations. This division limited the disaster system's ability to produce integrated emergency management systems. The treatment of each disaster as an isolated event made the entire disaster assistance system sensitive to political manipulation. To respond to these shortcomings, the President's Reorganization Project recommended that President Carter combine FDAA, FPA, and DCPA into a single, independent disaster assistance agency, an action he approved reluctantly (McIntyre, May 25, 1978: 6).

FEMA, created by Reorganization Plan No. 3 and implemented by Executive Orders 12127 and 12148, had operational difficulties from the start. The FPA, DCPA, and FDAA components remained physically separated for nearly two years. The two main directorates, National Preparedness (created from FPA) and State and Local Programs and Support (created from FDAA), had different organizational cultures that led to "stovepiping" or vertical integration and horizontal separation. Very little communication or support passed between the two directorates. This tendency was exacerbated by the culture of secrecy in National Preparedness and by the Reagan and George H. W. Bush administration's focus on national preparedness over disaster assistance. Despite these problems, agency response did not generate public criticism because no truly catastrophic disasters occurred between 1981 and 1988. The strongest hurricane was Gloria (Category 3) in 1985. The most powerful earthquake was the Coalinga quake in 1983. Although both caused extensive damage, neither produced the level of catastrophic damage that would occur under the George H. W. Bush administration.

Appendix III:
Methodology

Research Questions

In this study, the researchers investigated the evolution of the disaster assistance programs of FEMA from the George H. W. Bush administration to the Clinton administrations. Public perceptions of agency performance improved between the two administrations (Schneider, 1995). We investigated the following broad research questions:

- Do the improved perceptions reflect real improvements in agency performance?
- If real, do the improvements appear to be short term or long term?
- Do the improvements reflect technological breakthroughs, changes in leadership, managerial improvements, or some combination of these factors?

To answer the first question, the authors examined previous evaluations of agency performance by the National Academy of Public Administration (NAPA), the U.S. General Accounting Office (USGAO), and the FEMA Inspector General's (FEMA-IG) office. We also analyzed the agency's 1997 strategic plan (FEMA, Sept. 30, 1997). The second question required an investigation of the change in the agency's organizational culture. The third research question required the identification of the sources of the transformation, which can serve as a model for enhancing the business of government.

Study Methods

Given the six-month period of the grant, the researchers used the case study approach to focus the investigation. The researchers compared FEMA's readiness and response to three catastrophic disasters during the George H. W. Bush administration (Hurricane Hugo, the Loma Prieta Earthquake [both in 1989], and Hurricane Andrew in 1992) to the agency's reaction to two catastrophic disasters during the Clinton administration (the Great Midwestern Floods of 1993 and the Northridge Earthquake in 1994). This research allowed a comparison of disaster responses for which the agency received considerable criticism to ones that generated very positive public relations.

The three George H. W. Bush administration disasters were evaluated from disaster records in the White House Central Files of the Bush Library in College Station, Texas, and published documents. The two Clinton administration disasters were assessed from FEMA records, documents, and Internet material, and interviews with FEMA staff in Washington, D.C., especially the Mitigation, Preparedness, and the Response and Recovery Directorates.

The principal issues relate to differences in management style, technological developments, and performance enhancements that occurred between the administrations. This information will allow the identification of best practices that distinguish the current FEMA effort and will also provide advice to future presidential administrations on the broader questions of policy implementation.

List of Interviews *(positions held in 2000)*

Rob Alexander, Senior Legislative Assistant, U.S. Senator Barbara Boxer (D) – California.

Mike Armstrong, Associate Director, Mitigation Directorate, Federal Emergency Management Agency.

Kris Balderston, Deputy Assistant to the President, Deputy Cabinet Secretary, Clinton administration.

Keith Bea, Specialist in American National Government, Congressional Research Service.

Jane Bullock, Chief of Staff, Federal Emergency Management Agency.

Bryan Giddings, Legislative Assistant, U.S. Senator Bob Graham (D) - Florida.

Morrie Goodman, Director, Office of Public Affairs, Office of the Secretary, Department of Commerce.

Kay Goss, Associate Director, Preparedness and Training Directorate, Federal Emergency Management Agency.

George Haddow, Deputy Chief of Staff, Federal Emergency Management Agency.

Ann Hearst, Director of Special Projects, U.S. Senator Dianne Feinstein (D) – California.

Berke Kulik, Associate Director of Disaster Assistance, Small Business Administration.

Fran McCarthy, Acting Deputy Director, Office of Congressional and Legislative Affairs, Federal Emergency Management Agency.

Bill Medigovich, Director, Office of Emergency Transportation, U.S. Department of Transportation.

George Opfer, Inspector General, Federal Emergency Management Agency.

Marcus Peacock, Senior Professional Staff Member, Subcommittee on Oversight, Investigations, and Emergency Management, Committee on Transportation and Infrastructure, U.S. House of Representatives.

Lacy Suiter, Associate Director, Response and Recovery Directorate, Federal Emergency Management Agency.

James Lee Witt, Director, Federal Emergency Management Agency.

List of Abbreviations

ARC	Alaskan Reconstruction Commission
DAC	Disaster Assistance Center
DCPA	Defense Civil Preparedness Agency
FDAA	Federal Disaster Assistance Administration
FEMA	Federal Emergency Management Agency
FEMA-IG	Federal Emergency Management Agency, Inspector General's Office
FPA	Federal Preparedness Agency
HHFA	Housing and Home Finance Agency
NAPA	National Academy of Public Administration
NARA	National Archives and Records Administration
NPR	National Performance Review
OCDM	Office of Civil and Defense Mobilization
ODM	Office of Defense Mobilization
OEP	Office of Emergency Planning (Preparedness)
PCSD	President's Council on Sustainable Development
USGAO	United States General Accounting Office
WHORM	White House Office of Records Management

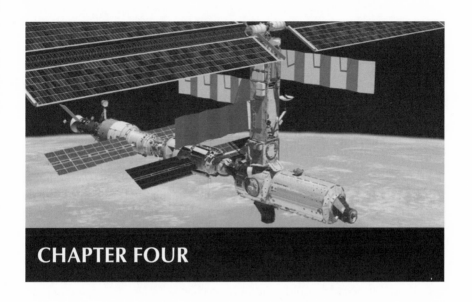

CHAPTER FOUR

Transforming the National Aeronautics and Space Administration: Dan Goldin and the Remaking of NASA

W. Henry Lambright
Professor of Political Science and Public Administration
Director, Center for Environmental Policy and Administration
The Maxwell School of Citizenship and Public Affairs
Syracuse University

Lessons Learned from the National Aeronautics and Space Administration (NASA)[1]

Lesson 1: Who Is Appointed the Agency Executive Matters

The 1990s were a time of turbulence for NASA. The Cold War ended in 1991 with the dissolution of the Soviet Union, taking from NASA its primary referent since *Sputnik*. NASA had to have a new rationale. At the same time, there was a huge budget deficit and agreement between the President and Congress to bring that deficit down. President Clinton and Congress later reinforced this imperative with the aim of balancing the budget. NASA was caught in the middle of changing times and had to adapt. Whoever came in to lead NASA in this decade would have to have change as his top priority and the temperament of a change agent. Such an individual would ideally have certain personal characteristics—a sense of vision; the intellect and managerial experience to run a huge technical organization; political skills; a high tolerance for controversy, since change implies conflict; and a willingness to persevere, given the opportunity, since the task would take many years.

The choice of Dan Goldin was fortuitous given the need. He was a good match for the organization and times. He replaced a man who was forced to leave because he was not viewed as the right person for the challenges facing the agency. There were certainly some rough spots where Goldin was concerned. He was not always sensitive to others' feelings insofar as his administrative style was concerned. He lacked Washington experience and had to learn quickly. On the whole, however, his original appointment and retention by Clinton were good for NASA and the country.

Lesson 2: Make the Most of a Mandate for Change

It helps an administrator if he or she has a clear mandate for change. It is the equivalent of the honeymoon that a President gets following election—a time of grace, when more discretion is granted a leader than usual, and some political constraints are temporarily lifted.

Goldin had a mandate, throughout his tour with George H.W. Bush and Clinton, to align NASA with administration priorities. How he did that was very much left to him as long as he showed results. This alignment was in large part a painful budget process—a downsizing. A "good face" was put on this process under Clinton—called "reinvention." However, it was still painful to the agency.

Beyond this budgetary alignment, there was a policy alignment of historic significance. Whoever was administrator would have to deal with the foreign policy need of the United States to forge a new relationship with the Russians and the world. Goldin, through the Space Station, made NASA a positive instrument of this policy need, elevating NASA to a component of presidential foreign policy and making it more relevant to the times. Goldin had the budgetary mandate handed to him when he arrived. The policy mandate evolved over the 1990s and beyond. Goldin helped forge the policy mandate to which he then responded.

Lesson 3: Adopt a General Strategy of What Needs to Be Done

It is important for an administrator to have a plan of action, however general and vague, when he or she takes command of an agency. If the President chooses a good match, he assures that the individual is knowledgeable about the agency and can hit the ground running. This general strategy, or "mental model," provides the administrator with at least an initial agenda and sense of priorities.[2]

Given the budget constraint Goldin faced when he first was appointed, he was forced to deal with the question, "What do I do to bring NASA's expectations into line with likely funding?" His answer was not to eliminate programs. Rather, he intended to promote technological and managerial reforms that would allow the agency to carry out all its existing programs and even provide funds to make new starts. This basic orientation guided Goldin throughout his tenure. All the major space programs he inherited were still there in 2001. However, they were all vastly different. While critics would say he was unnecessarily ruthless in carrying out his reforms, the fact is that NASA still had high expectations, but operated from a much leaner organization.

In having a mental model, he also had priorities. He saw the agency's top priority as human space exploration, and gave emphasis to pushing the frontier of research and development and abandoning more routine functions. He gave unqualified priority to the Space Station as the linchpin upon which NASA's future depended. And he kept his long-term sights on a manned Mars mission as the next great goal of NASA, the United States, and planet Earth. He knew he would not be around when such a mission became national policy, but he wanted to move NASA in the direction of that mission.

In developing a plan, a leader brings his own background and perspectives. However, he should seek a range of advice from outside and inside the organization, and listen to that advice. There are strategic and tactical dimensions to any plan of action, and some executives are more skilled in one aspect or the other.

The leader needs a general strategy at the outset. He must be willing to adapt that approach as time goes on, depending on events. Goldin generally held to his strategy, but his tactics were critical in the short term, requiring a number of side trips and delays on his way to NASA's future.

Lesson 4: Implement a Change Process Quickly, Instilling Urgency and Gaining as Much Organizational Support as Possible

Translating the leader's general strategy or mental model into agency action requires enlisting the organization. There are two methods for doing so. One is the slower, participatory approach, in which the leader, organization, and its external constituencies come together into a consensus. What results is a policy compromise, but it tends to be more acceptable to those who must carry it out or live with it indefinitely. The other approach is a top-down technique, in which change is forced on the agency and participation yields to the administrator's agenda and timing. Both the bottom-up and top-down approaches require an internal coalition of officials to carry out change. In the bottom-up approach, this cadre would be largely drawn from inside the organization. The top-down approach implies a cadre of the administrator's choosing, often drawn from outside the organization.

Goldin brought no one with him when he took NASA's reins. He initially sought change through the bottom-up strategy. He wanted the organization to reach a consensus and then interact with the public in creating an even larger consensus for change. Unfortunately, this participative strategy was coupled with financial costs. He ordered "red and blue" teams to counter one another in downsizing various programs even as they sought a vision statement and engaged in strategic planning. Cutback planning was a threat to many inside officials. Because it was late in the George H.W. Bush term, many thought they could wait out Goldin through "passive resistance."

Goldin countered with a top-down strategy that reorganized offices and replaced personnel. He made preemptive cuts, heading off budget reductions from his political masters. He felt an urgency to act on the budget, whereas many NASA officials believed growth was still possible. When he made his moves, he did not have a coalition of mid-level leaders ready to help him. Moreover, external political factors constrained him in making changes in the Space Station, NASA's lead program.

The basic lesson is that the ideal change strategy (bottom-up and consensual) takes time, and the leader may not have the time if there is an urgency to act. However, it is incumbent on the leader to communicate that urgency to his organization so that his top-down moves do not appear arbitrary and unnecessarily authoritarian.

Lesson 5: Turn Crisis into Opportunity

A leader can be aided by a threat from the organization's environment in conveying the requisite urgency for change to the organization. The key is the clarity and immediacy of the threat. Goldin felt the threat in the last year of the George H.W. Bush administration, but his organization did not share his perception. In the first year of the Clinton administration, when the Space Station was in jeopardy first from the White House and then from Congress, NASA knew it was in deep trouble. At this point, the threat became a crisis to the viability of the agency.

A crisis situation creates an organizational need for leadership and willingness of the organization to go along, at least for a while. Goldin proved an effective crisis manager. He seized command of Space Station decision making from those formally in charge and created what was, in effect, a parallel unit under his direction, which redesigned the Space Station. Then he gained White House support by linking the Russians with the Space Station. A "summit" between the President and Congress stabilized the budget for the "new" Space Station, which now bore the stamp of Goldin.

In addition, Goldin seized another moment in 1993—the failure of the $1 billion *Mars Observer*—to push through his "faster, better, cheaper" approach to planetary exploration. The Mars program was to be the flagship, de facto, for demonstrating technological and managerial reforms. It would allow NASA to do more while saving money.

Goldin additionally used the *Hubble Telescope* crisis, which also came to a head in 1993, to advantage. *Hubble* had to be fixed or NASA would have no credibility insofar as Space Station construction was concerned. Again, Goldin took command of *Hubble* repair decision making. He gave it organizational and budgetary priority. When *Hubble* was repaired and shown to work in early 1994, Goldin and NASA gained enormously in credibility from the success.

The lesson is that a crisis can help the leader in forwarding major change. Crisis allows the leader to pull power up to himself. Because he spans the boundary across organizational programs and negotiates the space between organization and environment, he is in a strategic position to seize the initiative. He can use a crisis to go beyond incremental to radical change. A leader who successfully leads his organization through a crisis can secure his position, neutralize rivals, and enlarge the change coalition within the organization through his appointees and insiders, who become believers.

Lesson 6: Build on Success

Successful response to crisis can create momentum for further change. Subsequent threats and opportunities in the environment provide occasions for action. For Goldin, "faster, better, cheaper" became his mantra, which he communicated inside and outside the organization—constantly.

He used budget constraint to trigger more change—structural change (focusing on research and development, privatizing Shuttle "operations," decentralizing authority from headquarters to field centers, downsizing personnel especially in headquarters, etc.). However, he held to his initial overall strategy. That is, he would protect existing programs and cut costs through managerial and technological efficiencies, as well as personnel reductions. Also, he would find the money to start new programs with an aim to NASA's future. NASA's future required "faster, better, cheaper" access to space. Hence, he initiated the X-33 program in 1996 as a potential replacement for Space Shuttle.

NASA also required a new mission beyond the Space Station. In the mid-1990s, opportunities opened with the discovery of planets orbiting distant stars. This exciting knowledge helped galvanize the Origins program to explore the cosmos and search for evidence of potential life. The disputed discovery of possible fossilized life in a Mars meteorite also helped boost interest in the Mars planetary exploration program. Goldin made a Mars soil sample return mission a relatively near-term goal. The remarkable success of *Pathfinder* in 1997 seemed to legitimate the acceleration of Mars exploration and Goldin's faster, better, cheaper strategy in general.

Lesson 7: Be Aware of the Limits of Change and Modify Strategies When Flaws Are Detected—Preferably Before They Lead to Organizational Setbacks

A leader has to know the limits of change. A change process pushed too far can lead to failure. A great success (e.g., *Pathfinder*) can give rise to over-optimism as to what can be accomplished. The 1999 Mars failures showed the limits of faster, better, cheaper. If not the limits of the management approach, they certainly showed limits in either how that approach was communicated or heard. A lesson to be drawn is that there are limits to change where technical, financial, and human resources are involved. A leader needs to detect those limits sooner than later. How can a leader get early feedback on a program pushing those limits? He needs good information, and that information must flow upward from those closest to the work.

A hard-driving administrator with a confrontational style can shut off the flow of communication, especially if he gets a reputation for killing the messenger of bad news. Mid-level officials will contribute to the communication blockage due to their own desire to show a "can do" attitude to the boss. Finally, even those at the project level will share the blame for technological over-optimism. Because they succeeded once, they believe they can succeed again, even faster, better, cheaper than before.

A leader and those below have to guard against hubris born of success. Communication, communication, and more communication in an organization is the answer to heading off disaster. The communication has to flow freely and candidly from the bottom to the top and vice versa. A leader has to work overtime to assure he gets such communication and feedback. This is especially the case where the change process is so strongly pushed from the top. If a leader is perceived as closed-minded by his officials and staff, he will be a barrier to his own reforms.

Moreover, if an administrator stays in office long enough, he will see not only success, but also failure in some of his policies, at least if he is innovating and taking risks. The aim is to minimize the failures through realism based on adequate communication within the agency and between the agency and contractors. It is also to learn from mistakes and make timely corrections in hardware, management, and, if need be, the administrator's personal style in dealing with the agency.

Lesson 8: Anticipate Future Needs

An administrator needs to anticipate the future in a range of ways. There are agencies with programs having long lead times, but perhaps none with lead times as long as NASA's. Missions have to be planned a decade or more in advance. Many long-term missions—such as human spaceflight to Mars—will require the creation and development of technological capabilities that do not now exist. The Origins program will need a telescope with strengths well beyond those of *Hubble*. Access to space necessitates a successor to Shuttle. Rockets have to be eventually replaced with a far better technology. In virtually every program of NASA, there are limits to success based on knowledge and human resources, as well as money.

A leader of an organization who thinks beyond a decade's length will emphasize basic research and the education of the next generation of professionals. The lesson is that not only must a leader fight today's battles, he must also look far ahead to coming challenges. It is not enough to provide visionary rhetoric about the future. To turn dreams into reality requires new ideas, understanding, and, above all, a share of the coming generation's best and brightest. Goldin, like most of NASA's leaders, is a child of the first Space Age, whose locus was in the Cold War. The Space Age of the 21st century will need a new generation of leaders, and they must be prepared today.

Leaders of organizations must "think in time."[3] They are individuals who step into an ongoing river of action. They may divert the flow this way or that, but must realize they have but a brief moment to make a difference, for the river moves on. Thinking in time implies a capacity for the longer view, understanding where the river began and envisioning where it may (and should) be headed. By seeing the present with past and future perspectives, a leader is more likely to make positive changes in an agency's course that last.

The NASA Case Study

Introduction

Daniel Goldin, administrator of NASA, stood nervously outside the House legislative chamber June 23, 1993, as lawmakers voted on the future of the Space Station, NASA's lead program. As Goldin saw it, if the Space Station went down, so would NASA as a significant agency and his career at NASA as well. As the vote began, Goldin could see the count recorded on a board outside the chamber. The vote was nip and tuck, with one side and then the other pulling ahead. At 214-214, voting stopped. John Lewis, an African-American congressman from Atlanta who had marched with Martin Luther King, rushed down the hall to enter the chamber and break the deadlock. "Say something to him," whispered Goldin's legislative aide, Jeff Lawrence. "Remind him you are from an ethnic neighborhood in New York City. Maybe you can connect with him. You've got to make your case in 10 seconds." All Goldin could blurt out as Lewis rushed past him was, "Please vote for the Space Station."

Lewis did vote positively, and the Space Station survived, 215-214. "It's a win," a relieved Goldin told the media. But to Lawrence, he confided, "It's exciting to win by one vote, but I never want to do it again."[4] The Space Station vote was the most dramatic of many tests faced by Goldin over what has been the longest continuing tenure in the history of any NASA administrator. The Space Station endured and Goldin survived, and over the years he remade NASA.

Daniel S. Goldin was appointed NASA administrator by President George H.W. Bush in 1992 and served through both Clinton terms. Without question, he has been the most change-oriented administrator since James Webb refashioned a small and weak NASA into a super-organization capable

Sojourner, *the Mars rover, near the Rock Garden on Mars.*

of taking America to the moon in the 1960s. Whereas Webb led an agency that was young and flexible, Goldin dealt with one that was middle-aged and in many ways calcified. It was his task to reinvent NASA in the post-Cold War era and take it into the 21st century. A self-proclaimed "agent of change," Goldin has made a substantial difference. The most influential NASA administrator since Webb, he was also the most controversial leader that NASA has had.

When Goldin became administrator, many observers saw NASA as a bloated bureaucracy pursuing missions that took too long, cost too much, and used technology that was old by the time it was put into space. Goldin instituted a "faster, better, cheaper" approach that increased the number of launches, reduced costs, and put a premium on employing innovative, usually smaller, technology. The technical and public relations returns from space and earth science missions increased substantially. The high point for faster, better, cheaper reforms came in 1997 when *Pathfinder* reached Mars and its tiny *Sojourner* robot separated to inch along the surface. The mission cost a fraction of the expense of previous Mars probes.

Also, Goldin rescued the *Hubble Telescope*, turning despair into triumph, and brought the Space Station back from the brink of political demise. By enlisting the Russians as a partner in a redesigned International Space Station, he elevated the program to the level of presidential foreign policy interest, and gave it new excitement with Congress and the media. He made dramatic moves to privatize the Space Shuttle, and launched the X-33 program to develop the Shuttle's successor.

Further, he cast NASA as a model for the Clinton-Gore reinventing government campaign, creating a long-term vision and strategic plan for the agency. In doing so, he streamlined NASA's civil service workforce by approximately one-third, with the headquarters' civil service and contractor workforce reduced by more than half—without forced layoffs. Finally, he gave a new priority to Mars and launched the Origins program, by which he aimed to create an appealing rationale for space exploration. Its purpose was to understand the universe's past and future, and detect evidence of life beyond Earth.

For his work, Goldin received strong plaudits from the White House and Congress, Democrats and Republicans alike. Vice President Gore called him "the most impressive NASA administrator I have ever worked with." *Aviation Week and Space Technology* said he "delivered on his promise to reshape NASA into a model government agency." The *New York Times* praised Goldin and credited NASA's revitalization "to the influence of Dan Goldin."[5] Long-time NASA space policy analyst John Logsdon lauded Goldin for seeking "great accomplishments" in space and moving the agency in the right direction for the 21st century.[6]

Yet, Goldin has many critics, and his record is not perfect. He has been called inconsistent and impetuous, "Captain Crazy," "paradoxical," and a man with a "dark side."[7] Charming one moment, he can attack another, especially subordinates. His impatient, demanding, intimidating management style engendered a "Goldin-watch" website within NASA where he was criticized incessantly. His reputation for "slaying the messenger" has hurt free communication within the agency and may have contributed to mission failures.[8] There has also been concern that his personnel cutbacks have created potential safety risks for the Space Shuttle. His program to develop a Shuttle successor has proved a bitter disappointment. Faster, better, cheaper turned out to be not necessarily better after *Pathfinder* when *Mars Climate Orbiter* and *Mars Polar Lander* both failed in 1999. Critics of Goldin also say he too easily accepted lower budgets for NASA, whereas other agency heads fought harder for increases. While admitting Goldin helped save the Space Station by linking its fate to the Russians, critics call it a Faustian bargain that caused delays and huge overruns in funding for the International Space Station (ISS).

Thus, Goldin has his supporters and detractors. But historians are more likely to see positive than negative in his overall record. He has been responsible for significant needed change at NASA, and clearly turned around an agency headed downward in reputation and performance. Most of his decisions have been correct, and he has accepted responsibility for errors. While his personality is volatile, the passion in that personality has effectively helped move NASA forward from the Cold War to a new century.

Approach

In understanding Goldin's leadership and change strategies at NASA, it is useful to consider, analytically, the process of policy innovation. One model may be called the evolutionary process.[9] In this model, change is straightforward and incremental. Once a performance gap is recognized, there is a search for options in how to address the problem. The leader selects an option, which is given legitimacy through formal policy-adoption procedures. This policy is then implemented. At an appropriate point, evaluation occurs and modifications are made as required. In time, the change is incorporated into the routines of the agency. There is consolidation and stability while the organization digests the innovation prior to initiation of another policy-change process.

This incremental, evolutionary model of policy change may apply to a number of situations, but not all. There is another model that may be called the radical or discontinuous-change process. The signature of this model is accelerated change.[10] It involves not just one policy innovation, but a sequence of innovations that produce a total effect registering a break with the past. The stages of policy innovation move quickly, sometimes erratically. Implementation of one change is barely underway before another is promulgated, overlapping the previous action. In the radical-change model, there is little time for consolidation. Stability for the organization is rare. The leader is much more assertive than in evolutionary change, forcing the process forward. The leader is entrepreneurial in style, championing change almost as an end rather than the means.

The radical-change model describes NASA under Goldin. While Goldin espouses theories of "total quality management," with its notion of "continuous improvement," and speaks of "non-linear thinking" and even "management by chaos," he also understands the value of stability for implementing innovation. However, in the real world of public management, a leader must deal with not only the administration, but also the politics of change. Much of what Goldin has done has entailed coping with internal resistance and especially reacting to pressures from outside the agency. NASA's politically turbulent environment created conditions under which NASA needed a leader with the temperament of a radical-change administrator. Goldin surely had that kind of temperament. And while he coped with short-term pressures and spoke of participation, he always held to a strategy geared to his strong-willed view of NASA's future. He was himself a prodigious force for change, constantly seeking to maintain initiative and control of his organization.

The Setting: NASA, an Agency in Trouble

In 1992, when Goldin came to NASA, the space agency was in deep trouble. To some extent, the trouble went back to 1986, when *Challenger* exploded shortly after launch. However, the Reagan administration provided funds to replace the lost Shuttle and gave support to NASA to help it recover. NASA's budget was going up when George H.W. Bush became President in 1989, and he continued to back NASA. In fact, he proclaimed, on the anniversary of the Apollo moon landing, a new mission: back to the moon and on to Mars. This mission, known as the Space Exploration Initiative, had no timetable and seemed hopelessly too expensive when NASA estimated the cost at one-half trillion dollars over 30 years.[11] The economy, meanwhile, was suffering and the budget deficit growing. NASA's lead program, the Space Station, begun in 1984, was years behind schedule, billions beyond the projected cost, with no hardware ready.

Worse, the *Hubble Telescope*, launched in 1990 amidst enormous media hype, turned out to have blurred vision. NASA had been roundly criticized after *Challenger*, but the reaction to *Hubble* was in some ways worse, as the space agency now became the subject of ridicule. With numerous other problems involving Shuttle glitches and space science launches, with many programs competing for funds without a sense of priority, NASA seemed adrift. *Time* magazine described NASA as "under siege, its reputation tarnished, its programs in disarray, its future clouded."[12]

A 1991 blue-ribbon presidential commission, headed by former Lockheed Martin Chief Executive Officer Norman Augustine, recounted NASA's many ills and recommended an infusion of new money that would have raised NASA's budget of $14 billion in 1991 to $30 billion in 2000.[13] However, a budget agreement by the President and Congress to rein in expenditures made that kind of increase impossible. Moreover, there was growing concern that NASA Administrator Richard Truly, an admiral and ex-astronaut, was not the man to turn NASA around. He was in constant combat with the National Space Council, a White House coordinating committee headed by Vice President Dan Quayle, and seemed unable to prevent congressional micromanagement and internecine strife among NASA's programs and field centers. The Office of Administrator was weakening as a force for central control. In 1991, Quayle and Presidential Chief of Staff John Sununu decided Truly had to go. This view was endorsed by three former NASA administrators. In early 1992, President George H.W. Bush reluctantly agreed and forced Truly to resign.[14]

Enter Dan Goldin: A Mandate for Change

On April 1, 1992, Daniel Goldin became NASA administrator. He was an "outsider" in terms of the Washington civil space establishment.

Fifty-one, Goldin was vice president and general manager of TRW's Space and Technology Group. Born in New York City, he had received a B.S. in mechanical engineering from City College of New York in 1962. Fascinated with space from boyhood, he had been captivated by *Sputnik* and was anxious to help America win the "space race." He wanted to be an astronaut, but his poor eyesight precluded that option. Instead, he went to work for NASA's Lewis Research Center immediately after college. He intended to help NASA with its next big program beyond Apollo, which he expected would be Mars.

After a few years at Lewis, he felt constrained and sensed the country losing interest in the space program. He put his Mars dream on hold and left NASA in 1967 to join TRW. There, he worked mainly on classified defense programs, rising through the ranks of the giant aerospace company. In the mid-1980s, he became heavily engaged in the nation's top-priority Strategic Defense Initiative, or SDI ("Star Wars"). The National Space Council, which presided over military as well as civil space, took note of Goldin's dynamic and innovative policies at TRW. In the "black" world of military space, Goldin was a rising star with a reputation as a hard-driving innovator. He, in particular, was winning attention by using very advanced microelectronic technology to launch smaller spacecraft.

National Space Council staff saw Goldin as what NASA needed. He was known to be abrasive, but the Council believed NASA required a "shaking up." The biggest issue was whether Goldin could move from the relatively cozy classified-weapons world to the goldfish bowl environment of NASA. He was inexperienced in the political world of Washington.[15]

Why did Goldin take the job? There was no guarantee he would survive beyond January 1993, even if George H.W. Bush won a second term—a victory hardly guaranteed. He had a wife and two grown daughters, a huge salary in industry, and a lot of good reasons to stay in California. But Goldin was ready for a move, flattered by a presidential offer, anxious for public service. He had participated on national aerospace committees and spoken out on the need for greater innovativeness in U.S. technology policy. Perhaps most importantly, he had maintained, from a distance, his love affair with space, especially exploration. He still wanted America to go to Mars—his concept of the country's next great frontier. In agreeing to lead NASA, he felt he was coming home.[16]

In conversations with the White House, he was assured that he—not the National Space Council—would be in charge of NASA. The President wanted Goldin to align NASA's program with budget reality. That reality, he was told by White House staff and senior lawmakers in Congress, was grim. NASA could not expect much more than steady-state funding in the 1990s. Goldin thought about what he would do and how. In spite of the financially pressed environment, he decided that he would maintain all major programs and centers and even try to initiate new starts. His reforms would be technical and managerial. In his senatorial confirmation hearings, he stressed his intent to exercise firm control of NASA and to be in command of civil space policy. "I detect a backbone in the nominee," then Senator Al Gore, chair of the subcommittee conducting the hearings, declared.[17]

Goldin came in with a mandate for change from the White House and Congress. The fact that he was a NASA outsider was regarded as a plus by many observers. The fact that he was a virtual unknown to most of the Washington community and media meant that they did not know what to expect from Goldin.

A Fast Start

Joining NASA April 1, Goldin immediately established himself as a man in a hurry. In his first month, Goldin traveled to all the NASA centers around the country and met with upper managers and employees. He talked with White House officials and legislators, read numerous reports on NASA and its problems, and engaged in wide-ranging conversations with Carl Sagan and other space luminaries. Everywhere, he searched for ideas while pondering the tight budget he faced.[18] His most important formal appointment, not made until November, was General John Dailey as acting deputy director. Recently retired from his post as second in command of the Marines, General Dailey provided a steady internal hand, while Goldin focused largely on the outside role and occasional major decisions affecting internal activities.

In addition, Goldin relied closely on the advice of George Abbey, a NASA veteran on leave to the National Space Council. He also worked closely with the Space Council's staff director, Mark Albrecht. Goldin's proximity to the National Space Council enhanced the impression NASA officials had of him as the Space Council's man, rather than their man. Goldin saw himself chiefly

as the President's man,[19] although George H.W. Bush was seemingly unin-
volved with space policy including his Space Exploration Initiative.

Believing change required a vision, Goldin set about defining what that
vision would be. He also spoke about empowerment with the notion being
the vision would come from a wide-ranging participative process. The problem was that long-term vision making could not be disassociated from
immediate budget cutting. In May, he established at headquarters a set of
teams charged to produce a new direction for NASA. The teams were organized so that each program area would be reviewed by two teams ("red"
and "blue"), with one serving as a critic of the other. He directed the teams
to streamline NASA programs by as much as 30 percent. The results were
to be integrated into the next budget submission in the fall.[20]

Goldin accepted budget constraint as inevitable for NASA in the 1990s,
and his strategy was to have NASA control program cuts rather than have
Congress and the White House impose priorities on the agency. It was a
preemptive-cut strategy, but he found many NASA program officials unwilling to join him in this course of action.

To help the internal teams set priorities, he brought in various external
management experts, even the elderly W. Edward Deming, founding father
of Total Quality Management. Goldin spoke of "cultural change" and "if
you can't measure it, you can't manage it." He also wanted to involve the
public in NASA planning through town meetings after NASA had finished
its own planning.

Goldin heralded the coming of a "new NASA," but officials in NASA
saw an inconsistency. He replaced the existing NASA logo with the insignia
used during the Apollo era. If Goldin wanted NASA to look ahead rather
than back, why return to the Apollo logo? The answer, he said, was that he
wanted to remind NASA of what it could be again.[21] Also, what was perceived as another inconsistency was that while Goldin stressed participation
and empowerment in his rhetoric, he was perfectly willing to make decisions by himself when he thought them necessary. The red-blue team process
was not producing the revolutionary change he believed was required. He
understood the desire of senior officials to wait him out, figuring he would
be gone with the upcoming election. But Goldin did not wait.

In September, six months after his arrival, Goldin announced a significant reorganization that sent a shockwave throughout NASA. While the
decision could be rationalized in strictly organizational terms, the widespread perception in NASA was that Goldin was making a statement about
power—his power vis-à-vis that of other senior officials.

The NASA unit most affected was the Office of Space Science and
Applications (OSSA). OSSA was second only to the manned space program
in NASA in budget and prominence. Len Fisk, leader of OSSA, was an

astute bureaucrat who fought hard for his projects. Influential inside NASA, he had a considerable outside constituency in the scientific community.

Goldin spoke of a "vicious cycle" afflicting OSSA and other NASA entities. He said NASA loaded a large number of experiments onto a few big, expensive machines launched into space. The scale of the enterprise made it take a long time to get the spacecraft developed and operating. Because it took so long to get these spacecraft built, they incorporated obsolete technology by the time they reached orbit. With so much incorporated into these expensive machines, NASA could not afford to lose any of them. The agency had become risk-averse, he said, and emphasized extra-reliable (i.e., less innovative) technology. If anything ever did go wrong, NASA took a huge political hit because so much money and time appeared to have been wasted.

Goldin's solution was faster, better, cheaper technology, taking advantage of the many technical advances outside civil aerospace to produce smaller spacecraft that could be built more quickly, launched more frequently, and cost less. The faster, better, cheaper policy was not new to the world—the National Space Council and SDI had used the concept and Goldin had implemented it at TRW. However, it was new to NASA. Such a policy could allow NASA to take greater risks and fail occasionally. Also, there was a certain public relations value in showing Congress and the American people that NASA was active, an energetic organization launching spacecraft often, rather than at long intervals.

Also, in reorganizing OSSA, Goldin wanted more visibility for the earth observation and life science elements of the enterprise. The former was politically salient given its environmental mission and was particularly of interest to then Senator Gore, whose support NASA needed. The life science element was increasingly vital to the Space Station and its mission. Moreover, the budget crunch made OSSA competitive with Space Station for funds, given its future funding trajectory. Finally, while at TRW, Goldin had crossed swords with OSSA over its designs for large-scale Earth-observing space satellites. Goldin argued that smaller was better. OSSA management had strongly disagreed and told TRW to keep Goldin quiet or risk losing NASA work.[22]

As administrator, Goldin was now in a position to get his way. He split OSSA into three offices.[23] This decision meant that astronomy, Earth observations, and life sciences would each have its own director, but each would preside over a relatively smaller and weaker operation. Fisk was summarily reassigned to a new role as chief scientist, with no program and budget authority. Fisk, whose treatment seemed unnecessarily harsh to many observers, soon left the agency, while Goldin personally reduced the Earth-observation budget by $750 million beyond cuts already absorbed.[24]

As Goldin moved other executives around, in the manner of Fisk, NASA veterans worried about being "Fisked." To those who criticized him for forceful moves that contradicted his talk about participative management, Goldin responded defiantly that some decisions were not subject to debate.[25]

Goldin wanted to also make changes in the Space Station's design and management. But here he was told to hold back by Space Station proponents in the White House and Congress. They told him support in Congress was so tenuous that any change could cost votes on the Hill. What an executive might do in the private sector, or even in the defense world, was limited in the more visible and politicized arena of NASA, at least where the Space Station was at issue.[26]

The Clinton Transition: Turning Crisis into Opportunity

In January 1993, Bill Clinton became President. He disbanded the National Space Council, but the Vice President remained the principal White House official overseeing space. Al Gore, a space enthusiast, was a potential friend of NASA—and Goldin. Exactly where Clinton stood on space was uncertain, but it was clearly not a priority for him. To his surprise, Goldin was retained, in part perhaps because Clinton could not get others to take the job. Whatever the reason, he let Goldin continue, and Goldin was determined to finish the task of change he had started under George H.W. Bush.

There were three crises that occurred over the ensuing year to which Goldin responded decisively and effectively. The way he handled these situations allowed Goldin to strengthen his hand at NASA as a change agent. The first crisis concerned the Space Station. In February, Leon Panetta, director of the Office of Management and Budget, summoned Goldin to the White House, where he told him that the administration intended to cut NASA's budget and perhaps terminate the Space Station. Goldin argued that without the Space Station, the Shuttle had little purpose. With both Station and Shuttle down, there was no manned space program. NASA would lose its core mission and could be broken up, with its parts distributed to other agencies. He pled for time to see if he could bring Space Station costs down to a point acceptable to the Clinton administration.[27]

On March 9, the President formally directed Goldin to find alternative ways the Station's projected bill over the next five years could be cut from the planned $14.4 billion to an administration goal of $9 billion. Goldin established an independent review group, headed by MIT President Charles Vest, to review NASA's recommendations.[28] In early June, NASA provided three approaches for redesign at varying costs, none of which met the

Backdropped against white clouds, the International Space Station moves away from the Space Shuttle Discovery.

President's $9 billion target. After listening to a variety of views, the President chose a hybrid of two of the options, which incorporated much of the work already done on Station design, estimated to cost $10.5 billion over the next five years.[29] While Goldin did not get the precise design option he might have preferred, he did get redesign—which he could not obtain under George H.W. Bush. Moreover, he also was able to commence a major management overhaul he believed essential. These management changes involved personnel reductions, reorganization, and replacement of officials in charge with managers of Goldin's choosing.

The Space Station crisis was not over, however. It now moved to Congress, where the battle was again one of life and death. With Goldin making pleas until the last second, and the White House adding its weight, the Station survived the House vote of June 23 by only one vote.[30] Then, it was back to the executive branch and on to a foreign policy front for Goldin.

The United States and Russia had been talking about joint ventures in space since the Cold War ended in the early 1990s. Under George H.W. Bush, Goldin had gone to Russia to discuss technical options. In the Clinton administration, Russia proposed, in a way more serious than previously, a partnership involving the Space Station. Goldin and Clinton saw the Space Station as a symbol of the new relationship with Russia. But Clinton wanted Russia to agree not to sell certain missile technology to India in order to stem possible proliferation. The two policy interests collided, and while the Space Station debate took place within Congress, the Clinton administration sought a compromise with the Russians. Goldin was a strong proponent of a Space Station partnership. He saw Russia as having technology and experience from which NASA could learn. He even could envision saving money on the Station given Russian cooperation.

On November 29, the Space Station crisis reached a climax with a "summit" meeting at the White House involving the President, various other top executive branch officials including Goldin, and congressional leaders.

Goldin and the Space Station

1992   Goldin appointed; he inherits a Space Station program that is behind schedule and over cost. Goldin moves to redesign the Space Station but is directed to cease doing so by Space Station supporters in the George H. W. Bush White House and Congress.

1993   Goldin is warned by OMB that the Space Station may be terminated due to budget problems. He is ordered by President Clinton to redesign the Space Station to save money. Goldin lobbies the House of Representatives, which comes within one vote of terminating the Station. Goldin helps bring the Russians into the program and agrees to cap yearly spending at $2.1 billion as part of a presidential-congressional "summit" decision to maintain and stabilize the program.

1995– As part of the "new" International Space Station program,
1997   U.S. astronauts train aboard Russian Mir. A series of accidents in 1997 cause great concern about the safety of Mir and put the U.S.-Russia relationship in jeopardy. Goldin defends the Russian partner. Following his assessment of the risks, Goldin sends an astronaut to Mir in spite of public opposition from the NASA Inspector General and House Science Committee Chairman James Sensenbrenner. The overall Space Station program moves ahead.

1998   Continuing Russian financial problems cause delays in the Space Station's development. Although Goldin develops a contingency plan in case Russia does not deliver needed equipment, he continues to support Russian involvement. The President agrees to further subsidize Russian participation. The $2.1 billion annual cap for the Space Station is breached. At the end of the year, the U.S. and Russia launch the first two components of the Space Station, and assembly in space begins.

2000   Following another year of delays and controversy, a U.S.-Russian team is launched to the Space Station to occupy a newly assembled module for living quarters. "Permanent" human habitation of the Space Station begins.

They agreed that the redesigned Space Station be rechristened the International Space Station (ISS), with Russia a new partner—the primary partner—in a venture already featuring Europe, Canada, and Japan. Russia would cancel the impending missile technology transfer with India and would get $100 million a year for four years from NASA for ISS work to compensate for the abrogated missile arrangement. The President and Congress agreed to stable support for the Station over the ensuing five years, provided NASA held ISS costs to $2.1 billion a year.[31]

The second crisis with which Goldin had to deal was the *Hubble Telescope*. The Space Station's prospects could not be totally separated from *Hubble* repair. Goldin regarded *Hubble* repair as make or break for NASA, since if NASA could not repair *Hubble*, how could it build the football-field sized ISS?[32] His strategy was to lift *Hubble* repair from its existing and somewhat conflicted bureaucratic setting and devote to it special managerial priority and resources. He appointed an overall director for this specific mission and made it clear that this director could get to Goldin to overcome any administrative roadblocks. He ordered unprecedented astronaut training for what would be extraordinary work in space. At the turn of the year, the mission was carried out superlatively, with high public attention, and in January 1994, an ebullient Goldin announced *Hubble* repair was a complete success.[33] That summer, with NASA's credibility strengthened by *Hubble*, and a year of Goldin lobbying behind, the vote on ISS came up. The House margin of victory expanded from the one vote of 1993 to 123 votes in 1994.

While ISS and *Hubble* were the most visible crises Goldin faced in the early Clinton administration, there was a third that also marked his unusual capacity to turn adversity to advantage. In August 1993, just three days short of its orbital rendezvous with Mars, the *Mars Observer*, a $1 billion spacecraft, lost contact with Earth. This had been the first Mars probe since *Viking* in 1976, and *Observer's* demise caused great chagrin in NASA, but not for Goldin. While the Space Exploration Initiative of George H.W. Bush was a casualty of first congressional and then Clinton budget cuts, Goldin still fervently wanted to go to Mars. He would keep a focus on Mars through unmanned probes that were faster, better, cheaper than anything planned before. He directed NASA to develop a new Mars effort, with more launches, reoriented to demonstrate his faster, better, cheaper approach.[34]

Becoming a Model for Federal Reinvention

Early on, the Clinton administration proclaimed the need to "reinvent government." Goldin pointed out that he had already been reinventing NASA, starting under George H.W. Bush, and would continue doing so. Goldin's reforms included new procurement rules that threatened cancellation of projects if contractors experienced overruns beyond a certain point. Those reforms were increasingly appreciated by Clinton and Gore. They asked Goldin to do more, and he enthusiastically took up the cause. Goldin declared that he emphasized not the 95 percent of NASA work that was excellent, but the 5 percent that needed improvement. Officials who did not share his enthusiasm for change did not survive. While Goldin continued under Clinton, many others at NASA did not. Before too long, more than half the senior managers—program and center directors—were Goldin's appointees.

In November 1994, the Republicans, for the first time in decades, gained control of Congress. Led by Newt Gingrich, they declared they had a "contract with America" and vowed action. Chastened by this surprising political defeat, Clinton, in January 1995, went beyond "reinvention" to proclaim "the end of Big Government." He promised tax relief, a future balanced budget, and cuts in federal spending. His strategy was one of preemption, a means of holding policy initiative rather than letting Gingrich decide what was cut and by how much. This was the same strategy Goldin had been exercising in his domain. However, as used by the President in relation to agencies, preemption took Goldin by surprise.

With no prior consultation with Goldin, Clinton asked NASA to find $5 billion in additional savings in its spending plan for the next five years. Since the ISS summit had "fenced off" funding for the Space Station, such a cut meant all other NASA programs were in jeopardy. Goldin had hoped his earlier moves had bought him breathing space. For two weeks, he was utterly depressed.

Then, he bounced back, determined once again to be proactive, and declared he would use the cuts as an opportunity to complete the revolution he had begun.[35] From February to May, NASA conducted a strategic planning exercise aimed at determining how NASA could maintain all its programs on far less funds than it had expected. The faster, better, cheaper strategy was not enough. There had to be a restructuring of the agency.

The restructuring strategy had at least four major dimensions: "back to basics," privatizing, decentralizing, and downsizing. While these aspects related to one another, there were differences. "Back to basics" meant focusing on the primary business of NASA, which was research and development (R&D), not operations. The latter was the job of the private sector or other non-R&D agencies. This view led to consideration of what functions NASA could let go and to whom. In February, Goldin commissioned a study that recommended "privatizing" the Shuttle, by which was meant turning over much of the routine work NASA civil servants did to a private contractor.[36] Such action was projected to save program money through efficiencies business could introduce. In November, NASA announced it

---

NASA's Budget in the Goldin Years

Fiscal Year	Total Appropriations (in Billions of Dollars)
1992	14.317
1993	14.310
1994	14.570
1995	13.854
1996	13.886
1997	13.711
1998	13.649
1999	13.655
2000	13.602
2001	14.254

Source: The Budget for Fiscal Year 2001, Historical Tables
(http://w3.access.gpo.gov/usbudget/fy2001/pdf/hist.pdf) pp. 88-90

---

would negotiate a sole-source contract with United Space Alliance, a partnership of the Lockheed Martin and Rockwell corporations specifically formed for Shuttle "operations."[37]

Restructuring also meant decentralizing. In February 1996, for example, Shuttle management was shifted from headquarters to Johnson Space Center in Texas. The decision prompted the resignation of the highly regarded Shuttle chief, Bryan O'Connor, who was at headquarters. O'Connor, a former astronaut, charged that NASA was returning to the organizational design that contributed to the *Challenger* disaster.[38]

Goldin countered that having too many civil servants sign off on flight readiness "represents a threat" to safety, rather than a guarantee of it, because the layering of bureaucrats obfuscated responsibility. Goldin insisted safety was his number one priority. Nevertheless, this element of the restructuring strategy received White House review, which ultimately supported Goldin's move to decentralize.[39]

All these changes eventually led to personnel downsizing, especially at headquarters. Goldin's view was that headquarters was overloaded with

Space Shuttle Endeavour *landing at Edwards.*

unnecessary personnel, since headquarters should be focused on policy related functions of agency-wide relevance and not perform work others in NASA or outside could handle. In April, Goldin announced a major cut in headquarters personnel, a cut so severe and rapid as to constitute a shift in downsizing strategy. Rather than downsize through attrition, this new tact appeared to involve actual layoffs.[40]

Senator Barbara Mikulski of Maryland, the most influential democrat on NASA's Appropriations Committee, "went ballistic." With many NASA employees in her constituency, she placed language in NASA's legislation preventing the announced cutbacks and called Goldin before her committee to explain what he had in mind. Goldin claimed errors in communication and said he would proceed slowly and humanely.[41] No reductions-in-force (layoffs) did take place, and reassignments and attrition became the means to accomplish the downsizing end, which was eventually accomplished.

Nevertheless, the incident reinforced the view in and outside NASA that Goldin might well be correct in his strategies, but the way he went about achieving them—the tactical details—were unnecessarily harsh and insensitive. He wanted to reinvent NASA so it would be stronger, but his methods contributed to morale problems.

Making New Starts

In spite of the criticism, Goldin persevered and had more admirers than detractors among his political masters. Remarkably, these included elected officials as diverse as Clinton and Gingrich. These adversaries both saw Goldin as an able man driving for positive change in an environment marked by financial constraint, partisan wrangling, and even government shutdown.

For Goldin, most of his change strategies had been in management, "how" to carry out existing programs: faster, better, cheaper; restructuring; ISS redesign and Russian partnership. However, he was after even greater changes in "what" NASA would do. He wanted new programs, new starts, or radical redirections of key efforts that would take NASA into the 21st century. There were three dramatic decisions in 1996 that stood out as most central to this strategy.

Goldin was sincere in wanting his agency "to dream again," and his speeches reveal a man of vision capable of looking far ahead. While some of his subordinates were intimidated by his style, others were inspired by his encouragement that they think imaginatively and "big." He engaged in yearly strategic planning with his officials not only to satisfy administration reinvention requirements, but also to get them to envision the future and how they could get there.

As before, events affected the timing of many executive actions. In the mid-1990s, there were striking new discoveries of planets circling stars beyond the sun. Might "other Earths" be out there—with life? NASA's Office of Space Science had in Goldin an administrator who shared its curiosities about the cosmos. In early 1996, Goldin announced a new program called Origins that would seek knowledge about the beginnings and destiny of the universe—and also look for life. This program envisioned a new emphasis on biological research and what was called "astrobiology." There would eventually be an astrobiology institute established at NASA, with a director who was an eminent scientist.[42]

In a related move, in 1996, Goldin used an apparent meteorite discovery to stimulate a second reorientation in the Mars exploration program—which he had first redirected in 1993. Reputable scientists associated with NASA claimed that a meteorite from Mars, found in Antarctica, contained evidence of ancient life. This claim was disputed by other scientists. However, the meteorite statements excited the White House, elements in Congress, the media, and Goldin.[43] He redirected the Mars program from more general science goals toward a search for life (present or past) on Mars.

In effect, Goldin reinvented the Mars program again and made it complementary to Origins (though organizationally separate). NASA would now launch a series of orbiting spacecraft and landers that would go to Mars every two years, culminating in the return of a soil sample to Earth in 2008. This program would also push the faster, better, cheaper philosophy further than ever before to accomplish as much as possible.

Another new start Goldin promoted in 1996 involved launch technology. Human exploration was stymied by launch costs. The Shuttle had not lived up to its promise of frequent, inexpensive, and reliable launches. Goldin badgered aerospace chief executives and his own manned space officials about the need for a breakthrough in launch technology. The Shuttle was aging. Something had to be done.

In 1996, Goldin went to California with Vice President Gore to announce that NASA and Lockheed Martin were forming a partnership in a new program called X-33. The X-33 would be an experimental vehicle, projected to cost $1.4 billion, developed primarily with NASA funds, but also some industry money. Its aim was to demonstrate new technology essential to a Shuttle successor. Once X-33 proved out that technology, Lockheed Martin would develop the operating vehicle, VentureStar, for which it presumably would largely pay.[44]

There were many space analysts who believed the single biggest problem NASA faced in the immediate future was to make human access to space faster, better, cheaper—and safer. Goldin intended, through the X-33/VentureStar program, to deal with this central challenge in a way that innovated technically and managerially. The X-33 involved high risks, as it pushed both frontiers—but that was what Goldin said NASA was all about.

Legitimating Faster, Better, Cheaper

In 1997, President Clinton began his second term, retaining Goldin, who was now a valued member of his administration. The NASA administrator had been in office long enough that he could see the results of some of his early initiatives. Most significantly, there was *Pathfinder*. On July 4, the *Pathfinder* spacecraft landed on Mars. This was a $171 million successor to the $1 billion *Mars Observer*. Almost universally, *Pathfinder* was heralded as legitimating faster, better, cheaper.

People everywhere could experience the Red Planet on television. They also had access to a *Pathfinder* website on their home computers as the *Sojourner* roving vehicle was released and crawled along the Mars surface. Skeptics now grudgingly admitted that faster, better, cheaper could work. Goldin received considerable praise. *Pathfinder* marked the high point of Goldin's personal reputation as a NASA change agent. Many supporters who had heard him criticized over the years felt he had been vindicated.[45]

Not only did *Pathfinder* legitimate faster, better, cheaper and help Goldin, but it also gave NASA and its contractors confidence to push ahead with the Mars sample return program, of which *Pathfinder* was an integral part.

Goldin and Mars

1992 Goldin appointed Administrator; he inherits George H. W. Bush's Space Exploration Initiative (humans to the moon and Mars) and unmanned Mars program.

1993 The Space Exploration Initiative is terminated by Congress and Clinton. The *Mars Observer*, a $1 billion spacecraft, is lost. Goldin uses this loss to capture momentum for reorienting the Mars program toward "faster, better, cheaper" philosophy.

1996 A Mars meteorite is claimed by some scientists to contain ancient bacterial life. Goldin uses the meteorite publicity and excitement to accelerate the Mars program with the aim of finding evidence of life, present or past. The Clinton administration issues a policy statement supporting Goldin by committing to a "robotic presence" on Mars by 2000, and endorsing the faster, better, cheaper philosophy. However, the statement says nothing about human exploration, for which Goldin is a strong advocate.

1997 The *Mars Global Surveyor* orbits Mars; *Pathfinder* lands and releases *Sojourner*, a rover that moves on the surface. This mission cost less than half that of the *Mars Observer*. Goldin's faster, better, cheaper approach is hailed as successful.

1999 The *Mars Climate Orbiter* and *Mars Polar Lander* fail. NASA is brought under intense scrutiny. Investigations by expert panels suggest faster, better, cheaper was pushed too hard, too soon by Goldin and there are limits to this strategy.

2000 Goldin accepts responsibility for setbacks and appoints a new Mars program director. The new director and his associates slow down the Mars program and allow costs to grow. However, the basic goals for the pro- gram remain the same and the faster, better, cheaper approach is retained in what employees perceive as a less doctrinaire form.

Coping with the Russians

While *Pathfinder* indicated the Mars program was going well, the situation with the International Space Station was not so positive. By 1997, it was abundantly clear that Russia was going downhill economically and also not proving particularly reliable as a partner in ISS.

Between 1995 and 1997, U.S. astronauts—as part of the U.S.-Russian arrangement—had traveled to and stayed aboard the Russian space station, Mir, as a way of learning from Russian experience. In 1997, however, Mir suffered a sequence of mishaps, including a fire, collision, computer outages, power failure, and a leak from the *Soyuz* escape capsule docked for Mir. NASA's inspector general and Rep. James Sensenbrenner (R-Wis.), chairman of the House Science Committee, warned Goldin about risking U.S. astronauts on future Mir missions. Goldin had good relations with many in Congress, but Sensenbrenner was a critic who repeatedly scored the decision to partner with Russia.[46]

Goldin asked for an independent review of the risks. With positive recommendations from two sets of experts, he decided to let astronaut David Wolf go to Mir in September. All went well.[47] While safety was paramount in the decision, preservation of the ISS partnership was also important. This was a way to show confidence in the Russians and Mir.

The Mir phase soon ended, giving way in 1998 to even greater worries about Russia and its ability to deliver on its promises. NASA was depending on Russia for certain components that put Russia on what NASA called a "critical path" for development. As delays occurred, Goldin admitted that the decision to allow the United States (and ISS) to be so dependent on Russia was a mistake. While continuing to stand by the Russians publicly (although imploring and badgering them privately), he allowed that Russia would have to be subsidized and the $2.1 billion annual cap on the U.S. Space Station budget imposed at the 1993 summit exceeded. Following the much-heralded Shuttle launch of Senator John Glenn in November 1998, President Clinton acknowledged that the administration would cover additional Station expenses arising from Russia's problems.[48]

At the end of 1998, the U.S. and Russia launched the first two components of ISS and they were linked in space.[49] Another key component to be supplied by Russia continued to be delayed, setting back the overall program. Goldin, pressed hard by Congress, had NASA develop a contingency plan involving new hardware to protect ISS from abrogation of its agreement by Russia. Goldin continued to support his Russian partner, but he was not going to bet the future of ISS on the troubled nation.

Suffering Major Setbacks

In 1999, Goldin saw more problems with ISS delays. Also, the X-33 ran into technological barriers that put it at acute risk as key to post-Shuttle access to space. Shuttle problems also brought about an internal evaluation that indicated personnel cutbacks and reduced government supervision might be raising safety issues. The number of Shuttle flights would have to increase to get ISS assembled, enlarging risks.[50] With White House approval, Goldin reversed course on downsizing and decided to hire employees in key areas. This decision to rethink personnel policy also related to serious setbacks in the Mars program.

First, the *Mars Climate Orbiter* (MCO) in September failed to find the proper trajectory around Mars. Second, the *Mars Polar Lander* (MPL) in December apparently crashed. Third, two microprobes carried on MPL that were to radio data after penetrating several feet into Martian soil did not function. This triple failure, so visible and so unexpected, appalled NASA and its constituents. It was the most serious setback for Goldin of his tenure. He had dealt with troubled programs before, but those were generally inherited from a previous regime. The Mars program bore his personal stamp and embodied not only his greatest hopes for NASA's future, but symbolized the faster, better, cheaper approach. These failures put his overall change strategy in question and tarnished his reputation.[51]

To find out what went wrong, he appointed a number of investigating panels. The most prominent was the Mars Program Independent Assessment Team headed by retired Lockheed Martin executive and former NASA executive Tom Young. The panels determined that the MCO accident was due to human error, confusion in English/metric units that caused navigation software mistakes. The likely cause of the MPL failure was a premature shutdown of landing engines, leading to a crash. No "most probable cause" could be identified for the microprobe failure, but it was concluded that due to inadequate testing the microprobes were not ready for flight in any event.

Beyond the technical issues were the management problems, which were specifically addressed by the Young Panel. Reporting in March 2000, it said that the two spacecraft were underfunded by about 30 percent and suffered from understaffing, inadequate margins, and unapplied institutional expertise. Communication among the principal organizational units was "highly ineffective." The contractor, Lockheed Martin, did not tell NASA's Jet Propulsion Laboratory (JPL), which was managing Lockheed Martin's work, about the risks it saw, and JPL did not adequately inform headquarters about cost problems, or perform its own risk assessments as it should have.[52]

Did the Mars failure mean that Goldin's faster, better, cheaper strategy had not worked? There was much soul-searching on that issue. Goldin went out to JPL and addressed the employees in the wake of the Young report. Afterward, he told the media:

> I asked these people to do incredibly tough things, to push the limits. We were successful and I asked them to push harder and we hit a boundary. And I told them that they should not apologize. They did terrific things and I pushed too hard. And that's why I feel responsible.[53]

NASA made a number of immediate changes in the Mars program, including a delay in follow-up missions pending corrections. NASA also announced a new headquarters post of Mars program director to serve as a single point of contact and deal with communication and other administrative problems.[54]

Congressional hearings followed, along with innumerable editorials and other media comment. It became clear that faster and cheaper were not necessarily always better. While no one stated it was possible or desirable to go back to "the old days" of billion-dollar unmanned Mars spacecraft, there seemed to be agreement that there would have to be adjustments upward in cost. The faster, better, cheaper policy was retained as a general guide. The problem was stated to be one of implementation. But implementation meant dealing with NASA staff stretched too thinly, often young and under-mentored—a function of personnel cutbacks and retirements of senior technical people. It also extended to issues of unrealistic expectations by NASA and its contractors. In addition, fear and distrust were rife within the implementation system. Goldin had indeed pushed too hard. Contractors and center officials worried that if they raised issues of cost to headquarters, they would have their programs killed or risk their own careers.

Goldin deliberately began softening his words, attempting to create a new image and work environment, showing a "kinder, gentler face."[55] He did not look for scapegoats and accepted responsibility. He seemed painfully aware that he was part of the problem. At the same time, he declared he still believed in the central thrust of his management reforms and would continue on his course.

A Final Push for Change

The year 2000 moved forward with Goldin knowing that his record-setting tour at NASA was likely to end with a new President. How was he to use the time remaining? While chastened by the Mars failures, he signaled no letup in his efforts to make NASA stronger for his having been its leader. His strategies included: (1) reorienting programs that had not gone as he had hoped or that required adaptation because of their inherent technical evolution; and (2) launching a new initiative that would make it possible for the space enterprise to have a long-term future.

The reorienting strategy was seen in the Mars and X-33 programs. In November, NASA unveiled a new 15-year blueprint for Mars exploration. It allowed more science, but at a slower and more cautious pace. It sought to identify "the most compelling places from above, before moving to the surface," and thus delayed the sample return—the prime goal sought from the previous program. Moreover, the cost would be approximately one-third greater during the ensuing five years than previously projected. The revamped Mars program was not as fast, not as cheap, but hopefully would be better.[56]

A second reorientation, even more drastic than that of Mars exploration, although not as visible to the general public, concerned the research and development program for a Shuttle successor. Goldin in 2000 all but admitted that the X-33 effort was failing. This government-industry partnership was at a virtual standstill due to a costly test stand failure and other technology problems. The government had already sunk $900 million into the X-33. Goldin decided he had to look for alternatives.

Hence, in 2000, he proposed a $4.5 billion five-year Space Launch Initiative. Conceivably, X-33 could compete for funds under that program, but the Space Launch Initiative was seen as a new activity, one that would attract different innovative concepts that would help take NASA to the Shuttle successor it eventually required. Goldin commented on the irony he

faced, saying he had come to NASA to lead the agency to Mars, but "we've had a little diversion because we can't build launch vehicles."[57]

The Mars and launch vehicle changes were due to failures in implementation. The third major reorientation in 2000 was because of belated success. In November, a huge milestone in ISS progress was reached—a U.S.-Russian team was launched to

X-33, Reusable Launch Vehicle in simulated flight.   ISS, heralding a new era of "permanent" human habitation of space. Still years from being complete in assembly, ISS was judged ready enough for a living quarters, and the expectation was that the first crew would be replaced by succeeding crews for the next 15 to 20 years, and probably beyond. It was a huge moment for Goldin, who had lived and suffered with the Space Station and its "perils of Pauline" virtually from the day he had arrived.[58]

That moment underlined for Goldin the importance of reorienting NASA for the permanent human habitation phase. Using ISS had to get the same priority as building it did now. Goldin consequently shifted personnel and reorganized for the ISS-utilization era. He established a Biological and Physical Research Enterprise on a par with the other major NASA programs. He declared that "it was time for the research for the station to be at the same level as the head of the space flight program."[59]

Also, Goldin announced the launch of a new initiative. He said that NASA was going to establish a stronger relationship with universities. NASA already had relationships with universities, but they were fragmented, limited in scale, and not linked in any strategic way to what NASA needed long term. The generation of space scientists and engineers that had come to NASA in the 1960s was aging, and many senior people had already left. Fifty-seven percent of all present NASA employees were eligible to retire in the next five years. NASA needed to nurture a new generation that would breathe life into the space program in the 21st century.

NASA had had a substantial university program in the Apollo era and then let that program atrophy. The agency had become inbred, with much of its research focused in its centers. The kind of work NASA was going to do in the future, particularly that associated with long-duration human missions to Mars and the search for life in the universe, needed scientific and technical breakthroughs most likely to come from fundamental research performed in universities. Also, NASA desperately needed young people to select space as a focus for their careers.

This university initiative would mean a build-up of the percentage of NASA's research and development funds that went to universities in the future. It would involve establishing space research institutes in universities, graduate student fellowships, and more internships at NASA centers. Fields emphasized would include nanotechnology and physiological research on humans exposed to deep space. In addressing a meeting of university administrators in October, Goldin declared, "I'm here to talk about where we go in a decade, and that's where we have to be coupled with universities."[60]

Finally, in early January 2001, NASA released a new report that was, in effect, a final word on the Mars failures. Entitled, "Enhancing Mission Success—A Framework for the Future," the report stressed that faster, better, cheaper principles were still valid if properly applied. However, these were not always applied correctly. Admitting mistakes in communication, and that the Mars missions were "over-constrained," the document argued that the concepts of faster, better, cheaper had to "be better articulated" and incorporated into NASA procedures so as to have them applied in a more uniform way across the agency. It provided definitions and implementation guidance regarding the management approach, noting the need for flexibility in specific cases. The document spoke of "open communication" and "trust." It provided prescriptions for improving the agency atmosphere and mechanisms within which faster, better, cheaper could be carried out with or without Goldin at the NASA helm.[61]

Conclusion

Goldin's record as a change agent at NASA is mixed, but decidedly positive. His greatest achievement was saving the Space Station. While others were involved, he was central. Although ISS is controversial, it lies at the heart of NASA in the early 21st century. Without it, there would be little to NASA's core mission. ISS keeps manned spaceflight alive and gives NASA a chance someday to build on this program with a humans-to-Mars mission—Goldin's dream. Goldin lobbied Congress unceasingly for the Station. Also, bringing the Russians aboard was essential to saving the project, although the Russian connection has surely had its costs. Whether it is viable over the long haul depends on circumstances beyond the power of any NASA administrator to control. However, had Goldin not done what he did in 1993 and subsequently maintained the Russian-U.S. alliance, the ISS might well not have made it to the next century.

Goldin's second great legacy was his revamping of the unmanned space science program. He directed *Hubble* repair and turned the *Mars Observer* failure into a trigger for infusing faster, better, cheaper into all science efforts, especially Mars exploration. Pictures from *Hubble* helped spawn Origins, an awe-inspiring program dealing with some of the most profound questions of science. *Pathfinder* showed faster, better, cheaper could work—and gave the nation and world an emotional lift that is one of the intangible rewards of space. He maintained the Earth observations effort, also using faster, better, cheaper techniques, and thus put it into a position to serve planet Earth in the future.

Third, Goldin streamlined NASA, an agency that was considered bloated and bureaucratic when he took it over. This streamlining was done in a way that linked NASA to Clinton administration reinvention goals, thus turning necessity into a political and public relations gain.

14. Bryan Burrough, *Dragonfly: NASA and the Crisis Aboard MIR* (New York: Harper Collins, 1998), 239-243.

15. The sense of need for change in NASA was pervasive in the media. "Fresh Air for the Space Agency," *New York Times* (March 13, 1993); "Confirm Bush's Choice for NASA," (Commentary) *Space News* (March 16-22, 1992).

16. Interviews with Daniel Goldin, December 16, 1999; October 21, 1999; November 12, 1998, Washington, D.C. "Bush Nominates TRW Executive Goldin to Succeed NASA's Truly," *Aerospace Daily* (March 12, 1992).

17. Nomination of Daniel S. Goldin to be Administrator of the National Aeronautics and Space Administration, U.S. Senate, Committee on Commerce, Science and Transportation, 102 Congress, 2d Session, (March 27, 1992) (Washington, D.C., USGPO, 1992), 7, 12.

18. Goldin interviews.

19. Goldin interviews.

20. NASA Administrator Daniel S. Goldin, "The New NASA—Faster, Better, Cheaper, Without Compromising Safety," document summarizing NASA Senior Management Team Meeting (May 18, 1992), NASA History Office Files, Wash. DC.; James Asker, "Goldin Orders Sweeping Review of NASA Programs, Eyes 30% Cut," *Aviation Week and Space Technology* (June 1, 1992), 29-30.

21. Eliot Marshall, "Making Less Do More at NASA," *Science*, Vol. 258, No. 5079 (Oct. 2, 1992), 20-23.

22. Theresa Foley, "Mr. Goldin Goes to Washington," *Air and Space* (April/May 1995), 36-43.

23. Ibid. Initially, he split OSSA into two offices, but it was clear that a third office would emerge. Shortly after the first two came into being, the third did also.

24. Kathy Sawyer, "The Man on the Moon," *Washington Post* (July 20, 1994). W. He nry Lambright, "Downsizing Big Science: Strategic Choices," *Public Administration Review* (May/June 1999).

25. Eliot Marshall, "Space Scientists Get the Jitters," *Science*, Vol. 258, No. 5086 (Nov. 20, 1992), 1296-98; Foley.

26. Marshall, "Making Less Do More at NASA."

27. Goldin interviews.

28. "Space Station Redesign Advisory Members Named," *NASA News* (Washington, D.C.: NASA, April 1, 1993).

29. Andrew Lawler, "Gore, Panetta Dispute Shaped Space Station Fate," *Space News* (July 26-August 1, 1993); Andrew Lawler, "Clinton Picked Station Matching His Vision, Priorities," *Space News* (Aug. 2-8, 1993); William J. Broad, "US To Cut Costs, Seeks Russian Role in Space Station," *New York Times* (April 7, 1993).

30. Lawrence interview.

31. William Broad, "Impasse is Broken on Space Station," *New York Times*, Dec. 1, 1993.

32. Joseph Tatarewicz, "The Hubble Space Telescope Servicing Mission," in Pam Mack, ed. *From Engineering Science to Big Science* (Wash., DC: NASA, 1998), 365-396.

33. Ibid.

34. Foley, 40.

35. David Morrison, "Low-Rent Space," *National Journal* (April 29, 1995), 1028-1072.

36. *Report of the Space Shuttle Management Independent Review Team* (Washington, D.C.: NASA, 1995).

37. Sean Holton, "Shuttle Deal Has Panel Asking NASA for Answers," *Orlando Sentinel* (Dec. 1, 1995).

38. "Shuttle Chief Resigns in Management Dispute," *Space News* (Feb. 5-11, 1996).

39. "Safety Panel to Conduct Space Shuttle Program Review," NASA News Release (May 31, 1996).

40. Seth Borenstein, "NASA Headquarters Job Cuts Slice Deeper," *Orlando Sentinel* (April 18, 1996).

41. Kathy Sawyer, "Goldin Takes the Heat," *Washington Post* (May 3, 1996).

42. Interviews with Gerald Soffen (May 12, 1999 and February 18, 1999, Washington, D.C.

43. Michael D. Lemonick, *Other Worlds: The Search for Life in the Universe* (New York: Simon and Schuster, 1998), 136; "Goldin Chooses Logic Over Emotion," *Space Views* (August 8, 1996), http://seds.lpl.arizona.edu/spaceviews/hotnews/goldin.960808.html.

44. Charles Petit, "Lockheed to Build Next-Generation Spaceship," *San Francisco Chronicle* (July 3, 1996).

45. Sharon Begley, "Greetings From Mars," *Newsweek* (July 14, 1997), 27.

46. Larry Wheeler, "Goldin's Decision Destined for History," *Florida Today* (Sept. 25, 1997); Paul Recer, "NASA Chief Bore Weighty Burden," *Buffalo News* (Sept. 26, 1997).

47. Burrough, *Dragonfly*; Kathy Sawyer, "NASA Decides to Send Another Astronaut to MIR," *Washington Post* (Sept. 26, 1997).

48. Chuck McCutcheon, "Lost in Space: NASA's Quest for a New Direction," *CQ Quarterly* (June 6, 1998), 1494-1502; "The Way It Is, Walter," *Aviation Week and Space Technology* (Nov. 2, 1998), 23; Joseph Anselmo, "Clinton Raises Hopes for NASA Bailout," *Aviation Week and Space Technology* (Nov. 9, 1998), 40-41.

49. "Dawn of a New Era for Space," *Syracuse Post-Standard* (Nov. 21, 1998); Craig Covault, "US, Russia Modules Link to Begin Station," *Aviation Week and Space Technology* (Dec. 14, 1998), 22-25.

50. Independent Assessment Team, *Report to Associate Administrator, Office of Space Flight, Space Shuttle,* (Wash. DC: NASA, March 7, 2000); Craig Covault, "Shuttle Quality Control Now a Major Concern," *Aviation Week and Space Technology,* (Dec. 20/27, 1999), 10.

51. Leonard David, "NASA's Mars Losses Spark Anger and Opportunity," *space.com* (Dec. 20, 1999), wysiwyg://17http://www.space.com/...arsystem/NASA-Marsloss-991220.html.

52. Leonard David, "Mismanagement Blamed for NASA/JPL Mars Failures," *space.com* March 28, 2000; *Mars Program Independent Assessment Team Summary Report* (March 14, 2000), NASA History Office files, Washington, DC. Michael A. Dornheim, "NASA Says MPL was Too Cheap, Too Fast," *Aviation Week and Space Technology* (April 3, 2000), 40.

53. Andrew Bridges, "Goldin Accepts Blame for Lost Mars Missions," *space.com* (March 29, 2000).

54. Michael Dornheim.

55. Andrew Lawler, "'Faster, Cheaper, Better' on Trial," *Science* (April 7, 2000), 32.

56. Andrew Lawler, "A More Cautious NASA Sets Plans for Mars," *Science* (Nov. 3, 2000), 915-916; "NASA's Reworked Mars Exploration Plan," *Aviation Week and Space Technology,* (Oct. 30, 2000), 24.

57. Leonard David, "NASA Chief Predicts Scientific Tsunami," *space.com,* (Oct. 11, 2000); Brian Berger, "Activists Say Lockheed Should Not Compete for X-33 Funds," *Space News* (Oct. 16, 2000), 21.

58. Craig Covault, "ISS Finally Manned as Challenges Abound," *Aviation Week and Space Technology*, (Nov. 6, 2000), 30-31; Remarks after launch of Expedition 1 crew to the ISS, (Oct. 31, 2000), http://www.nasa.gov/bios/goldin_speeches.html.

59. Brian Berger, "Funding Still Unclear For New BRP Mission," *Space News* (Oct. 16, 2000), 4.

60. Ron Southwick, "NASA Outlines Plans For Closer Collaboration with Colleges on Research Projects," *Chronicle of Higher Education* (Nov. 10, 2000), A29.

61. "Enhancing Mission Success—A Framework for the Future, A report by the NASA Chief Engineer and the NASA Integrated Action Team," Dec. 21, 2000 (Washington, D.C.: NASA, 2000).

62. Peter Senge, *The Fifth Discipline: The Art and Practice of the Learning Organization* (New York: Doubleday, 1990), 8-9.

63. James Webb was quite conscious about this need to think about the organization as a constituency to be won, much as any external constituency. Webb was an excellent manager in part because he was such an able politician. Goldin had political skills, as noted, but he apparently did not direct them internally, a circumstance that is one of many paradoxes about his leadership style. For Webb, see W. Henry Lambright, *Powering Apollo: James E. Webb of NASA*, (Baltimore: Johns Hopkins, 1995).

Appendix:
A Conversation with Daniel S. Goldin, Administrator, National Aeronautics and Space Administration

(In May 2001, The PricewaterhouseCoopers Endowment for The Business of Government hosted a seminar with Daniel Goldin to discuss the Endowment report "Transforming Government: Dan Goldin and the Remaking of NASA." Mark Abramson, executive director of the Endowment, and W. Henry Lambright, author of the report and professor of political science and public administration at Syracuse University, moderated the discussion. Excerpts from the conversation are presented below. The full transcript is available on the Endowment's website: endowment.pwcglobal.com.)

On His Major Accomplishment at NASA

Freeing up the NASA people to dream, telling them that failure is okay in spite of the constant hammering they take. I remember early in my tenure, I was going home at about 9:00 o'clock, 9:30 at night. There were still offices lit at NASA headquarters and, contrary to popular belief, federal employees are terrific. They work long, hard hours, and it's very easy to take shots at them, and with NASA, it's an even bigger bull's-eye.

One of NASA's employees said to me, "I'm so depressed. The harder I work, the more we get criticized." And I said to him, "There is a new kid in town. You'll work hard, you'll get criticized, but you'll have fun because failure will be acceptable and you can dream again."

And I feel, based upon what NASA has done, the employees are really dreaming. That in my mind is more important than anything else. There were good people at NASA before I came, there are good people there now, and there will be outstanding people when I leave.

All that a leader can do is create an environment, pick good people, nurture and train those people, and support the hell out of those people and take personal responsibility for the problems so those people aren't afraid to fail. That in my mind is the most enjoyable thing that I had at NASA.

On NASA in 1992

I felt that NASA, in a very honest attempt to deal with their environment, had gone into a survival mode. What was important then was how many jobs did people win in what part of the country—rather than what those jobs were about—and that more and more their budget was going into operations in near-term things because of the criticism over the *Challenger*, the *Hubble* being blind, *Galileo* being deaf, and I could go on and on.

People lost their confidence and were doing more and more mundane things. The Space Station was dead man walking. They spent $8 billion or $10 billion in eight years. There wasn't a piece of hardware, but the contractors were having a good time. I could cry.

So I resolved that I would free up NASA employees from these burdens and try and get a process in place that would focus on performance, not style, that would focus on what needs to be done to fix things instead of putting our heads in the sand and transitioning NASA from near-term safe things into long-term high-risk things.

On Risk-Taking at NASA

... the most important message I wanted to get ... failure is good. Failure is really the process that you learn.

...10 out of 10 failures is bad. On the other hand, zero out of 10 failures is worse, zero failures out of 10 attempts, because if you tried 10 things and had zero failures you set such mediocre goals you don't deserve being part of the space program. Getting that message across was the fundamental essence of what faster, better, cheaper was, and I came with this passion to do it.

If you have a few big things managed by a few powerful individuals, you suppress the creative process. Second, if you have a few big things managed by a few powerful individuals, you are terrified of failure because you risk the whole program.

So the concept of faster, better, cheaper that's not well understood is to get a large number, a diversity in number and function, so no one failure takes you down, and then to empower a broad range of people and develop the next generation and create competition of ideas, not emotions, within the organization.

On Positioning NASA for the Future

Every new day is jeopardy. You can never position yourself. Look at what happened to Nortel. Look at what happened to Lucent. Look at what happened to some of the dot-coms. We live in a world of change, and people like to think of government as this slow, lumbering, momentum model where you set things up right and you can coast for 10 years. That's not what it's about.

When you get out there on that ledge, you've got to be ready to jump off, and the change is going to happen and you cannot control the environment. Now, if you take a get-safe policy and you set mediocre goals and you say, "Boy, I'm setting these." It's like Babe Ruth, instead of pointing to the stands for a grand slam, he says, "I'll try for a bunt."

I mean, if you try for half a dozen bunts in the game, you could probably get away for five or 10 years, but there is no way young people are going to want to come to work for the agency. You've got to be out there. You've got to take risk.

On Getting Started at NASA

I'm a right side of the brain person. I'm intuitive. In fact I just heard a talk by Meg Whitman, who is the chairman, CEO, and president of eBay, and she talked about the fact that she was proud ... she said she was proud that she had a mid-40s management team because they were intuitive, because they could have an intuition based on their experience, and she said that a lot of the dot-com companies got started by kids in their early 20s who are brilliant but didn't have this intuition.

... what I am saying is I had been in the business. I was 51 years old. I was no spring chicken. I understand the aerospace business. I know how to pick up a phone, and I decided I would call the brightest, most informed people in the country.

And I called everyone from senators to congressmen to Nobel laureates. I talked to people in industry, executives. I called executives that had nothing to do with the aerospace business and I got a very clear picture.

I said there is a new way of doing it. I'm a new kid in town. I have been empowered by the president of the United States. I know exactly what his policy is. I know exactly what he wants to get done and I will go do the homework myself, and then after I do the homework, I'll then throw it open.

On Striving for Consensus

... I tried an experiment that failed. I wanted to have consensus management. I wanted to try it. I knew what I wanted. You can't do consensus management unless you know what you want to do first, and then you just make a note to yourself and say these are the things I want. Let me now throw it open and see how I can enrich what I have.

So I asked the people in the agency. First of all, I came to the agency by myself. I didn't so much as bring a secretary with me because I wanted to send a signal to the NASA employees that I trusted them. There are a whole bunch of people who wanted to come with me. I didn't want that.

And the second signal I wanted to give them was I wanted them to meet what I had signed up to do. That was to transform the agency. So rather than telling them what to do, I said why don't you form these red teams and blue teams and go take a look at all of these different areas.

And I said I want you to find 30 percent cut in the budget—not to give back anywhere but to reprogram so we could start a lot of new exciting things, and they didn't meet the mark. And many of the discussions we had were more of resistance, what do you know, rather than what could be done.

But in the process of doing the red teams and the blue teams, I saw who the real leadership at NASA was. It was not necessarily the people who have the appointed leadership positions, but they were people two and three and four levels down. It is amazing. When you give people a chance to shine they glow in the dark. And from the red team and blue team exercises, even though it didn't achieve the goal, I found out who the movers and shakers in NASA were.

And the other message is I brought in very few people from the outside. Relative to the total number of Senior Executive Service (SES) promotions that we have had at NASA, I'll bet 90 percent of them are from within the organization. And it really came as a result of these red team and blue team activities, so that was the process that I used.

On Accountability

Hyman Rickover was criticized for his success, but he had as a statement ... that fundamentally you don't know who is responsible unless you can take your finger and point at that person and that person says "I'm responsible."

And one of the problems I had when I arrived at NASA, I tried to find out who was responsible for anything. People do a wonderful job and, again, these are good people. These are not bad people. But people were so afraid of failure no one wanted to say I'm responsible when something occurred.

So I decided I would tell them hey, look, when there is a major problem don't worry. The administrator will say he's responsible. I have a letter of resignation in my desk and the very minute it's necessary because I serve the American people I'm ready to go. I won't fight to stay. You've got to have the ability to do that, and once you do that everything is okay.

On Working with Congress

... the big lesson that I learned out of this job is we have a wonderful democracy. From the outside looking in, you don't see how well it works. And a democracy doesn't need everyone supporting you, and you don't need cheerleaders to make a democracy work. In fact, you need skeptics.

So if you go to the hearings—I go up on the Hill—we don't have cheerleaders. I could assure you that, but that's good. That's not bad. And in fact there is a story that I recollect. We faced the senator from Arkansas, Dale Bumpers. I mean, he got pretty graphic on the floor of the Senate about how upset he was with the Space Station.

And after the next to the last vote before he left the Congress I had been looming outside the Senate chambers watching the vote. And I walked up to him and I said, "How are you doing, Senator Bumpers?" He says, "Dan, you're talking to me?" I said, "Yes." He says, "I always go after the Space Station." I said, "Senator Bumpers, do you know what you don't realize? More than anyone else, with your criticism of the Space Station you have made us more determined to do a better job."

And people always think of the debate up on Capitol Hill as being bad. It's good. Go to some other countries and see where everyone talks together and votes together, and you lose the ability for a democracy.

Having the open press, having the press criticize us, it gets depressing for the employees, but I keep telling them this is good; this is not bad. Because if you believe in what you're doing, deeply believe in what you're doing, you have a passion for what you're doing. You're not doing this to get promoted. You're not doing this to get a job after you leave the government. You're doing this for the benefit of the American people. You could stand up to the criticism, and the criticism makes you better.

Now, that takes an enormous amount of time, but that's called listening to your customer, and it is the job of the NASA administrator to understand what the customer wants. Now, the customer is the American people. I can't talk to each American person, but by talking to all of their representatives in the Congress and going to the districts and meeting with people, I got a sense of what the American people wanted and expected from NASA.

On Working in a Public Environment

It's more difficult than running a corporation without that glare, but there is another story that comes to mind. I did a lot of work in the highly classified area of our government while I was at TRW, and I used to read articles about NASA in the paper. And you would see about all of the warts and blemishes. I mean, right out there every day.

"God," I'd say, "how incompetent those people look. Why can't they be perfect like us, where we get no criticism?" You begin to drink your own bath water. You feel omnipotent and then I got a chance to come to this great agency.

I don't think there is any other place that has the kind of scrutiny that NASA does. Everyone is a rocket scientist. Everybody loves the space program. And even your friends start criticizing you because they know how to do it better.

I submit, and then now being at NASA, I would stack our employees against any corporation, any of the highly classified units of the Department of Defense, against any corporation in the world, because they have a thick skin because of the public scrutiny.

So my point is this is a system full of checks and balances and don't fight the checks and balances. Don't search for the guilty. Don't see who talked to members of Congress. If you're coming in as a presidential appointee, look upon this great democracy as helping you. It's important. Once you recognize that, you can be at peace with yourself.

On Rewards in Government

Let me explain to you what are rewards. Reward is when the NASA team celebrated fixing the *Hubble* space telescope. The reward was hugging Yuri Kopchev on the plains of Kazakhstan when we launched the service module. Reward—seeing Bill Sheppard, who personally helped me redesign the Space Station, as the commander of *Expedition I* holding hands with two Russians in space, Russians who worked in places that I targeted with ballistic missiles.

When you come to NASA, rewards are landing on Mars when at NASA many people in the NASA alumni league said, "Goldin, you're crazy, you'll never do it." Reward—Jim Martin, our biggest critic, who did the *Viking* mission, walked up to me at mission control at the Jet Propulsion Laboratory, and said, "Dan, you were right. I was wrong." That is reward.

On Budgets in Government

... let's analyze how democracy works and let's analyze how government works—because there is no return on assets employed, because there is no return on sales, because there is no bottom line measurement like you have in capitalism. The only measure for reward in the federal government is how big does your budget go up.

That's sinful. That's sinful. It's wrong. What you want to say is, "What have I done for the American people and how have I gotten efficient?" NASA turned back $40 billion from 1993 to 2000 in the projected budget runout that we had in the '93 budget.

That's a reward because now that money is going into curing cancer. That money is going into educating children. The reward for working for the federal government is not the increase in the budget of money you don't own.

Now, should NASA have more money? It would be nice, but that's not the important issue. The important issue is what are you accomplishing and what are you doing for the American people. Are your employees engaged in exciting things?

I am proud, although we would have liked to have had more money, and we get beat up all of the time. We were asked, "Why are you overrunning, why are you incompetent?" You show me one agency that does that [turns back $40 billion over seven years].

On "Pushing" Too Hard

If I were God, I'd know how not to push too hard at times, but I'm not. I'm a human being and I have to make my best judgment. It's more of a sin to push too little, because you don't know where you'll get to. Now, keep in mind the concept of faster, better, cheaper. Increase wherever possible the number and diversity of the projects you have to allow failure.

You sometimes spend too much money being cautious by not pushing hard enough and when failure occurs, you've got to be prepared to say, "I pushed my team too hard." We're bright. We'll come back and we'll figure out how to fix it. You could never push too hard.

On His Weaknesses as a Leader

I care too much and sometimes I get my emotions involved in what I do and it scares people. That's my biggest failure. And it's not that I don't care. When I care too much, you feel some of my intensity. This is me. It's not play acting. This is the most important thing I have ever done in my life.

I view the space program as one of the most important things that this nation does in the broader sense. And in the last nine years, living through all the potential to lose the program scares me, and it causes me to operate with an even greater intensity and I have done a better job.

Sometimes there is a kinder, gentler me, but every once in a while my intensity pops out, and it scares some of my subordinates, scares the hell out of some of our executives in the corporations that work with us, but I need to control that more. That's a concern about myself.

On the Space Station

You have to be able to work with all these different countries and all of their different cultures and it's very hard but it's wonderful.... That's a reward.

Getting together with the heads of agencies, I walk into a room with people who we duke it out every day, but there is such a level of respect. And when I first started, I thought in America we did everything. We had infinite knowledge.

The Russians taught us humility. The Russian space program, contrary to what the perception is in America, is unbelievable. Yuri Kopchev has to run that program, I think, on 140 million American dollars each year, if you want to talk about a budget problem for us.

Think about what those poor Russians have to go through to make their program work. So you learn about culture, you learn that there are other ways of doing things, and you get a sense of humility.

There are a few Russians I don't like, and there are a few Russians who don't like me. But the fact of the matter is I think the world is less prone, although it's still there, to go to war when people break bread, work together towards a common goal.

And with the Space Station we're building something where technology is being used to better the position of the human species on this planet, and that's a goal that you could wrap your arms around.

And the Space Station—God, it's hard—but the Space Station just because it was built. I want it to do research—the researchers, don't get me wrong. But [it has value] even if we just build it and sit on the ground and look at it and say, "We did it together, we made this place a better planet."

CHAPTER FIVE

Transforming the Veterans
Health Administration:
The Revitalization of VHA

Gary J. Young
Senior Researcher
Management Decision and Research Center
Veterans Affairs Health Services Research
and Development Service
and
Associate Professor of Health Services
School of Public Health
Boston University

Lessons Learned from the Transformation of the Veterans Health Administration (VHA)[1]

In 1995, the Veterans Health Administration, a primary operating unit of the U.S. Department of Veterans Affairs, embarked on a large-scale transformation. VHA is a federally funded and centrally administered health care system for veterans. The agency is also one of the country's largest providers of health care services. In 1999, VHA's health care system included 172 hospitals, 132 nursing homes, 73 home health care programs, 40 residential care programs, and more than 600 outpatient clinics. In addition, VHA oversees substantial health-care-related research and educational programs, and serves as a contingency backup for the Department of Defense medical care system.

VHA's transformation was in response to several external events and trends that threatened its future viability. In particular, the agency had become out of sync with prevailing trends in the delivery of health care services. VHA also faced the prospect of budgetary cuts and potential competition for patients from private-sector health care organizations. At the same time, the agency's complex mission and highly centralized decision-making structure were substantial impediments to its ability to adapt to these external threats.

A longitudinal case study of the VHA transformation was conducted to gain insight into the opportunities and problems organizations face when attempting large-scale organizational change. As part of the case study, VHA employees at all levels of the agency were interviewed, as well as individuals who observed the transformation as members of organizations that interface with VHA. Information for the case study was also obtained by conducting employee surveys and by examining VHA internal documents and data sets.

As a general finding, VHA's transformation has been highly successful. Since the transformation began in 1995, the agency has made substantial improvements on a number of important performance indicators. The transformation also has had limitations that reflect the challenges and tensions of conducting a large-scale organizational change. Although each organizational transformation is somewhat unique, VHA's experiences offer a number of lessons for future transformation efforts. Based on the case study, the following seven lessons have been identified.

Lesson 1: Appoint Leaders Whose Backgrounds and Experiences Are Appropriate for the Transformation

As is often the case with organizational change efforts, VHA's transformation began with new leadership. Toward the end of 1994, Dr. Kenneth W. Kizer assumed the position of under secretary for health, the highest-ranking position within VHA, with a mandate from Congress to transform the agency. Dr. Kizer, a physician trained in emergency medicine and public health, proved to be a highly effective leader for the VHA transformation. His effectiveness, as many of those interviewed repeated, was largely a result of the match between his professional experience and qualifications and the needs of the transformation.

Interviewees referred to three of Dr. Kizer's qualifications as being particularly relevant to his effectiveness. First, he was an outsider. Unlike many of his predecessors, he assumed the under secretary position without progressing through the agency hierarchy. Because of his outsider status, he was not a captive to entrenched interests within the agency. According to interviewees, when previous VHA leaders proposed making large-scale changes to the agency, they would find themselves constrained from going forward by loyalties to old colleagues who opposed the changes. Dr. Kizer was beholden to no one inside the agency. After assuming the under secretary position, Dr. Kizer selected several insiders for his senior leadership team, an action that reportedly helped him compensate for his own limited knowledge of the inner workings of the agency.

Second, although Dr. Kizer was new to VHA, he did have substantial leadership experience in the public sector. In particular, Dr. Kizer had served as director of the California Department of Health Services, where he reportedly learned how to work effectively with both policy makers and career civil servants. Dr. Kizer also had experience as a medical school department chair, a position that helped prepare him to manage VHA's important but complicated relationships with its affiliated medical schools.

Third, Dr. Kizer was an astute student of innovations in the financing and delivery of health care services. He had witnessed many innovations firsthand through his professional experiences in California, a state that has led the country in many innovations in the delivery of health care services. Dr. Kizer brought this spirit of innovation and experimentation to VHA.

VHA's transformation highlights the importance of having leaders whose backgrounds and experiences fit the needs of the transformation. For some organizations undergoing transformation, new leadership may be necessary, but the focus should be on ensuring that selected leaders have the right background and experiences for the transformation.

Lesson 2: Follow a Focused and Coherent Transformation Plan

Most transformations encompass many different activities and initiatives. Although this is also true of VHA's transformation, the senior leadership team for the transformation focused on four interrelated initiatives that formed a coherent and effective transformation plan. These initiatives were the following:

Creation of a Vision for the Agency

The senior leadership team developed and disseminated a series of documents that presented the vision for the transformation. These documents articulated the basic philosophy, principles, and organizational framework to which a transformed VHA would adhere.

Adoption of a New Organizational Structure

Within the first year of the transformation, VHA's senior leadership team implemented a sweeping change in the agency's basic organizational structure. The new structure decentralized decision-making authority within the agency and created new operating units for carrying out planning and budgeting. The agency's resource allocation system was also changed so that an operating unit's budget was based on the number of veterans it served rather than its historical costs. The individuals selected to oversee these new operating units were given primary responsibility for achieving transformation goals.

Establishment of an Accountability System

As the centerpiece of a new accountability system, the senior leadership team established performance contracts with upper-level managers. Each manager was required to sign a contract that stipulated a set of performance goals to which he or she would be held accountable. The performance goals related logically to the agenda set forth in the vision documents.

Modification of Agency Rules and Regulations

The senior leadership team sought and obtained reforms to a number of long-standing agency rules and regulations. These reforms provided VHA managers with greater operational flexibility for achieving the goals of the transformation. Some of these reforms entailed changes by the senior leadership team in the agency's own policies while others entailed changes by Congress in legislatively defined regulations for VHA.

These four initiatives formed the basic transformation framework for the agency. Other activities undertaken during the transformation were typically linked to one or more of the initiatives. The senior leadership team's ability to develop and implement each one of the four initiatives was central to the overall success of the transformation.

Lesson 3: Persevere in the Presence of Imperfection

All transformations generate controversy and criticism. Such criticism and controversy often distract leaders of transformation from focusing on the central goals of the change effort. In the case of VHA, the senior leadership team kept its sights fixed on key transformation goals while making mid-course corrections to address technical problems as they were recognized.

For example, VHA's senior leadership team became deeply embroiled in controversy over the accountability system it had established for upper-level managers. The new accountability system entailed the development of new performance measures and data sets. Initially, managers complained bitterly about the adequacy of the data sets, reliability of the measures, and potential opportunities for gaming the accountability system. They also raised objections based on the number and attainability of performance goals.

Certainly many of the complaints were valid, and efforts were made to improve databases and measures. The senior leadership team, however, believed the value of the new accountability system exceeded its functional capabilities. Indeed, the new accountability system's emphasis on performance data reverberated throughout the agency. Managers at lower levels of the agency began developing data sets for monitoring the performance of their own units in ways that supported the transformation agenda. Moreover, interviewees commented that the senior leadership team appeared less concerned about whether upper-level managers met precisely each and every performance goal in their contracts than whether they met the spirit of their contracts in the sense that performance was moving in a direction that promoted the transformation agenda.

No transformation will be perfect, and those who oppose the changes will seek to exploit flaws or limitations to derail the effort. Leaders of transformation need to be responsive to legitimate criticisms, but they also must avoid being swallowed up in technical details.

Lesson 4: Match Changes in the External Environment with Changes in the Internal Environment

Leaders of transformation are often consumed with managing the internal changes of an organization. VHA's transformation reveals the importance of managing external changes to complement internal ones. VHA's senior leadership team collaborated with other interested parties to secure from Congress a number of legislative reforms that were central to the transformation.

For example, the senior leadership team collaborated with veterans service organizations to change patient eligibility requirements that had limited the agency's ability to treat patients on an outpatient basis. Dr. Kizer reportedly played an important role in winning support for these reforms from certain key members of Congress who had long been opposed to them. He gained their support by presenting the reforms as a necessary step to achieving agency accountability for the goals of the transformation. In addition, the reforms expanded VHA's authority to contract with private-sector entities, facilitating the agency's ability to build its infrastructure for outpatient care.

Lesson 5: Develop and Manage Communication Channels from the Highest to the Lowest Levels of the Organization

VHA's transformation offers another of many examples where conventional communication strategies did not work to keep frontline employees informed during a large-scale change effort. To inform employees about the transformation, the senior leadership team distributed written notices and videotapes, held town meetings, and conducted video conferences. However, the survey data collected as part of this study indicate that these methods of communication were not reaching frontline employees.

What strategies can managers use to communicate effectively with their employees during a transformation? Some management consultants advocate that organizations plan for communication to be handled face-to-face between frontline employees and the supervisors to whom they report directly. Along these lines, at Ford Motor Company the CEO has embraced the concept of what change expert Noel Tichy calls the teachable point of view. This philosophy calls for a carefully planned initiative whereby managers at each level of an organization, from highest to lowest, spend time with the employees they supervise directly to convey and discuss key organizational principles. Under this approach, frontline employees meet to discuss a change effort with their immediate supervisors, who have had similar meetings with their own immediate supervisors.[2]

Lesson 6: Do Not Overlook Training and Education.

By implementing, as part of the transformation, a sweeping change in the agency's organizational structure, VHA's senior leadership team created in a sense a test case for a long-standing debate over how quickly a transforming organization should implement major changes in organizational structure. Some experts on organizational change recommend that organizations make gradual changes in structure to allow employees an opportunity to adjust to new work requirements. Others contend that sweeping changes in organizational structure can "unfreeze" the organization from its existing state and allow the transformation to proceed.

Although the VHA experience cannot resolve this debate, it does point to an important role for training and education in transformation efforts. For VHA managers, the sweeping change in organizational structure thrust them into a trial by fire situation. Many managers reportedly struggled to adapt to a management system that now called for them to make innovative and strategic decisions in a turbulent environment. Such decision making was not the common experience of most VHA managers who had spent much of their careers carrying out directives from agency headquarters. Some managers adapted, some did not. Interviewees repeatedly noted that many managers lacked the skills to operate effectively in the new environment and that there were few educational or training resources available to them. Although VHA's senior leadership team did plan for several educational and training initiatives as part of the transformation, most of these initiatives were not in place at the time the agency was undergoing its sweeping change in structure. It appears that in setting priorities, VHA's senior leadership team placed too little emphasis on training and education.

Accordingly, in situations where swift change is deemed necessary, senior managers should not overlook the importance of training and education to support employees in developing needed skills in a timely manner.

Lesson 7: Balance Systemwide Unity with Operating-Unit Flexibility

Leaders of all multi-unit organizations struggle with the issue of how much decision-making authority should be given to operating units and how much should be reserved for headquarters. The issue is frequently central to transformations, which are often undertaken by organizations in part to improve the fit between their decision-making structure and business requirements. The management literature recommends a number of factors that organizations should consider in addressing this issue, such as the magnitude and pace of technological and market changes in the external environment.[3]

In the case of VHA, a dramatic push occurred to decentralize decision making after years of micromanagement on the part of headquarters. However, the swing from centralized to decentralized management appears to have allowed little opportunity for careful planning in the reorganization of certain functions and programs at agency headquarters. Some programs were left in disarray without clear lines of responsibility or systemwide criteria for coordinating activities across operating units. There also appeared to be an absence of central oversight mechanisms to ensure that operating units followed consistent data collection and reporting procedures. This problem was noted in reports by the Senate Committee on Veterans' Affairs, the General Accounting Office, and VHA's own Office of the Inspector General.[4] Interviewees from within and outside the agency also expressed concern that the new decentralized decision-making structure provided limited opportunities for sharing best practices among the agency's operating units.

VHA's experiences reveal the need to carefully plan decentralization efforts so that an appropriate balance is struck between system-level coordination and control and operating-unit flexibility.

The VHA Case Study

Introduction

During the 1990s, many U.S. organizations in both the public and private sectors underwent large-scale transformation to improve their performance.[5] This report presents findings from a longitudinal case study of the transformation of the Veterans Health Administration. VHA's transformation, which began in 1995, is worthy of careful study for several reasons. First, the transformation overcame substantial obstacles to achieve many impressive results and is a potential source of best practices for other organizations undergoing transformation. Second, VHA's transformation, while generally a success, has not been without shortcomings that offer insight to the challenges and tensions that underlie many transformations. Third, VHA is one of the largest agencies in the federal government, and the size and scope of its transformation is itself a remarkable story of large-scale organizational change in the public sector.

This chapter consists of four primary sections. The first section provides background information on VHA. The next section presents the context in which the VHA transformation was launched. The third section focuses on the appointment of new leadership for VHA as the beginning of the transformation effort. The fourth and final section discusses four key initiatives that define the VHA transformation.

VHA Background

VHA is a federally funded and centrally administered health care system for veterans.[6] The agency is one of three primary components of the U.S. Department of Veterans Affairs, which was formed in 1988 as a cabinet-level department within the executive branch of the federal government. The Department subsumed the former Veterans Administration, which was established in 1930 to consolidate most veterans programs within a single agency. Through its two other primary components, the Department of Veterans Affairs administers on behalf of veterans a program for benefits and a national system of cemeteries.

VHA has a four-part congressionally mandated mission: patient care, research, teaching, and contingency backup for the Department of Defense medical care system. With respect to patient care, VHA is one of the country's largest health care delivery systems. In 1999, VHA's health care system included 172 hospitals, 132 nursing homes, 73 home health care programs, 40 residential careprograms, and more than 600 outpatient clinics. Through this nationwide health care system, VHA provided services to 3.6 million veterans in 1999, approximately 14 percent of the more than 25 million veterans in the U.S. Most of the veterans who use the VHA system meet at least one of two criteria that affords them priority status under the agency's patient eligibility rules, namely a low income or a disability that is connected to military service.

VHA's research and teaching activities are also quite extensive. The agency manages research programs in biomedical sciences, rehabilitative medicine, and health services delivery systems. These research programs have produced numerous medical innovations in such areas as cardiac care and hypertension. VHA fulfills its teaching mission through academic affiliations with many of the country's medical schools and schools of allied health professions. In particular, the agency is an integral component of the country's system for graduate medical education, providing financial support and clinical training to approximately one-third of the country's medical residents.

In terms of its role as a contingency backup for the Department of Defense medical care system, VHA has two primary responsibilities. One is to provide support to the Department of Defense medical system during times of war. The other is to assist the Public Health Service and the National Disaster Medical System in providing emergency care to victims of natural and other disasters.

As noted, VHA is a federally funded health care system. However, in contrast to Medicare, which is a federal health insurance program for the aged, VHA is not an entitlement program for its beneficiaries. The agency's funding is subject to discretionary appropriations from Congress. In 1999, VHA operated with a medical care budget of over $17 billion. The agency's workforce, which has undergone substantial reductions in recent years, now consists of approximately 180,000 individuals. A large percentage of the agency's workforce consists of clinical personnel such as physicians, nurses, and therapists. The senior official for the VHA, who carries the title "under secretary for health," is appointed by the president of the United States for a term of four years. By law the under secretary must be a physician.

VHA operates in a highly politically charged environment where its activities are closely monitored by a variety of organizations. As part of a cabinet-level department, the agency is subject to particularly close scrutiny by both the General Accounting Office and the Office of Management and Budget, as well as by congressional oversight committees. VHA also is under the close scrutiny of several different veterans service organizations (VSOs) that represent the interests of various veteran constituency groups. Two internal oversight groups—Office of the Inspector General and Office of the Medical Inspector—also oversee agency activities.

Context for VHA Transformation

The impetus for most transformations is a set of external events or trends that threaten the transforming organization's future viability. At the time VHA embarked on its transformation in 1995, several external developments had placed its future in peril. At the same time, however, VHA faced significant internal barriers to changing itself to adapt to these developments.[7]

External Threats
Shifting Priorities in the Delivery of Health Services: By the early 1990s, VHA had become out of sync with prevailing trends in the delivery of health care services. The advent of health maintenance organizations and developments in medical technology had been shifting resource priorities in the delivery of health care services away from inpatient-based tertiary care medicine to outpatient-based primary care medicine. At this time, however, much of VHA's material and intellectual resources were invested in the delivery of inpatient care. Most of VHA's hospitals, which historically have served as the agency's primary operating units, were large, technologically intensive, and often underutilized facilities. VHA physicians who staffed these hospitals were medical specialists with little expertise or interest in primary care medicine. Moreover, VHA lacked a well-developed infrastructure for providing services in the community.

Prospect of Competition: VHA also faced the prospect that it could lose many of its patients to the private sector. More than 50 percent of the veterans who use VHA services have low incomes and thus typically lack alternative sources of health care. However, during the early 1990s national and state-level health care reform proposals were advanced that included provisions to expand the accessibility of low-income individuals to private-sector health care. Although these health care reform initiatives did not come to pass, VHA officials were left to ponder the agency's ability to compete with private-sector health care organizations should such reforms come to pass in the future. VHA officials knew the agency would have to its advantage a strong reputation for excellence in many areas of specialty medicine, but they also realized that unless changes occurred, the agency would have to its disadvantage a reputation for long waiting times, fragmented care, and a cumbersome bureaucracy for accessing services.

Other external threats: VHA confronted at least two other substantial threats to its viability. One such threat concerned the efficiency of the agency's operations. Although VHA had been searching for ways to achieve cost savings for some time, the issue became much more pressing in 1995 when Congress indicated its intention to freeze the agency's budget. Another threat was an unfavorable demographic trend in the agency's patient population. Over time VHA's patient population has become increasingly older and sicker than the U.S. population generally. In the absence of any future military conflicts, this trend would result in the agency caring for a sicker but dwindling patient population.

The sum total of these external threats created a black cloud over VHA's future. To ensure its viability into the next century, VHA needed to significantly change the way it provided health care services, improve patient satisfaction, and increase the efficiency of its operations.

Internal Problems and Barriers to Change

Centralized and Bureaucratic Decision-Making Structure: Like many large, established organizations, VHA was not oriented to flexibility and change. The agency's management systems and culture were deeply rooted in a command and control, military-style mind-set. In particular, decision making was highly centralized and bureaucratic. VHA headquarters tended to micromanage many of the decisions and activities of the agency's hospitals and other operating units. This decision-making structure impeded operating units from adapting to local circumstances in a timely manner. Additionally, VHA's system for allocating resources to operating units, which was based largely on units' historical costs, did not provide incentives for the efficient and effective delivery of health care services to the patient population.

Multiple Stakeholders: As a public-sector health care system, VHA has multiple stakeholders who have different and sometimes conflicting interests regarding the agency's activities. This has presented a substantial complication to any agency change effort. Congress, a primary stakeholder, has long wanted to see the agency provide veteran constituents with more accessible and cost-effective health care services, though its individual members have also been wary of any changes that might have a negative impact on VHA facilities in their own districts. VHA's affiliated medical schools are also stakeholders. They have had a strong interest in maintaining the agency's capacity to provide high-tech inpatient care, since this capacity supports their residency programs and faculty research. Indeed, approximately 70 percent of VHA physicians have faculty appointments at the affiliated medical schools, an arrangement that has reinforced the agency's inclination toward high-tech inpatient care. The previously noted veterans service organizations are also major stakeholders with their own agencies and constituents. In addition, several different unions represent much of VHA's workforce and have an interest in protecting the jobs of employees within the agency.

Legal Barriers: As a federal agency, VHA operates within a framework of legislatively defined rules and regulations. At the time of the transformation, a number of these rules and regulations were barriers to the agency's ability to adapt to its changing circumstances. In particular, complex patient eligibility rules limited the agency's ability to treat patients on an outpatient basis. The agency also operated under rules that limited its ability to contract for services with private-sector organizations. This restriction impeded VHA from expanding community-based services to meet the needs of its patients.

Appointment of New Leadership

Many experts on organizational change view leadership as the most important factor for launching a successful large-scale transformation. These experts typically define a "transformational leader" as an individual who is capable of developing a vision for the transformation and who also can secure the necessary commitment from employees to pursue the vision.[8]

As is the case with many transformation efforts, VHA's transformation began with new leadership. Toward the end of 1994, Dr. Kenneth W. Kizer was appointed as VHA's under secretary for health and given a mandate by Congress to transform the agency. The appointment of Dr. Kizer, a physician trained in emergency medicine and public health, was, in essence, the beginning of VHA's transformation.

Dr. Kizer proved to be an effective leader for VHA's transformation. While not the originator behind all of the key ideas and initiatives that defined the transformation, he was, in the opinion of virtually everyone interviewed, a tireless champion for the transformation who was able to keep it moving forward despite formidable obstacles. In this respect, he possessed several attributes that were relevant to his effectiveness as the leader of the VHA transformation.

Outsider Status: Unlike his most recent predecessors, Dr. Kizer had not built his professional career within VHA. According to interviewees, when previous VHA leaders had proposed large-scale changes to the agency they were constrained from going forward by loyalties to old colleagues who opposed the changes. By contrast, Dr. Kizer was beholden to no one inside VHA. He did select several insiders to form a senior leadership team for the transformation. These insiders, in the words of one former VHA official, "provided Kizer, a newcomer, with needed guidance about the inner workings of the agency."

Relevant Experience: Although Dr. Kizer was new to VHA, he did have substantial leadership experience in the public sector. In particular, he had served as director of the California Department of Health Services, where he reportedly learned to work effectively with both policy makers and with career civil servants. In his discussions with members of Congress about VHA's transformation, Dr. Kizer was reportedly "unusually candid and direct for an agency official." But he also gained the trust of many members of Congress by keeping them well informed of all major changes he was planning to make at the agency. Dr. Kizer also had prior experience as a medical school department chair, a position that helped prepare him to manage VHA's important but complicated relationships with its affiliated medical schools. Dr. Kizer was, as noted by a staff member of the Senate Committee on Veterans' Affairs, "exceptionally well qualified for the job."

In addition, Dr. Kizer was an enthusiastic and knowledgeable student of private-sector innovations in the financing and delivery of health care services. Through his professional experiences in California, a state where managed care organizations have a strong presence, he developed an expertise in managed-care principles and practices. Dr. Kizer brought a spirit of innovation and experimentation to VHA. Because of his affinity for and knowledge of such private-sector innovations, Dr. Kizer developed a reputation within the agency as a private-sector disciple, despite the fact that he had worked in the public sector most of his career.

Good Timing: In the words of one interviewee: "Timing may not be everything, but Kizer certainly had his timing right." Dr. Kizer took the helm of VHA at a time when Congress, the veterans service organizations, and many of the agency's own employees were ready to see the agency undergo change. As a result, Dr. Kizer had a window of opportunity to remake the agency without some of the constraints and close scrutiny that would have certainly impeded his predecessors. Dr. Kizer appears to have capitalized on this opportunity to its fullest. Nevertheless, the difficulties of reconciling the interests of so many different stakeholders also took their toll on him politically. His reappointment to another term as under secretary proved to be a contentious matter in Congress. As the end of Dr. Kizer's initial appointment approached, members of Congress extended the appointment nine months so they could further deliberate on the matter of reappointment. When the nine-month period expired without resolution about his reappointment, Dr. Kizer, rather than endure the process further, stepped down.

Transformation Framework

Most transformations encompass a wide range of activities and initiatives. Because of the difficulty of delimiting a transformation effort, it was important to identify those initiatives of VHA's senior leadership team that were *central* to the transformation.

Four initiatives were identified that formed the basic framework for the transformation. These four initiatives, presented in Figure 5.1, are: the creation of a vision for the future, the adoption of a new organizational structure, the establishment of an accountability system, and modification in agency rules and regulations.

Collectively, the four interrelated initiatives played a central role in VHA's ability to achieve a number of impressive results during the first five years of its transformation (1995 to 1999). These results, which speak to the general success of VHA's transformation, are presented selectively in Figure 5.2. In general, they reveal a substantial shift in agency priorities and activities relative to outpatient care and primary care. The General Accounting Office, which has monitored the VHA transformation closely, recently reported to Congress that the VHA transformation has made "significant progress."[9] Additionally, a recent national survey of veterans, commissioned by the National Partnership for Reinventing Government, points to the success of the transformation. The survey used the American Customer Satisfaction Index (ACSI), which tracks customer satisfaction for more than 170 private and public sector organizations and is produced by a partnership among the University of Michigan Business School, the American Society for Quality, and Arthur Andersen. Approximately 80 percent of the survey respondents reported that the care provided by VHA had improved in the last two years. Further, VHA's satisfaction scores compared very favorably to the scores of other organizations that had been surveyed using the ACSI.[10]

Figure 5.1: VHA's Transformation Framework

> • Creation of a Vision for the Future
>
> • Adoption of a New Organizational Structure
>
> • Establishment of an Accountability System
>
> • Modification in Agency Rules and Regulations

The remainder of this section of the report discusses VHA's experiences with each of the four initiatives that comprised the transformation framework.

Creation of a Vision for the Future

It has become a well-established principle that successful transformation requires a clear and comprehensive vision of the organization's future.[11] Early in the transformation effort, VHA's senior leadership team developed such a vision. After his appointment as under secretary, Dr. Kizer held several months of planning meetings that included representatives from different parts of the agency. Based on these meetings, the senior leadership team prepared a document entitled *Vision for Change*.[12] The document articulated the basic philosophy, principles, and organizational framework to which a transformed VHA would adhere. As a follow-up to *Vision for Change*, the senior leadership team prepared two other related documents that provided greater operational guidance to VHA managers regarding the transformation.[13]

Clear Purpose and Goals: The vision documents provided a comprehensive statement of the purpose and goals of the transformation. The documents made clear that the "transformation would fundamentally change the way veterans health care is provided" and that this would include "increasing ambulatory care access points and a marked emphasis on providing primary care, decentralizing decision making, and integrating the delivery assets to provide a seamless continuum of care." Interviewees referred to the documents as forming a "true charter" for the transformation.

High Standards: The vision documents established high standards for the transformation. VHA was to provide care at a level that "must be demonstratively equal to, or better than, what is available in the local community." Although VHA officials had always spoken with pride of the quality of care that the agency offered veterans, interviewees repeatedly referred to the vision documents as presenting a direct challenge to the agency to provide the best care available anywhere in the country.

Figure 5.2: Selected Transformation Results

- **Orientation to Outpatient-Based, Primary Care:**
  - Annual inpatient admissions have declined by more than 32 percent while outpatient care visits have increased by more than 45 percent.
  - Percentage of surgeries performed on an outpatient basis has increased from approximately 35 percent to over 70 percent.
  - Approximately 60 percent of hospital beds have been eliminated.

- **Convenience and Accessibility of Care:**
  - Over 300 new community-based out-patient clinics have been established.
  - Telephone-linked care has been established at all hospitals.

- **Operational Efficiency:**
  - The number of full-time equivalent employees has been reduced by more than 14 percent while the number of patients treated per year has increased by more than 25 percent.

- **Patient Satisfaction:**
  - Patient satisfaction scores for outpatient care (based on VHA's own national surveys of patients) have improved by more than 15 percent.

- **Quality of Care:**
  - Percentage of patients receiving cancer screening for early detection of several types of cancers has increased substantially (e.g., colorectal cancer screening from approximately 34 percent to 74 percent).
  - Percentage of patients receiving treatments for preventing or controlling disease has increased substantially (e.g., cholesterol management for heart disease from approximately 74 percent to almost 100 percent).

Source: VHA internal documents and databases; General Accounting Office, Veterans' Affairs: Progress and Challenges in Transforming Health Care, GAO/T-HEHS-99-109 9 (April 1999).

Difficulties in Reaching Frontline Employees: VHA experienced the same difficulty that many transforming organizations do when trying to communicate a future vision to frontline employees. VHA's senior leadership team used several conventional strategies to communicate the transformation goals throughout the agency, including town meetings, video conferences, written notices, and videotapes. These communication efforts were not effective in reaching frontline employees. The employee surveys

conducted for this report indicate that after the first year of the transformation, frontline employees, including physicians in non-supervisory positions, had substantially less understanding of the purpose and nature of the
transformation than did those to whom they reported. For example, one of
the questions on the survey asked employees to indicate on a five-point
scale the degree to which they understood the goals the transformation was
intended to accomplish (where five was very strong understanding and one
was no understanding). The mean score for frontline employees on this
question was slightly below two, whereas the mean score for employees
occupying managerial or supervisory positions was approximately four. The
interview data also indicate that VHA's communication efforts had limited
success in reaching frontline employees. In a series of focus groups conducted for the case study, frontline employees repeatedly expressed their
frustration with communications. One employee appeared to sum up the
sentiments of many of the focus group participants when she remarked that
"[frontline] employees had too much rumor and too few facts about the
change process."

Adoption of a New Organizational Structure

Within the first year of the transformation, VHA's senior leadership team
implemented a sweeping change in the agency's organizational structure.
The new structure entailed the reorganization of all VHA operating units
into 22 networks known as Veterans Integrated Service Networks. The
design of the networks was intended to reflect actual and potential patient
referral patterns among VHA hospitals and other service organizations.

Within this structure, the networks replaced the hospitals as the primary planning and budgeting units within VHA. In addition, much of the
authority for operational decision making was effectively transferred from
headquarters to the networks. The role of VHA headquarters, which as part
of the transformation had its staff cut by more than a third, was to set overall policy and to provide technical support to network managers. The
senior leadership team selected a director for each network. Of the first
group of 22 directors, about one-third were drawn from outside the
agency. In addition, changes were made to the agency's internal resource
allocation methods so that a network's budget depended on the number of
veterans served rather than its historical costs (which was the case for hospitals in the past).

By implementing this sweeping change in structure at such an early
point in its transformation, VHA became, in a sense, a test case for a long-
standing debate over how quickly a transforming organization should
implement major changes in organizational structure.[14] Some experts argue
against dramatic changes in organizational structure or management systems

on the ground that employees will be mentally and emotionally unprepared to adapt to the new job requirements that such changes entail. These
experts often recommend that organizations make gradual changes to
allow employees to adjust to their new circumstances. Other experts, however, contend that dramatic changes in structure are sometimes needed to
overcome the inertia that often attends transformation efforts. These
experts contend that sweeping changes in organizational structure can
"unfreeze" the organization from its existing state and allow the transformation to proceed.

In general, VHA's sweeping change in organizational structure had a
positive impact on the transformation, though certain problems did in fact
emerge.

Affirmation of a New Era: The sweeping change in organizational structure appears to have affirmed the emergence of a new era in VHA's history.
Prior to the transformation, VHA employees had witnessed other attempted
change efforts only to see them abandoned before they were fully implemented. The expression "this too shall pass" became a rallying cry for VHA
employees who opposed the transformation. However, the dramatic change
in structure could not be overlooked; it provided a strong signal that the
transformation was not a passing fad. One longtime VHA manager summed
up the comments of many of the interviewees about the sweeping change
in structure: "VHA needed clear, decisive action that would ensure that the
agency would never return to its past." Still, there were many examples
where longtime headquarters staff tested the boundaries of the new power
structure by attempting to impose central policy initiatives on network
directors. Interviewees commented that when such circumstances arose,
the senior leadership team stepped in and reaffirmed the transfer of decision-making authority to the network directors.

Effective Platform for Change: By giving network directors substantial
decision-making authority, the new structure by design created an opportunity for experimentation. The result was a wave of new ideas and entrepreneurial activity. For example, in an effort to save money and streamline
care, network directors consolidated hospitals in more than 45 locations
where two or more facilities operated in close proximity to each other.
Network directors also implemented many innovative organizational
arrangements to coordinate patient care across operating units within the
same network. These arrangements often featured managed-care principles
related to primary care and preventive services. One network director, a
longtime VHA manager with over 20 years' experience with the agency,
commented, "I saw more innovation at the agency during the first three
years of the transformation than I had seen during all my previous years
combined." Another network director, who had been a longtime hospital

manager, remarked, "The new freedom I had to make decisions was absolutely invigorating."

Problems of Adaptation to the New Structure: Although the new organizational structure helped achieve credibility for the transformation and stimulate innovations, not all network directors and lower-level mangers were prepared for the new challenges ahead of them. Many managers struggled in their efforts to adapt to a system that now called for them to make innovative and strategic decisions in a turbulent environment. Such decision making was not the common experience of most VHA managers, who had spent much of their careers carrying out directives from agency headquarters. Interviewees noted that in the new structure, managers needed but often lacked the background to conduct sophisticated analyses for strategic and marketing plans, capital investment decisions, and contract negotiations with private-sector organizations. In a report to Congress, the General Accounting Office was particularly critical of VHA managers' efforts to plan and conduct feasibility studies for hospital consolidations.[15]

Interviewees repeatedly noted that few educational or training resources were available to managers to help them develop the necessary skills for adapting to the new structure. Although VHA's senior leadership team did plan for several educational and training initiatives as part of the transformation, most of these initiatives were not in place at the time the agency was undergoing its sweeping change in structure.

Problems in Lack of Uniformity: VHA's sudden swing from centralized to decentralized management appears to have allowed little opportunity for careful planning in the reorganization of certain functions and programs at agency headquarters. Some programs were left in disarray without clear lines of responsibility or systemwide criteria for coordinating activities across networks and operating units. Functions and activities were also sometimes eliminated without careful review and evaluation. There also appeared to be an absence of central oversight to ensure that networks followed consistent data collection and reporting procedures. As noted by one VHA manager who played a prominent role in the transformation process: "We were moving so quickly that we probably in some instances could not help but throw out the baby with the bathwater."

The problem was noted in reports by the Senate Committee on Veterans' Affairs, the General Accounting Office, and VHA's own Office of the Inspector General.[16] The report by the Senate Committee on Veterans' Affairs criticized the agency for not maintaining a cohesive, systemwide quality management program, noting, "headquarters does not require that its hospitals and clinics use uniform methods for collecting data."[17]

Members of several federal agencies who were interviewed also commented that the transformation had resulted in substantial problems with the comparability of operational and performance data among VHA operating units.

Although problems in the comparability of data among VHA operating units had existed before the transformation, the network structure had both exacerbated and magnified these problems.

Interviewees also remarked that the new structure provided limited opportunities for sharing best practices among the networks. Although VHA headquarters holds monthly group meetings for network directors, these meetings have largely focused on administrative matters.

Establishment of an Accountability System

As another key transformation initiative, the senior leadership team established an accountability system for network directors. Performance contracts were the centerpiece of the new accountability system. Each director was required to sign a contract that stipulated a set of performance goals to which he or she would be held accountable. The contracts provided directors with financial incentives in the form of a bonus for achiev- ing performance goals. The goals changed each year to reflect new agency requirements and priorities. Some performance goals required network directors to develop core competencies in such areas as interpersonal effec- tiveness; some called for directors to implement programs or functions; and other goals called for directors to achieve quantitatively measurable improvements in key efficiency and quality indicators for their network (e.g., patient satisfaction). It was also Dr. Kizer's intention that each network director would negotiate certain elements of his or her performance con- tract with the senior leadership team so that performance goals would reflect the variation among directors and networks in terms of capabilities and limitations.

To monitor performance, the senior leadership team used existing data sets and measurement systems and also created new ones. Reports were rou- tinely generated and disseminated to provide feedback on each network's relative performance on key measures and indicators for the transformation.

Alignment of Goals and Behaviors: The accountability system strategi- cally linked a network director's performance goals to the agenda set forth in the vision documents. The agency had not previously had an account- ability system that integrated the performance goals of operating units with agencywide strategic goals. As one interviewee noted, "The accountability system created a very sustained focus on the ultimate goals of the trans- formation at levels of the agency where the goals could best be translated into action."

Symbolic Value: The new accountability system had as much a symbolic role in strengthening performance management in VHA as it did a functional role. Initially, the functionality of the new system was subject to much criticism from network directors and other agency managers who complained bitterly about the adequacy of data sets, reliability of measures, and potential opportunities for gaming the system. There were also complaints about the number and attainability of performance goals.

The senior leadership team was responsive to but not deterred by these criticisms. Certainly, many of the criticisms were valid, and efforts were made to improve databases and measures. The senior leadership team, however, believed the value of the accountability system exceeded its functional capabilities. Indeed, the new accountability system's emphasis on performance data reverberated throughout the agency. Managers at lower levels of the agency began developing data sets for measuring the performance of their own units or departments in ways that supported the transformation agenda. These new performance systems often came to be known by such clinically-oriented nicknames as pulse points and vital signs. The result was a substantial shift in focus among VHA managers, a shift away from inputs (i.e., how large my budget is and how many staff do I have) to that of outputs as defined by the goals in network directors' performance contracts. Moreover, interviewees commented that the senior leadership team appeared less concerned about whether network directors met precisely each and every goal stipulated in their contracts than whether they met the spirit of their contracts in the sense that performance was moving in a direction that promoted the transformation agenda.

Problems of Implementation: The performance contracts were not implemented as fully as they were intended. As noted, Dr. Kizer intended the performance contracts to be negotiated agreements between network directors and the senior leadership team. In addition, it was the hope of Dr. Kizer that performance contracts would become a widely used concept throughout the agency for managing performance. He envisioned that the concept would diffuse throughout the agency. However, there was reportedly little negotiation around performance contracts and little diffusion of the performance contract concept. The reasons for this are not entirely clear. Some interviewees commented that the senior leadership team presented performance contracts to network directors without affording them an opportunity to negotiate performance goals; others remarked that network directors passively accepted the performance goals that were presented to them. Nevertheless, it does seem that inexperience with such concepts as performance contracts on the part of both the senior leadership team and network directors was a factor in the limited implementation of the concept. Many interviewees commented that negotiation of performance goals was very much outside "the traditional skill set of VHA managers."

Modification in Agency Rules and Regulations

The VHA transformation included reforms to agency rules and regulations. The primary reforms pertained to patient eligibility requirements that provided the agency with more flexibility to shift patient care to outpatient settings. These reforms also provided the agency with more opportunity to market its services to veterans who lacked priority status under the traditional eligibility requirements. Other reforms gave agency managers expanded authority to contract with private-sector organizations and to dismiss physician employees.

Effective Management of the External Environment: Although patient eligibility reforms had been in the planning stage long before the transformation began, VHA's senior leadership team worked closely and effectively with the veterans service organizations and other interested parties to win the approval of Congress for legislative reforms that became part of the Veterans Eligibility Reform Act of 1996.[18] In particular, Dr. Kizer reportedly won support for the reforms from several members of Congress whose support was critical to obtain the necessary votes to move the proposed reforms forward into legislation. These members of Congress initially opposed the reforms because of concerns that they might translate into increased service utilization and thus higher agency costs. Dr. Kizer countered this opposition by presenting the reforms as a necessary step to achieving agency accountability for the goals of the transformation, such as shifting service orientation from inpatient care to outpatient care. Interviewees familiar with these events noted Dr. Kizer's "political acumen in reframing the debate over the reforms from one of access and cost to one of agency accountability." These reforms also expanded the VHA's authority to contract with private-sector entities for various services, facilitating the agency's ability to build its infrastructure for outpatient care.

Hardball: The senior leadership team eliminated a long-standing agency policy that prevented dismissal of physician employees except for clinical incompetence. Although this reform created some bitter feelings on the part of VHA physicians, it reportedly conveyed a necessary message to all VHA employees that they needed to change their attitudes and behaviors to serve the goals of the transformation. On this point, Dr. Kizer remarked: "It always was our hope to achieve compliance by offering employees a carrot, but we could ill afford not to have a stick available to us."

Future Challenges: Network directors have generally capitalized on patient eligibility reforms to increase the number of veterans receiving services from the agency. However, it is not yet clear whether the agency has the resources and processes in place to care for more patients without compromising the quality of service.[19] The higher patient volume will undoubtedly test the ability of VHA managers to adapt to higher levels of workload.

The VHA Transformation As Viewed by Dr. Kenneth W. Kizer, Former Undersecretary for Health, U.S. Department of Veterans Affairs

(Dr. Kenneth Kizer's description of the VHA transformation originally appeared in Straight from the CEO: The World's Top Business Leaders Reveal Ideas That Every Manager Can Use *(Simon & Schuster, 1998), edited by G. William Dauphinais and Colin Price.)*

One of the most profound transformations of any organization in U.S. history has been happening at the Veterans Health Administration for the last couple of years. Replacing an older, monolithic, military-style top-down organization, this turnaround has involved a 180-degree shift in management philosophy and execution, plus an intense application of integrated management network systems.

The VHA's ambitious networks are the kind of new organizational structures that are rapidly coming to dominate the health care field. They have piqued the interest of management academics and researchers because these novel organizational links and architectures point to the way many large-scale institutions, both public and private, will be managed in the next millennium. The seed of the VHA's transformation came not from within government, but rather was inspired by such outside organizations as Kaiser Permanente and private health care groups.

However, what is remarkable at the VHA is that no other organization has heretofore applied the integrated network management concept on such a large scale. And none have had to first break down and reconstruct such a huge existing organization and aggregate of physical structures, while at the same time continuing to maintain good service delivery to the client population. Few entities anywhere have been at the nexus of as many forces of change.

Transformation Through New Alliances—Internal and External

What is an integrated service network? Conceptually, it is based on the simple idea that whoever controls and coordinates the supply, production, distribution, and marketing of service delivery will be a vastly more efficient producer than the non-integrated operator. An integrated network is a superior form because it has a higher rate of asset and service utilization. It can also bring to bear at one point and at one time a superior package of services.

Because it offers the opportunity to serve specific populations with uniform quality services at standardized prices, the relevance of this idea to the once highly fragmented U.S. health care market cannot be overstated. In an integrated health system, physicians, hospitals, and other components share the risks and rewards—supporting one another, blending their talents, and pooling their resources. The network requires management of total costs, plus a focus on populations with common needs rather than on disparate individuals. Furthermore, it requires a data-driven, process-focused customer orientation.

A second innovative organizing principle at work in the VHA's transformation is the concept of the "virtual health care organization," which first emerged in the 1980s. It is based largely on experiences in the biotechnology industry, when businesses invented integrated capabilities by creating a wide array of discrete corporate partnerships, alliances, and consortia to either develop or market specific products. A number of private health care companies have used this approach to form virtual organizations that are held together by (1) the operating framework—that is, the aggregate of agreements and protocols that govern how patients are cared for, and the systems that monitor patient flow; and (2) the framework of incentives that governs how physicians and hospitals are paid.

Virtual health care systems invest substantial resources in developing their provider networks, which have a strong focus on community-based networks of participant physicians. The skills demonstrated by these virtual organizations are likely to become increasingly important in all facets of the economy and society.

Chained to the Past

The VHA, at least in theory, was ripe for the application of the integrated service network and the virtual organization. And, in fact, all the necessary ingredients were buried within this monolithic, old-fashioned, hospital-centered organization. The first step was to liberate these serendipitous ingredients from their chains! It was clear that the VHA had to deconstruct its old organization simply to keep abreast of the frenetic pace of change in U.S. health care delivery.

Further pressure for action came from a Congress skeptical of the wildly skewed cost-benefits of the old hierarchical methods. Plus there were mounting complaints about inadequate and inconsistent VHA services from veterans' organizations. For years, these groups had been voicing their dissatisfaction over the long waits to see a doctor, being treated with a lack of respect, and long hospital stays for conditions better treated in an outpatient setting, such as the removal of cataracts.

The old VHA management was centralized to an absurd degree, and thus highly ineffective. Permission for leasing small amounts of space, or for such trivial expenditures as $9.82 for an individual's purchase of a computer cable, had to be approved at the CEO level. The center was so inundated with trivia that, by default, too much power had come to reside in the VHA hospitals. Given these handicaps, it's amazing that the VHA could have provided such a relatively good level of care and services to its constituencies.

But this is far more than a tale of a long-overdue cleanup of an inept government bureaucracy. This is a story of how we jump-started change thanks to a sweeping application of the integrated service network, and in the process lowered costs and improved services.

Contrary to popular belief, most of the nation's 26.1 million veterans are not eligible for care at the VHA. In essence, only veterans with service-connected disabilities or who are poor can receive care at the VHA. Nevertheless, the VHA grew to its present size in response to the enormous influx of wounded at the close of World War II. And 50 years later it was still trying to handle a completely different set of needs with the same structure.

Here's an idea of the magnitude of the problem: There are some 11.6 million eligible veterans who are 60 or over, and another 8.3 million who are between 40 and 55. Before its recent transformation, the VHA was treating some 900,000 patients a year at the 173 VHA hospitals. The average length of stay in fiscal 1993 was nearly three times greater than the U.S. average—with only a small part of this difference attributable to the advanced ages of these patients.

The system was convoluted, fragmented, and self-defeating. It emphasized medical specialization, high technology, biomedical research, and acute inpatient services at a time when all trends in health care were heading in the opposite direction, toward primary care, or basic services.

Even more importantly, the VHA lacked the ability to adequately serve its aging customers, many of whom were on the edge of poverty and suffering from non-war-related illnesses—the two most common medical problems among all veterans being alcoholism and schizophrenia.

A "Vision" for Dramatic Change

The challenge was clear: The VHA had to transform itself from a hospital-based, specialty-focused health care system to one rooted in ambulatory care. Accordingly, in October 1995, the VHA consolidated its 173 independent and often competing hospitals, over 400 clinics, 133 nursing homes, over 200 counseling centers, and various other facilities into 22 Veterans Integrated Service Networks, or VISNs (pronounced "visions").

This new operating system emphasizes efficiency, collaboration and cooperation, and the quest for productivity by eliminating layers of bureaucracy and streamlining communications. The goal: To have all patients assigned to a dedicated generalist physician, or physician-led team of caregivers, responsible for providing readily accessible, continuous, coordinated, and comprehensive care.

No sooner were the VISNs up and running than a number of service improvements were pushed through. For example, in 1994 only a few VHA facilities had telephone advice services; within two years, all of them did. Adding to the new momentum at the VHA was the elimination of some 2,626 types of forms (64 percent of those in use), and the marked simplification and automation of the remainder. In addition, many tens of millions of dollars in savings resulted from an aggressive program to increase the number of goods and services acquired through bulk-purchase agreements, and a pharmaceutical prime vendor program.

Under the VISNs strategy, the basic budgetary and planning unit of health care delivery shifted from the autonomous medical centers to the networks—with each of these networks being responsible for all VHA activities in a specified geographic region. The VISNs promote better integration of resources and the expansion of community-based access points for primary care. The paradigm under which they operate is made up of strategic alliances between neighboring VHA medical centers, sharing agreements with other governmental providers, and other relationships, including direct purchases from the private sector.

The Hospital Becomes Part of a Larger Picture

In this scheme, the hospital becomes a component of a larger and better-coordinated community-based network of care—embracing both ambulatory and acute and extended inpatient services. The superiority of the network is that it focuses on customer needs from primary to tertiary care.

The VISNs are a revolutionary organizational form, based on patient referral patterns, hospitals, and other VHA assets. Their mission is to conduct population-based planning, to increase patient access, and to pool and align local resources to provide a seamless continuum of care. The individual VISNs are like strategic business units. As the basic budgetary and planning components of the system, each one is measured against specific performance contracts.

The heads of the various hospitals and facilities report in to their VISN, which optimizes the networks and extracts the highest value for the resources allocated. All VISNs have procedures for input from the VA's internal and external stakeholders through a council that consists of facility directors, chiefs of staff, nurse executives, union representatives, and others. The council debates and makes recommendations to the VISNs directors.

The VISNs' big point of departure is that they are in part virtual health care systems—in that they may deliver services through contractual agreements with other institutions. Traditional, nonvirtual health care systems rely on ownership of assets and employment of their own professionals. In the new configurations, the once-central position of the VHA hospitals would be moderated by the needs of more coordinated, community-based care. The first outreaches of the network have already been built. The VHA has developed new joint-venture relationships with the Juvenile Diabetes Foundation, the National Cancer Institute, and the Shriner's Hospitals. Other such alliances are under discussion.

Changing the People—and the Culture

The VISNs had to be created out of whole cloth. As undersecretary it was crucial for me to have deep personal involvement in the networks' design, as well as in the recruitment of their leaders. I began by developing the questions to be asked of all candidates, and I personally interviewed all 90 finalists for the 22 positions. In the end, eight of these positions were filled by outsiders, some from private industry—a big break with VHA tradition.

The VISNs are the VHA's chief tools of transformation. In both image and substance, they are sweeping away the old view—prevalent inside and outside the VHA—that it was a kind of public works program in building construction and lifetime jobs. Such a culture of stasis is typical of large bureaucracies, which tend to focus on self-propagation at the expense of purpose. And in fact, even as the VISNs were being instituted, there remained the lingering attitude that, "Well, this too will pass. It won't be long before we get back to the old way of doing things." It took us a little while to stamp out passivity and negativity—much of it fostered by a reduction of staff from 205,000 to 181,000 and the elimination of 17,000 acute-care beds.

A New Role for Headquarters

If the VISNs are doing all the heavy lifting, what's the role of the Washington, D.C., headquarters? It has shifted its orientation away from hierarchical dominance to seeking ways to support the field—by offering governance principles and consulting advice, and by leading the system through the dynamic and turbulent changes ahead. To the degree that headquarters displays leadership capabilities and insights, the field managers will continue to seek its advice and counsel—not because of its position in the hierarchy. One of the chief missions of headquarters is to foster and demand new behaviors and attitudes that further the goals of the new overall structure.

A major block to change was a 1947 policy stipulating that VHA physicians could not be terminated for any reason short of malpractice. That law institutionalized complacency, and its repeal—which came in 1995—was essential for the success of the reorganization. Another block was that the VA's research arms had splintered into isolated pockets that placed researchers' personal agendas ahead of customer service. Under the new network regime there must be a demonstrable link between research and patient care. In 1994, the VHA implemented its first-ever customer service standards, and patient surveys in 1995 and 1996 indicated statistically significant improvements.

A Work in Progress

Systemic change at the VHA is still a work in progress. Challenges remain. There still needs to be more managerial accountability, and there still needs to be more flexibility and latitude to make tough decisions. Some of the old culture of insularity remains—but the message is getting out.

This is an era in which the entire health care industry is in transition. It's our belief that by the time the transformation of the VHA is complete, it will be a fully integrated health care provider—one capable of competing with private entities.

Endnotes

1. The case study that this report is based on was supported financially in part by the National Science Foundation (grant number–9529884). The author is grateful to several members of the Management Decision and Research Center for their help in conducting the case study—Martin Charns, Carol VanDeusen Lukas, and Geraldine McGlynn. The author is also grateful to Richard Coffey of the University of Michigan Hospitals who served as a co-principal investigator on the National Science Foundation grant. The views expressed in this article are those of the author and do not necessarily represent the views of the Department of Veterans Affairs or Boston University.

2. See T.J. Larkin and S. Larkin, "Reaching and Changing Frontline Employees," *Harvard Business Review*, 1996 May-June, 95-104.; S. Wetlaufer, "Driving Change: An Interview with Ford Motor Company's Jacques Nasser," *Harvard Business Review*, 1999 March-April, 77-88.

3. See, generally, P. Leatt, S. Shortell, and J. Kimberly, "Organization Design," in (S. Shortell and A. Kaluzny, eds.) *Health Care Management: Organizational Design and Behavior*, Albany, New York: Delmar (2000).

4. U.S. Senate, Minority Staff of the Committee on Veterans' Affairs, *Staff Report on Quality Management in the Veterans Health Administration*, Department of Veterans Affairs (December 1997); General Accounting Office, *Major Management Challenges and Program Risks: Department of Veterans Affairs*, GAO/OGC-99-15 (January 1999); U.S. Department of Veterans Affairs, Office of the Inspector General, *Quality Management in the Department of Veterans Affairs Veterans Health Administration*. Office of Healthcare Inspections, Report 8HI-A28-072, Washington, D.C. (February 1998).

5. Although no studies document comprehensively the proportion of transformations that actually fail, experts seem to agree that the majority of transformations fall very short of the expectations of those who initiated them. See, for example, J.P. Kotter, "Leading Change: Why Transformation Efforts Fail," *Harvard Business Review*, 1995 March-April, 59-67; G. Hall, J. Rosenthal, and J. Wade, "How to Make Reengineering Really Work," *Harvard Business Review*, 1993 November-December, 119-130. Some evidence suggests that transformation of public-sector organizations is less likely to succeed than transformation of private-sector organizations (P. J. Robertson and S. J. Seneviratne, "Outcomes of Planned Organizational Change in the Public Sector: A Meta-Analytic Comparison to the Private Sector," *Public Administration Review*, 1995, 55 [16]: 547-558).

6. Information contained in this section was drawn from both published sources as well as internal VHA documents. For published sources, see generally K. W. Kizer, "The 'New VA': A National Laboratory for Health Care Quality Management," *American Journal of Medical Quality*, 1995, 14: (1): 3-19; E. S. Fisher and H.G. Welch, "The Future of the Department of Veterans Affairs Health Care System," *Journal of the American Medical Association*, 1995, 273 (8):651-667; K.W. Kizer, "Re-engineering the Veterans Healthcare System" in P. Ramsaroop, J. Ball, D. Beaulieu, and J.V. Douglas, eds., *Advances in Federal Sector Health Care*, New York: Springer (in press).

7. Information contained in this section was drawn from a number of sources. See Paralyzed Veterans of America, *The VA Responsibility on Tomorrow's National Health Care System: Strategy 2000*, Washington, D.C. (1992); Mission Commission, *Report of the Commission on the Future Structure of Veterans Health Care*, Washington, D.C

(1991); E. S. Fisher and H.G. Welch, "The Future of the Department of Veterans Affairs Health Care System," and J.K. Iglehart, "Reform of the Veterans Health Care System," *New England Journal of Medicine*, 1996, 335 (18): 1407-1411; K. W. Kizer, "Health Care, Not Hospitals: Transforming the Veterans Health Administration," in (G.W. Dauphinais and C. Price, eds.) *Straight from the CEO*, New York: Simon & Schuster (1998); S. Findlay, "Military Medicine: The Image and the Reality of Veterans' Hospitals," *U.S. News & World Report*, June 1992; Department of Veterans Affairs (Management Decision and Research Center), "Analysis and Recommendations for Reorganization of Veterans Health Administration," (October 1993); Task Force on the Reorganization of VHA Central Office, "Veterans Health Administration Central Office Reorganization," (September 1994); Northwestern University (Kellogg Graduate School of Management), "Analysis of the Organizational Structure and Management Functioning of VA's Health Delivery System (1991); K.W. Kizer, "Re-engineering the Veterans Healthcare System" in P. Ramsaroop, J. Ball, D. Beaulieu, and J.V. Douglas, eds., *Advances in Federal Sector Health Care*, New York: Springer (in press).

8. A cornerstone of this literature is J. Burns, *Leadership*, New York: Harper & Row (1978).

9. General Accounting Office, *Veterans Affairs: Progress and Challenges in Transforming Health Care*, GAO/T-HEHS-99-109 9 (April 1999).

10. K.W. Kizer, "Re-engineering the Veterans Healthcare System" in P. Ramsaroop, J. Ball, D. Beaulieu, and J. Douglas, eds., *Advances in Federal Sector Health Care*, New York: Springer (in press).

11. For a recently published book that discusses the concept, see R.M. Miles, *Leading Corporate Transformation*, San Francisco: Jossey-Bass (1997).

12. Veterans Health Administration, *Vision for Change: A Plan to Restructure the Veterans Health Administration*, Washington, D.C. (February 1995).

13. Veterans Health Administration, *Prescription for Change: The Strategic Principles and Objectives for Transforming the Veterans Healthcare System*, Washington, D.C. (January 1996); Veterans Health Administration, *Journey for Change*, Washington, D.C. (April 1997).

14. See, generally, L. E. Greiner, "Patterns of Organizational Change," *Harvard Business Review*, 1967 May/June, 119-128; M. Beer, R.A. Eisenstadt and B. Spector, *The Critical Path to Corporate Renewal*, Harvard Business School Press, Boston (1990); D.A. Nadler, R.B. Shaw, and A.E. Walton (editors), *Discontinuous Change*, Jossey-Bass, San Francisco (1995); R.K. Reger, L.T. Gustafson, S. M. Demarie, and J. Mullane, "Reframing the Organization: Why Implementing Total Quality Is Easier Said Than Done," *Academy of Management Journal* 1994, 19 (3): 565-584.

15. General Accounting Office, *Major Management Challenges and Program Risks: Department of Veterans Affairs*, GAO/OCG-99-15 (January 1999).

16. U.S. Senate, Minority Staff of the Committee on Veterans' Affairs, *Staff Report on Quality Management in the Veterans Health Administration*, Department of Veterans Affairs (December 1997); General Accounting Office, *Major Management Challenges and Program Risks: Department of Veterans Affairs*, GAO/OGC-99-15 (January 1999); U.S. Department of Veterans Affairs, Office of the Inspector General, *Quality Management in the Department of Veterans Affairs Veterans Health Administration*. Office of Healthcare Inspections, Report 8HI-A28-072, Washington, D.C. (February 1998).

17. U.S. Senate, Minority Staff of the Committee on Veterans' Affairs, *Staff Report on Quality Management in the Veterans Health Administration*, Department of Veterans Affairs (December 1997).

18. U.S. Congress, "Veterans Eligibility Reform Act of 1996." Public Law. 104-262, Washington, D.C., 1996.

19. General Accounting Office, *Major Management Challenges and Program Risks: Department of Veterans Affairs*, GAO/OCG-99-15 (January 1999).

20. For example, I used as part of my framework a model of the change process that was originally proposed by Kurt Lewin. In this model, transforming organizations are conceptualized as moving through three stages or states of equilibrium—frozen, unfrozen, and refrozen. The model does not consider strategies or tactics that move organizations from one stage to another. K. Lewin, "Group Decision and Social Change" in *Readings in Social Psychology*, rev. ed., edited by G. E. Swanson, T. N. Newcomb, and E.L. Hartley. New York: Holt (1952).

Appendix I:
Kenneth W. Kizer's Key Principles
of Transformation

1. Clearly articulate your vision, intent, and principles of change.

The VHA's statement is about "why," not "how." With a clear end-purpose in mind, we used certain principles of modern health care to lay the framework for transformation at the VHA, as well as the new managerial system that would implement it:

- The VHA is in the business of health care, not of running hospitals.
- Health care is now primarily a local outpatient activity.
- The VHA's critical mandate is to provide good value.
- The success of future health care systems will depend on their ability to integrate and manage information.
- Health care must reorient itself to become more population-directed, community-based, and health-promotive.
- Health care must become more accountable and responsive to those who purchase it.
- Medical education and research must be accountable to the public good.

2. The process of change should be broadly inclusive.

The top manager should allow all members of the organization to have their say in some form or forum—and what they say should be taken seriously and sincerely. However, that inclusivity should be flexible enough to embrace partnerships and outside associations that can facilitate the new vision.

3. Change within an organization must move in harmony with environmental or externally focused change.

Top managers, particularly those in the public sector, cannot hope to stand against the "forces of nature"—this constitutes bad management. In the case of the VHA, that means being in sync with broad trends, such as the national revolution in health care, the explosion of biomedical research and knowledge, the shift to an "information society," and the aging of the eligible VHA population.

4. The top manager must make key personnel decisions.

Bad hires stay around to haunt you; good ones make you look good. Here are seven key characteristics of the good hire:
- Committed to change
- Shares the vision
- Experienced, knowledgeable
- Innovative, nontraditional
- Respected
- Empowered
- Willing to get his or her hands dirty

5. Set high expectations.

People will meet them—unless your system impedes their best efforts.

6. Focus on rigorous execution, including minimizing errors.

Innovative, nontraditional thinkers will make errors because errors are inherent to trailblazing. These should be openly discussed without instilling the kind of fear that engenders complacency. However, stupid, careless mistakes should not be tolerated.

7. Anticipate problems.

Change, by definition, is rarely neutral. It will create new problems—but they shouldn't come as a surprise.

Appendix II:
Study Methods

This chapter is based on a longitudinal case study of VHA's transformation. The study began in 1995 at the time the transformation began. The findings presented in this report are drawn primarily from the following sources of information.

Literature Review

A literature search was conducted to identify both conceptual issues and empirical findings that have emerged from previous research on transformations. These concepts and findings were used as a framework for studying VHA's transformation.[20]

Interviews

During the study period, interviews were conducted with more than 100 individuals who had been involved directly or indirectly with the transformation. These interviews were conducted using semi-structured interview protocols. The majority of interviews were with VHA employees at all levels of the agency's hierarchy, including the senior leadership team. Other interviews were with individuals who have observed the transformation as members of organizations that interface with VHA.

This included the General Accounting Office, Office of Management and Budget, and veterans service organizations. We also interviewed staff members of the offices of senators and representatives who have served on congressional oversight committees for VHA.

Secondary Data

Internal VHA documents, reports, and databases were examined. These secondary sources of data provided information about VHA's transformation activities and operational performance.

Surveys

During the course of the transformation, several surveys of VHA employees were conducted. These surveys focused on employee perceptions of the nature and impact of the transformation effort.

CHAPTER SIX

Transforming the United Kingdom's National Health Service and the United States Veterans Health Administration: Trans-Atlantic Experiences in Health Reform

Marilyn A. DeLuca
Doctoral Program
Robert F. Wagner Graduate School of Public Service
New York University

Introduction[1]

Health system reform is a topic of current worldwide interest. The confluence of economic pressures, growing demands, aging populations, and
rapidly developing technologies force governments and policy makers to
examine policy options, adjust the "public-private mix," and consider the
introduction of seemingly similar market mechanisms. While the recent
trend in reform demonstrates a reliance on market-based strategies such as
managed care and other competitive arrangements, growing evidence finds
such models often have unfavorable impacts on access to and the quality of
health services (*Health Affairs,* September/October 1997, January/February,
1998; *Journal of Health Politics, Policy and Law,* October 1999; Light 1995,
1997; Ikegami 1991).

This study examines the recent reforms in the world's largest public
healthcare systems, the 1991 reforms in the National Health Service (NHS)
in the United Kingdom and the 1995 reforms in the Veterans Health
Administration (VHA) in the United States Department of Veterans Affairs.
Although they differed in aims and specific strategies, the NHS and VHA
reforms were influenced by cross-national trends for market-based reform
and reflect the pressures and politics of the British and U.S. governments.
The NHS wanted to improve access to services and contain costs; the VHA
wanted to reduce costs and increase the number of veterans served.
Overshadowing the introduction of both reform efforts was concern over
the future viability of both systems.

The 1991 NHS reform policies emanated from a review established by
Prime Minister Thatcher in 1988 and were outlined in *Working for Patients*
(UK Secretaries of State for Health 1989). The NHS reforms, which were formally implemented in April 1991, introduced an internal market into the
NHS and were based on the work of Enthoven (1985) and managed competition, which "forces providers to compete for price, efficiency, and value
for money" (Light 1994, 1197), and General Practitioner fundholding (Maynard 1986). The NHS internal market split purchasers (NHS Health Authorities and GP fundholders) from providers (hospital and community service
providers and NHS Trusts).

The VHA reforms followed the failed U.S. health reform debates of
1993-94 and were outlined in *Vision for Change* (U.S. DVA 1995). The VHA
reforms, formally adopted in October 1995, were drawn from recommendations of earlier VHA appointed advisory groups and were based on managed-care models or "institutional arrangements whereby all (or nearly all)
services are coordinated under one administrative roof " (Light 1994, 1198)
and which use an array of techniques to contain costs. The VHA reform

techniques included cost reduction strategies, provider gatekeeping, use of performance measures, national price setting, and internal competition over fixed resources. The VHA centered its reform strategies on structural reorganization and the establishment of 22 Veterans Integrated Service Networks (VISNs), and, in an American technocratic fashion, developed an elaborate implementation plan that drove the reform objectives by linking them to performance measures.

The Health Systems

The NHS and VHA health systems share some features and have similar missions in delivery, medical education and training, and research. Both the NHS and VHA are government owned and operated systems that were established to ensure access to health services.

Both systems are primarily financed by general taxation.[2] However, the NHS is a large national health system in a relatively small nation; the VHA is the largest U.S. public healthcare system and exists alongside the mix of private and public U.S. health systems. Both the NHS and VHA provide health services to a disproportionate share of their respective populations that cannot afford health insurance.

The NHS

The NHS was created in 1948 following prior attempts for health reform, most notably the seminal proposal set forth in 1942 by Britain's Health Minister Beveridge calling for a national health service. Before the NHS was established, health services in the UK were uncoordinated and inadequate. The successful operation of England's Emergency Medical Service (EMS) during World War II brought together voluntary and area health authority hospitals under the direction of the British government and demonstrated the benefits of coordinated healthcare planning. This wartime experience helped to coalesce Britain's prior reform efforts for a national health system.

The NHS is an integrated national delivery system that provides inpatient and outpatient services free to all with the exception of small co-payments for select services, such as prescription co-payments, eyeglasses, and dental care. The NHS, a near monopoly, is available to all who reside in the UK. Of the 58 million people who live in the UK, 51.5 million people are residents of Britain, and the majority, 48.5 million, reside in England (UK OHE 1995). UK residents and visitors who want their care in the NHS register with a General Practitioner (GP), who is the point of referral for specialty and hospital services. There is a modest private health sector in the UK, which represented 3.4 percent of total UK health expenditures at the start of the reforms in 1991. The private sector primarily serves as a backup to the NHS and is used to bypass the long waiting lists in the NHS.

NHS health services are firmly based in primary care, with less emphasis on the provision of tertiary care and special services (Aaron and Schwartz 1984; Klein 1994) as provided by the VHA, which mirrors American medical practice with its comparatively high utilization of health services. The NHS provides health services to a proportionately larger number of women and children and offers maternity and pediatric services, which are not part of the VHA mission.

The VHA

Although the first mention of the U.S. government's responsibility for veterans was in 1636 in colonial laws, the Veterans Administration (VA) was formally established in 1930 to provide medical care and veterans' services for honorably discharged veterans. The VA underwent major expansion following World War II. Large numbers of returning veterans prompted the 1946 reorganization of VA medical programs from administrative to medical management under the VA's new Department of Medicine and Surgery (DM&S). At the same time, affiliation of VA hospitals with U.S. medical schools expanded the size, scope, and missions of the VA. In 1989, the VA was designated the Department of Veterans Affairs (DVA), the 14th cabinet department, which encompasses the Veterans Health Administration (VHA) as well as the Veterans Benefits Administration (VBA).

Market penetration differs between the VHA and the NHS. The VHA is an exclusive health provider that serves approximately 1 percent of the U.S. population and just over 10 percent of all living veterans. The VHA competes with other more dominant U.S. health systems. In recent years, the growth of managed care, which varies state by state, affects that competition. Veterans' use of the VHA is limited by misunderstanding of veteran eligibility for VHA care and public perceptions that VHA health services are only for the poor or those that cannot afford private health insurance. In recent years, there has been modest growth in the number of veterans who use the VHA. Over the years prior to implementation of the VHA reforms from FY 1991 to FY 1995, there was an increase of 100,000 veterans, representing 2.7 percent of veterans who received health services in the VHA.

A vertically integrated health system since its inception, the VHA provides care across the spectrum of health delivery from acute, state-of-the-art tertiary care and outpatient services to long term and home care services. The VHA services exclude pediatric and maternity care. To this day, and particularly in urban areas, the VHA serves as a safety net providing

Glossary of Terms

Consultants: Physician specialists who have training in specialty areas. Consultants are salaried employees of the National Health Service, but may also have private practices.

Cost Weighted Activity Index (CWAI): Introduced with the 1991 NHS reforms, CWAI is a weighted resource allocation formula that uses age, morbidity, local costs, and hospital utilization patterns to guide the local distribution of NHS resources.

General Practitioners (GPs): Self-employed physician practitioners paid out of public funds to provide primary care services to NHS patients who register on their lists.

GP Fundholders: As part of the 1991 NHS reforms, GPs with a certain patient list size could become fundholders and receive NHS appropriated funds to purchase select hospital and community services, prescription drugs, and provide salaries for non-medical practice staff.

Health Authorities (HAs): New organizational structures established by NHS in 1995 following the 1991 reforms. Each of the 100 HAs in the United Kingdom is responsible for the health planning needs of the area population and the purchasing the bulk of health services for residents of the community.

National Health Service (NHS): The United Kingdom's NHS is a government owned and operated healthcare system financed by general taxes. The NHS provides services free of charge, with the exception of small co-payments, to residents of the United Kingdom who register with a General Practitioner.

NHS Trusts: Established as part of the 1991 reforms, NHS Trusts include NHS hospitals and community service providers. These self-governing Trusts contract with purchasers of health services, namely Health Authorities and GP fundholders, to provide defined services. NHS Trusts are permitted to retain excess revenues from contracts to reinvest in patient services.

Primary Care Groups and Trusts (PCGs/PCGTs): As of 1999, under the Labour government's "new NHS," PCGs and PCGTs replaced GP Fundholders. PCGs of qualifying patient size could hold funds for purchasing services for resident populations.

Veterans Equitable Resource Allocation (VERA): A new resource allocation formula implemented by VHA in 1997, this capitation-based system uses national price per patient group, where average cost is used for national price.

Veterans Health Administration (VHA): The VHA is a federally funded public healthcare system. The VHA, the largest component of the Department of Veterans Affairs, provides healthcare to eligible veterans. A vertically integrated system since its inception, the VHA provides inpatient care, outpatient care, long term care, and home health services.

Veterans Integrated Service Networks (VISNs or Networks): The new organizational structure established in 1995 as part of the VHA reforms, the 22 Networks replaced the four prior Regions. The VISNs assumed responsibility for veteran population-based planning and health service delivery. The head of each VISN has budget control for the VHA hospitals and clinics in their areas.

health services to veterans with limited incomes and those who would otherwise be among the under-served. This role is of increasing importance in light of the recent U.S. health industry changes, growing costs of private health insurance, and the contraction in Medicaid and Medicare funding and local government spending.

Both the NHS and VHA provide major support to medical education, the training of allied health professionals, and basic and clinical research. The NHS supports all medical trainees in England; 60 percent of all U.S.-trained physicians have some part of their training in the VHA.

Study Findings

The NHS Reforms: Overview

The need to reform the NHS grew during the 1980s. In the early 1980s, the Conservative Thatcher government considered the introduction of private insurance schemes, but realizing the lack of popular and political support abandoned that reform plan. However, pressure for reform of the NHS increased due to problems over funding, reflected by long waiting lists and access issues. By the late 1980s, the pressures from professionals and the public reached a critical level. In 1988, Prime Minister Thatcher announced a review of the NHS. She pushed through the review of the NHS and won Parliamentary approval of the reforms before the runup to the 1990 election. The resulting policy paper, *Working for Patients,* which outlined the reforms, was approved by Parliament in 1990. The key goals of the NHS reform were to improve access and contain costs. Formal implementation of the reforms occurred in April 1991. However, despite the push for rapid approval, implementation of the NHS reforms was slow compared to the VHA reforms.

The NHS reforms were based on managed competition, which forces providers to compete for price, efficiency, and value for money. The reforms introduced an internal market into the NHS, which split the purchasers of services (Health Authorities and GP fundholders) from hospital and community service providers. NHS hospitals and community service providers could apply to become "quasi-independent" NHS Trusts and were promised more autonomy in hiring and firing staff and setting salary levels. As a last minute add-on to the reforms, General Practitioners could apply to become fundholders and purchase certain services for the patients on their lists. As part of the reforms, the Department of Health for the NHS introduced a new resource allocation formula—the Cost Weighted Activity Index (CWAI)—

which uses census data to allocate area funding.

The NHS reforms reflect the preference of Britain's Conservative government under Thatcher for a market model approach in public administration (Peters 1996, 19-25). The NHS reform efforts focused more on the process of setting new structures in motion (Trusts, GP fundholding, Health Authorities) rather than on outcomes. This emphasis differed from that in the VHA, where the reform strategies reflect a model of deregulating government (Ibid., 34-38), with a focus on results (Thompson and Riccucci 1998, 235-237).

1991 NHS Reforms

Precipitators:
Problems with access
Under-funding
Professional and public pressure

Policy document:
Working for Patients (1989)

Reform aims:
Improve access to services
Cost containment

Formal implementation date:
April 1, 1991

The Conservative government continued under the leadership of Prime Minister Major for seven years following the formal implementation of the reforms. These years were filled with challenges for Major as well as internecine struggles within the Conservative Party (Sullivan 1999, 41-42). Perhaps the implementation of the NHS reforms might have been more focused on outcomes had these confounding political pressures and distractions not clouded the reform implementation period.

The NHS reforms did not achieve all they set out to accomplish: waiting lists grew, and there was little change in patient choice, measures of clinical efficiency, or employee satisfaction. The most successful aspect of the NHS reforms was the separation of purchasers and providers. This finding was substantiated by both primary and secondary data. In a study of 22 Health Authorities in the West Midlands area conducted from 1989 to 1991, the initial years following announcement of the reforms, 87 percent of the District General Managers approved of the separation of purchaser and provider (Appleby et al. 1994).

GP fundholding, the "wild card" of the 1991 reforms, served as a large demonstration project that produced favorable outcomes and earned the confidence of the new Labour government. The experience with GP fundholding paved the way for Labour's current strategies for the "new NHS" and total commissioning (UK DOH 1997). In the long run, it may become evident that fundholding was the biggest success among the 1991 reform strategies. Despite the consensus from both primary and secondary data sources that regard the internal market as a failure, the purchaser provider

Features of the NHS Reforms
• Created an internal market to increase competition • Split purchasers of services from providers • Created Trust status for NHS hospitals and community service providers • Provided option for General Practitioners to become fund-holders

split was the winning strategy and remains central to Labour's new commissioning model (Dobson 1999, 40; UK DOH 1997). While commissioning is currently being touted as the replacement for competition, the value of such political word-smithing will reside in its ability to modulate the negative forces of market mechanisms (Light 1998) if lessons have been derived from the 1991 reforms.

There is less enthusiasm over the other aspects of the internal market (Appleby et al.1994, 32) and, in addition, evidence of the government's frequent need to manage the market. There were persistent pleas for close monitoring and critical evaluation of the reform impacts (Robinson and Le Grand 1994). The evidence indicates that NHS reform decisions were made for the short term. Yet, such short-term planning bypassed modeling the long-term impacts of the reforms, which would have helped anticipate the perverse incentives fostered by the reform strategies (Whitehead 1994).

The VHA Reforms: Overview

The antecedent for the VHA reforms was the 1993-94 U.S. attempt at national health reform. The VHA had participated in the national reform deliberations, and following those efforts, recognized the need to demonstrate improved clinical efficiency.

The VHA reforms were outlined in *Vision for Change* and approved by Congress in September 1995. The key aims of the reforms were to improve clinical efficiency and shift care from the hospital to outpatient settings. Formal implementation started in October 1995. Compared with the NHS, the VHA's reforms were fast-paced. They were timed for approval before the 1996 election campaign took off and were implemented quickly between election cycles.

The VHA reforms were based on managed care models, inspired by the recommendations of earlier VHA commissioned advisory groups. The VHA built its reform strategies around structural reorganization and the establishment of 22 Veterans Integrated Service Networks. Early in the plans for reform, Congress confirmed the appointment of a new Under Secretary for Health for the Department of Veterans Affairs from outside the VHA, Dr. Kenneth Kizer. Congruent with reinventing government techniques, the VHA developed an elaborate implementation plan that drove the reform objectives by linking them to performance measures.

The VHA's new resource allocation model VERA, which was adopted soon after the start of the reforms, fostered changes in resource distribution to Networks. As a result, VERA precipitated management practices that undermined

---

1995 VHA Reforms

Precipitators:
Perceived clinical inefficiency
U.S. national reform debate

Policy document:
Vision for Change (1995)

Reform aims:
Improve "clinical value" for expenditures
Shift care from hospital to outpatient settings

Formal implementation date:
October 1, 1995

---

access and equity for several vulnerable populations—namely, elderly veterans and those in need of long-term care, and complex and chronic patients such as the seriously mentally ill and substance abuse patients (US GAO 1999; US VSOs 1999). The VHA reduced the apparent demand from chronic patients by downsizing programs and cutting beds in response to performance measures and the VERA model and its use of national allocation rates. And, just as the effects of VERA varied across the country, the responses of managers and staff were often linked to the level of Network funding.

The rapid pace of the VHA reforms reflects the relatively brief window of opportunity that the VHA had for reform. Compared to the NHS reforms, which relied on a market model (Peters 1996, 19-25), the VHA reforms were based on a model of deregulating government (Ibid., 34-37). Yet, Peters (1996) urges caution in the use of deregulation in public program areas "that deal with the basic rights of citizens" (Ibid., 38). And while the VHA benefits are not basic rights, but part of discretionary government spending, they represent a government commitment to veterans for military service, a commitment that is perceived by veterans as an entitlement. Devolution of authority, results orientation and use of performance contracts, and emphasis on competition and customer service, despite questionable effects, reflect strategies common to reinventing government (Thompson and Riccucci 1998, 235-237). These strategies had bipartisan appeal and helped to support the opportunity for reform of the VHA.

The VHA was successful in changing the focus of VHA care from hospital care to healthcare. Aided by VA eligibility reform (U.S. Congress

---

Features of the NHS Reforms

• Adopted managed-care principles
• Created VISN structure and decentralized decision-making
• Recruited a new VHA Under Secretary for Health
• Relied on performance contracts and performance measures for change

---

1996)—which removed restrictions on the provision of outpatient services for most categories of veterans—and primary-care initiatives, more veterans are now treated by the VHA.[3] Yet, while the VHA was successful in decreasing costs in response to federal budget constraints and the reform strategies, these pressures spawned problems across the VHA missions of delivery, medical education and training, and research, and impacted the workforce.

The VHA achieved many of the stated reform targets. Yet, the VHA reforms were controversial among Veterans Service Organizations (VSOs). By late 1998, there was increasing political fallout over the effects of the VHA reforms. Dr. Kizer was not re-confirmed by Congress for a full term in October 1998 and resigned on June 30, 1999.

The NHS and VHA incorporated several shared strategies in their reform interventions: (1) adopted market-based reform strategies; (2) reshaped the organization and moved operational authority from the center (the NHS Executive and VHA Headquarters) to the periphery (Health Authorities in NHS and Networks in VHA); (3) introduced new weighted capitation models for resource allocation within fixed global budgets— CWAI in the NHS, VERA in the VHA; (4) set incentives to change clinical practice, which includes the expansion of primary care and adoption of clinical pathways, and tightly controlled drug formularies; and (5) modified missions through changes in the balance within and among delivery, medical education and training, and research.

The NHS expenditures increased gradually before the reforms, and continued to increase in a similar gradual pattern following the reforms. However, during the early years of the reforms, infusion of additional funds

---

Shared NHS and VHA Reform Strategies

• Adopted market-inspired reform models
• Reconfigured regions and devolved power
• Introduced new allocation models
• Established incentives to change clinical practice
• Re-evaluated missions

facilitated reform implementation. The VHA budget, which had very minimally increased before the reforms, completely flat-lined as a result of the 1997 Balanced Budget Amendment (Figure 6.1). And given the VHA's expansion into new outpatient areas as a result of the reforms, this amounted to a relative decrease in funding. After adjusting for inflation, the NHS expenditures increased 21 percent (1989-1993) and the VHA expenditures increased 3 percent (1994-1998).

Figure 6.1: NHS and VHA Expenditures
Constant Pounds/Dollars in Billions (1995)

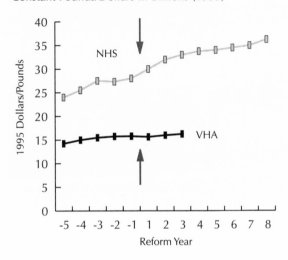

Structures

The establishment of NHS Health Authorities (HAs) came relatively late in the reforms. Health Authorities were key in shepherding change and serving as organizational anchors during times of flux; they served as the interface between policy and implementation and mediated new roles with Trusts and GP fundholders. The NHS Executive artfully devolved power and responsibility to Health Authorities, and the HAs responded with remarkable skill given their limited experience in the newly established quasi-markets. The NHS was primarily "being shaped, not so much by competition or consumer preferences as by Health Authority planners using purchasing as their tool" (Redmayne, Day and Klein 1995, 9). The future of Health Authorities is uncertain both with respect to their role and number. However, future evaluation of Health Authorities will be based not only on their role in health service planning, but also on measures of health outcomes.

Table 6.1: NHS and VHA Reforms: Areas of Convergence and Divergence in Health Policy

Health Policy/ Strategy Area	Convergence		Divergence	
	NHS	**VHA**	**NHS**	**VHA**
Planning the reform strategies			↓	♦↑↑
Funding			♦↑	♦=
Change in resource allocation model	♦	♦		
Population-based planning	♦	♦		
National allocation rate per patient			=	♦↓
Geographic shift in resource allocation	♦↑	♦↑↑↑		
Market mechanisms			♦	♦
New sources of private funding	♦	♦		
Use of performance contracts			=	♦↑↑↑↑
Use of performance measures			=	♦↑↑↑↑
Evaluation of reforms	♦↓↓↓↓	♦↓↓↓		

Key:

↑ = slight use/increase	↑↑ = moderate use/increase
↑↑↑ = great use/increase	↑↑↑↑ = extreme use/increase
↓ = slight use/decrease	↓↓ = moderate use/decrease
↓↓↓ = great use/decrease	↓↓↓↓ = extreme use/decrease
♦ = key reform strategy	= = unchanged

Arrows (↑) indicate the relative degree of reliance on or the direction of change a particular strategy elicited. The number of arrows assigned is an approximation based on the synthesis of the quantitative and qualitative data gathered and reviewed.

The long tenure of the NHS Executive and longevity of the Conservative party's dominance in the UK, compared with the leadership in VHA Headquarters and given the U.S. political structure, provided continuity to establish the NHS reforms and gain experience with GP fundholding.

The creation of Veterans Integrated Service Networks was key in the VHA reforms. The use of performance measures and contracts to achieve the objectives of the reforms introduced a new level of central control despite the flattening of the organization and the devolution of operational responsibility to the Networks. The Network structure was accompanied by a new form of competition that was compounded by scarce resources due to VHA's constrained budget and the adoption of VERA. Both secondary and primary data prompt questions over the pace and evaluation of the VHA reforms. These questions suggest that the VHA underwent substantive and rapid change, and in the context of the newly devolved authority to Networks and pressures for performance, the need existed for better information, national coordination and oversight of health services, and evaluation of the effects of reform at the local level.

Health Service Delivery

Changes in health service delivery were more pronounced in the VHA than in the NHS. In the VHA, the numbers of hospital admissions and beds dropped dramatically, whereas the number of patients and the provision of outpatient services showed marked increases. Both systems expanded primary care, with greater change in the VHA. And both the NHS and VHA introduced strategies to decrease clinical cost variations such as clinical pathways and controlled drug formularies.

Several factors constrain the ability to assess the NHS post-reform change in the delivery of health services. First, frustration exists among reviewers of the NHS reforms over the lack of information and the need for systematic evaluation of the reforms. Given the limitations of information, in general, the scope of the NHS health services are similar to those in 1989, if not 1948: Healthcare remains a local decision at the discretion of the provider (Klein 1995, 311). Exceptions to this are the erosion of government support for the NHS provision of long term care and the problems with coordination of community services in the care of the mentally ill despite the growing demand for services among the elderly and frequent crises in the care of the seriously mentally ill.

The reforms were not successful in improving waiting times in a significant and sustained way, and they were ineffective in increasing patient choice. They did achieve improvements in care, access, and quality for the

---

Changes in Clinical Practice

- Trends in health service delivery

	NHS (1989-1993)	VHA (1994-1998)
- hospital admissions	+ 7%	– 23%
- reduced beds	– 19%	– 48%
- increased number of patients	~	+ 20%
- increased outpatient services	+ 8%	+ 35%

- Expanded primary and outpatient care
- Introduced clinical pathways and drug formularies

---

patients of GP fundholders, demonstrating the efficiencies and value to be derived from organizational rearrangements that promote ownership and enhance the achievement of common goals. However, the lack of continuity of care from primary to tertiary settings raises concerns over future clinical efficiency and quality.

The evidence of the impact of the reforms on equity reveals mixed findings. The change in policy for non-acute long term care has adversely affected many individuals and precipitated financial hardship (Whitehead 1994, 231-240). However, claims of cream skimming have produced equivocal findings. Le Grand notes that, for fundholders, the policy provision to protect practices from the cost of expensive patients (above 5,000 pounds) reduced the incentive to limit complex patients from their lists (Le Grand 1999, 31).

The only evidence of change in overall efficiency is demonstrated by an increase in the cost-weighted activity index (CWAI), the overall indicator of NHS efficiency. The CWAI—which measures volume of health services, but not case-mix, quality, or effectiveness of outcomes—grew 4.4 percent from 1991 to 1995, compared to a 2.3 percent growth in the decade from 1980 through 1990. When adjusted for the changes in resources over these periods, the average annual change in productivity efficiency, or volume of health services, was 2 percent following the reforms compared to 1.5 percent in the decade prior to the reforms (Mulligan 1998, 24; Le Grand, Mays, and Dixon 1998, 120).

As summarized by Le Grand (1994, 259), much of the direct research on the reforms indicates little change in quality, efficiency, choice, responsiveness, and equity in the first two years following the reforms. Hunter

Table 6.2: NHS and VHA: Areas of Convergence and Divergence in Health Service Delivery Following Reform

Health Service Delivery/ Strategy Area	Convergence		Divergence	
	NHS	VHA	NHS	VHA
Reduced number of beds	♦↓	♦↓↓↓		
Reduced length of stay/ BDOC/1,000 pts	♦↓↓	♦↓↓↓		
Integrated/merged hospitals	♦↑	♦↑↑		
Change in number of patients treated/yr			=↑	♦↑↑
Change in number of enrollees			=↑	♦↑↑
Change in access to long-term care	♦↓↓	♦↓↓		
Change in access to mental health services	♦↓↓	♦↓↓		
Change in access to outpatient services	↑	↑↑↑		
Primary care: coordinated/ comprehensive			=	♦↑↑
Pharmaceutical controls	♦	♦		
National strategic planning	↓↓	↓↓↓		
Rationing	↑↑	↑		
Quality of care	?	?		
Quality Management Program			♦↑↑	♦↓↓↓
Waiting lists/times	↑/↓	? /?		
Patient satisfaction			=?	↓↓

Key:

↑ = slight use/increase   ↑↑ = moderate use/increase
↑↑↑ = great use/increase   ↓ = slight use/decrease
↓↓ = moderate use/decrease   ↓↓↓ = great use/decrease
♦ = key reform strategy   ? = uncertain
= = unchanged

Arrows (↑) indicate the relative degree of reliance on or the direction of change a particular strategy elicited. The number of arrows assigned is an approximation based on the synthesis of the quantitative and qualitative data gathered and reviewed for this research.

(1997) echoed this assertion later in the course of the implementation of the reforms noting however, that the NHS reforms suffer from the lack of systematic evaluation. In his most recent assessment of the NHS, Le Grand (1999, 32) reconfirmed his earlier observations that little change occurred. Perhaps this lack of change fits with the Conservative agenda: contain costs and satisfy public unrest over the NHS, but avoid cumbersome regulation. In the end, there was little measurable change in health service delivery in the NHS following the 1991 reforms.

The effects of the VHA reforms on the delivery of health services are mixed. While the VHA is now treating more patients than prior to the 1995 reforms, it does not appear that access for the more indigent veterans has improved. In fact, the evidence suggests that support of these patients eroded. The assumption by many managers was that the VHA was inefficient in all areas of health service delivery; this assumption may reflect a lack of appreciation among such managers for the differences between and among veteran populations.

The reforms fostered changes in the delivery of VHA health services. The number of veterans cared for increased and bed days of care fell. However, there is evidence of uneven access to costly programs and that the VHA must carefully reassess that balance among its clinical programs in light of the veterans it serves, their needs, and the recommendations of concerned interest groups (US VSOs 1999; US GAO 1998, 1999; Cohen 1999).

The VHA made strides in expanding primary care programs and integrating primary care through all levels of care. In terms of integrating care, the VHA and NHS differ. Most primary care providers are VHA employees and many VHA clinics are situated on the site of VA medical centers, which offers a geographical convenience that encourages communication. This differs from the NHS, where GP-provided care is distinct from NHS inpatient, acute, and specialty care. However, as the number of VHA Community Based Outreach Clinics (CBOCs) grows, and with many CBOCs staffed by non-VHA employees, the challenges that face the VHA may mimic those of the NHS in integrating primary and hospital-based care.

While the quality of VHA care appears good compared with other health systems, following the reforms, the VHA limited what they systematically measure and set aside established quality management programs that assessed the quality of care and detected sentinel events (US Senate Minority Staff 1997). The findings of recent reviews (US DVA OIG 1998, 1999; US Senate Minority Staff 1997) encouraged the VHA to rebuild its quality management programs to reliably assess access, equity, and outcomes of health services given the magnitude of changes the reforms introduced into VHA health service delivery.

In the NHS, following the reforms, the number of admissions continued to increase at the same rate as before. In addition, the number of day cases increased. The decrease in the number of VHA admissions reflects the VHA's shift in care from hospital to outpatient settings (Figure 6.2).

Figure 6.2: NHS and VHA Hospital Admissions

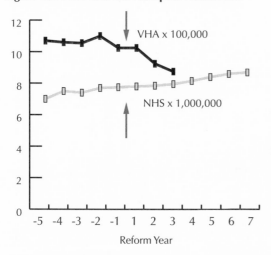

In both systems, there were noticeable bed reductions in the early years of the reform. Bed reductions in the VHA were much more pronounced than in the NHS (Figure 6.3).

Figure 6.3: Total Hospital Beds

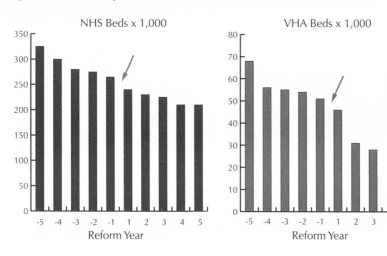

The reductions in mental health beds were more pronounced in the VHA than in the NHS (Figure 6.4). The adverse impacts of these rapid closures drew so much public criticism that in the VHA, control of mental health resources was recently re-centralized; in the NHS, there was a call for a national review.

Figure 6.4: Mental Health Beds

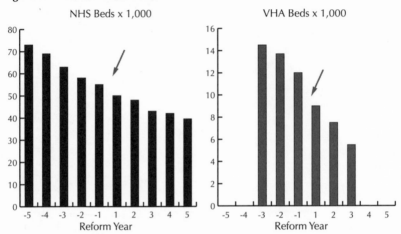

In the past, the NHS did not maintain data on the number of individuals cared for in the NHS. The NHS reforms had no incentive to treat more patients, and the number of patients, as can best be estimated, was essentially unchanged. The VHA increased the number of new veterans it cared for by 20 percent from 1994 to 1998 (Figure 6.5). One of the VHA's reform

Figure 6.5: NHS and VHA Patient Population (x Million)

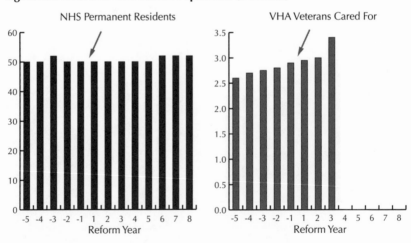

aims was to increase the number of veterans cared for to drive down apparent cost per capita and move more in line with a managed care setting. The VHA was successful in accomplishing that goal aided by eligibility reform. VHA officials won congressional support for eligibility reform early in the reforms, which rationalized the provision of outpatient care and allowed veterans to be cared for without prior hospitalization. In addition, the new VERA allocation model rewarded facilities similar to HMO models, with resources for treating new, especially inexpensive, patients.

Outpatient activity increased in both systems, but the increases were steeper for the VHA (Figure 6.6). These differences may be attributable to the VHA's goals and reform incentives, as well as pre-reform market penetration.

Figure 6.6: Outpatient Activity (x Million Visits)

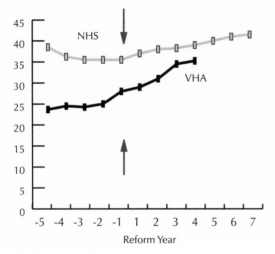

Medical Education & Training and Research

The reforms ushered in new pressures between the NHS and VHA and their affiliated universities and medical schools. In both settings, external changes in medical education, such as changes in training requirements and restricted work hours for trainees, confounded implementation of the reforms. Although the NHS environment differs from that of the VHA, where there are competing health systems to serve as affiliates, the confluence of the NHS reforms and growing pressures in medical education and training, and research impacted physician roles and affiliate relationships. Concerned over the impact of the reforms on medical education and research, the vice-chancellors of NHS affiliates, through lobbying efforts with Parliament, gained membership on Health Authority and NHS Trust

Boards. Among the more palpable changes in medical education and training, and research is the impact on individual faculty and consultants for clinical service, which infringes on academic time.

It will take a number of years to correct the current physician shortage in Britain given the recent approval to increase the number of medical trainee slots. More significantly, it appears that the British government needs to respond to current pressures to increase the NHS budget if they are to appease professionals and retain trained physicians in the UK. The current

Table 6.3: NHS and VHA: Areas of Convergence and Divergence in Medical Education and Training Following Reform

Medical Education and Training/Strategy Area	Convergence		Divergence	
	NHS	VHA	NHS	VHA
Number of medical education affiliates			NA	↓
Change in number of medical students			↑↑	↓
Change in number of medical residents			↑↑	↓
Change in number of allied trainees/programs			NA	↓
Change in support of faculty in medical education	↓	↓		
Pressure on faculty for delivery versus education	◆↑↑	◆↑↑		
Medical education emphasis on primary care	↑	↑↑		

Key:

↑ = slight use/increase   ↑↑ = moderate use/increase
↓ = slight use/decrease   ↓↓ = moderate use/decrease
◆ = use of strategy   NA = not available

Arrows (↑) indicate the relative degree of reliance on or the direction of change a particular strategy elicited. The number of arrows assigned is an approximation based on the synthesis of the quantitative and qualitative data gathered and reviewed for this research.

environment requires both political skill and wisdom to learn from the past strife between the government and clinicians over funding of health services.

The VHA reforms introduced change that has challenged the VHA's commitment to medical education and training, and research—two key missions that have helped define the VHA health system and contribute to the quality of its services. Like the NHS, funding pressures and dwindling

Table 6.4: NHS and VHA: Areas of Convergence and Divergence in Research Following Reform

Research/ Strategy Area	Convergence		Divergence	
	NHS	VHA	NHS	VHA
Evaluation of research mission	↑↑	↑↑		
Total research funding change	?	↑		
NHS and VHA research funding/operational support	?/↓	↑/↓		
Control of funds	◆	◆		
Change in research focus	◆↑	◆↑↑		
Increase in HSR&D	◆↑	◆↑		
National influences on research agenda (Prevention/institutional)	◆↑↑	◆↑↑		
Pressure on staff for clinical time over research	◆↑↑↑	◆↑↑↑		
New initiatives for research program planning	◆	◆		
New initiatives for research	◆↑	◆↑		

Key:

↑ = slight use/increase   ↑↑ = moderate use/increase
↑↑↑ = great use/increase   ↓ = slight use/decrease
↓↓ = moderate use/decrease   ↓↓↓ = great use/decrease
◆ = key reform strategy   ? = uncertain

Arrows (↑) indicate the relative degree of reliance on or the direction of change a particular strategy elicited. The number of arrows assigned is an approximation based on the synthesis of the quantitative and qualitative data gathered and reviewed for this research.

support of management for research and education followed the reforms and discouraged VHA clinicians. In addition to the reforms transforming the VHA, the scope and nature of the changes associated with the reforms have altered the historic and traditional relationships between medical schools and VHA medical centers (Cohen 1999). In 1998, out of concern for the tensions between the VHA and its academic affiliates, the Association of American Medical Colleges (AAMC) surveyed deans of medical schools on the health of their affiliations with the VHA. Half of the deans who responded indicated that they were extremely dissatisfied with their Network director and one foresaw the likely possibility of disaffiliating from the VHA. In November 1998, at the AAMC 109th annual meeting, a joint meeting gathered members of the AAMC's Council of Deans and Network directors for a half-day airing of views and discussion. The deans again reiterated the need for their involvement in VHA's planning processes (Ibid.).

Human Resources

The reforms generated anxiety for NHS and VHA staff. Fears over privatization or demise of each health system; change in roles and status; staff cuts; and changes in medical education and training, and research impacted the workforce in both systems.

Following the reforms, there were staff reductions, morale problems, and strained communications in both systems. The reductions in staff were more pronounced in the VHA and varied by VISN depending on the impact of the VERA resource allocation model (Figure 6.7).

Figure 6.7: Total Staff (x 1,000)

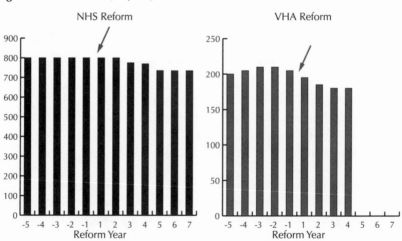

At the start of their respective reforms, the NHS was comparatively understaffed by physician specialists while the VHA was physician-rich. Following the reforms, the number of NHS Consultants was increased to reduce waiting lists and increase the availability of services. The VHA, after several years of hiring physicians, began to reduce physicians (Figure 6.8).

Figure 6.8: Medical Staff (x 1,000)

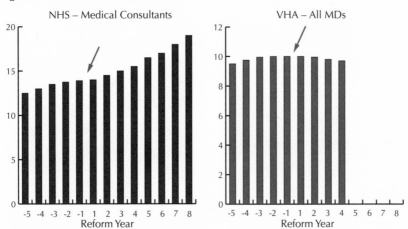

The NHS reforms were not successful in increasing employee satisfaction. The reform process and constrained resources seriously eroded employee and GP confidence and satisfaction. While professional gaps between GPs and Consultants improved, the future promises numerous interdisciplinary challenges as Primary Care Groups expand their roles and interactions with NHS Hospital and Community Trusts and Consultants. Moreover, the NHS faces crucial issues related to its workforce: professional staff shortages and recruitment problems persist, and training deficiencies, inequities in pay, and work conditions are inextricably linked to competencies and professional satisfaction. The health of the NHS depends on the ability of the government to rectify the past by thoughtfully tackling these areas, or suffer the ills of a disgruntled workforce and further staff losses.

The VHA reforms have had significant effects on their employees. In part because of the pace and goals of the VHA reforms, these problems were experienced as being more severe in the VHA than in the NHS. Rapid implementation of the reform strategies, large reductions in staff, and limited and poor communications impacted employee morale. While the evidence found that employee issues and low morale varied by geographic area, the overall morale of the VHA workforce suffered as a result of the reforms. There was little evidence of true empowerment of front-line staff.

Table 6.5: NHS and VHA: Areas of Convergence and Divergence in Human Resources Following Reform

Human Resource Area/ Strategy	Convergence		Divergence	
	NHS	VHA	NHS	VHA
Number of staff	↓↓	♦↓↓↓		
Early retirements	↑↑	♦↑↑↑		
Buy-outs incentives to leave system			?	♦↑↑
Staff morale	↓↓	↓↓↓		
Communications	↓↓	↓↓↓↓		
Professional staff involvement in reforms	♦↓↓	♦↓↓↓↓		
Staff empowerment	♦↓	♦↓↓↓		

Key:

↑ = slight use/increase   ↑↑ = moderate use/increase

↑↑↑ = great use/increase   ↑↑↑↑ = extreme use/increase

↓ = slight use/decrease   ↓↓ = moderate use/decrease

↓↓↓ = great use/decrease   ↓↓↓↓ = extreme use/decrease

♦ = use of strategy   ? = uncertain

Arrows (↑) indicate the relative degree of reliance on or the direction of change a particular strategy elicited. The number of arrows assigned is an approximation based on the synthesis of the quantitative and qualitative data gathered and reviewed.

Organizational Change

The window for reform appears to have impacted the organizational culture of the NHS more than the quantitative measures of health service delivery. The reforms provided the groundwork for the 1998 Labour government's move to a "softer," "new NHS," and adoption of total GP commissioning through the creation of Primary Care Groups and Trusts. The 1991 reforms "fast forwarded" the prior pace of incremental change in the NHS and made a significant statement regarding the diminishing role of the welfare state. Still, ubiquitous issues persist for the NHS: timeliness of services, equity, and underfunding. The current concerns over care of the chronically mentally ill and provision of long term care for the elderly and special populations highlight a sample of the inequities and resource needs.

> "... Even in an ideal world, there are rarely simple answers
> to apparently simple questions—usually because, as in this
> case, the questions are not actually simple. The reforms
> embrace a wide variety of organizational changes, each of
> which involves different aspects of the NHS, affects differ-
> ent players and agents within the service, and ideally
> should be subject to its own evaluation process."
>
> (Le Grand 1994, 243)

Labour's "new NHS" appears committed to integrating care, diminish-ing inequalities (UK Independent Inquiry 1998), and raising the quality of care by setting national standards through the National Institute for Clinical Excellence (NICE) and oversight by the Commission for Health Improvement (CHI) (UK DOH 1998). The message of the new government is for less com-mand and control and a commitment to increase NHS funding by 4.7 per-cent a year in real terms (Dobson 1999, 40-41). It remains to be seen if this proposed increase in funding will be both realized and sufficient.

The past accommodation of British medical practice to NHS appropri-ations raises the question of whether this method of rationing will continue to manage the increased demand for NHS services as advances in medical technology, coupled with better informed patients, compound the NHS "supply crisis." Today's young British generation expects a more affluent lifestyle than that of its parents'; it is unlikely that it will be as complacent a generation in its expectations for healthcare.

The experience from an earlier study of the effects of the 1991 reforms is instructive for the future (Salter 1994). The struggle between the old and new structures as prior Regional Health Authorities faded and District Health Authorities gained control created destructive tensions between ambitious managers and physicians over perennial concerns about the rationing of healthcare (Ibid.). As the NHS moves forward, it is essential to strategically plan and intervene as new vulnerabilities resurrect old ten-sions. Still, the overarching theme persists: The NHS is comparatively underfunded and, as such, is hard-pressed to face the coming challenges of technologically advanced heath care in the 21st century. Aesthetic repairs "at the margins," despite the dramatic reorganization, have not improved the fundamental ability of the NHS to provide timely, state-of-the-art care for all groups. While it was not expected that the reforms would decrease cost, it appears that value for money is improving in areas such as services to patients of fundholders. Yet, additional resources are required to continue that process. In the future, as it has been in the past, it will be important to distinguish "between political need to claim success and, on the other hand, evidence of improved efficiency—which is incomplete at best, and ambiguous and uncertain at worst" (Maynard and Bloor 1996, 607).

Finally, the NHS reforms have been described as an Americanized reform model: an emphasis on market forces; the use of the internal markets for contracting; the establishment of Trusts to transform hospitals similar to non-profits; and efforts to promote health (Mechanic 1995). As a counter argument, another perspective of the 1991 reforms proposes that the NHS has been Americanized by the use of tax breaks that provide discounts on health insurance at taxpayers' expense; the fostering of two-tier access to vital services; the transfer of public property to investors at favorable rates; the use of public dollars to pay for private services with built-in profits; and the erosion of services for individuals with chronic problems despite an increase in those requiring such support (Light 1997, 333-334). Perhaps the current change that is underway in the NHS will provide the evidence to settle this policy debate.

The questions remain: Can the British government sculpt constructive incentives, adequately fund the NHS, and provide sufficient guidance to improve access, efficiency, and quality in the NHS? Time and better information are needed to determine the answers. The 1991 reforms generated significant change and set a foundation for future improvements of the NHS that mostly will depend on adequate resources, effective strategies, and organizational will. While many of the stated objectives of the reforms were not achieved, progress was made in several areas. The essence of the 1991 reform experience is that the NHS continues to reinvent itself and that the lessons learned over the past 10 years have enabled the imminent changes in the NHS under Labour's plan for a "new NHS."

One of the most successful aspects of the VHA reforms was to move the VHA further into the mainstream of the mix of U.S. health systems. Through the use of market principles and initiatives to improve the utilization of health services, the reforms advanced several changes that improved patient care and fostered continuity, which include expanded access to outpatient services and community-based clinics. In addition, the reforms revitalized the agency's energy and introduced an unprecedented process of change that some thought not possible. The VHA reforms, like the NHS reforms, shifted the organizational balance. And, as in the NHS, power shifted away from the professionals to the managers. The VHA relied on managers rather than clinicians, perhaps more so than in the NHS, to adjust health-service planning and delivery to budgetary appropriations. In this regard, the VHA differed from the NHS, where the tradition has been to rely on British medical practice to accommodate available NHS resources and to allow comparatively more professional input.

Still, like the NHS, the VHA has significant issues still to address. Waiting times remain problematic and new challenges have developed regarding access and equity for some veterans.

The NHS and VHA reforms were associated with convergent and divergent reform strategies and consequences in the areas of health policy; health service delivery; medical education and training; research; human resources; and byproducts or unexpected consequences of the reforms (Tables 6.1-6.6). The NHS reforms reflect the Conservative government's market model orientation in public administration (Peters 1996, 19-21), while the VHA reforms best fit with a deregulating model of government (Ibid., 34-37), which matched the bipartisan U.S. objectives associated with the "reinvention of government" (US National Performance Review 1993; Osborne and Graebler 1992).

Byproducts of the Reforms

Both the NHS and VHA reforms precipitated byproducts and unexpected consequences, and several of these consequences were similar: power shifts, changes in organizational culture, dominance of area planning over national coordination, changes in communications, and impacts on staff morale (Table 6.6). The evidence from both cases suggests that the NHS and VHA reforms were dependent on a window for reform, but circumstances around the windows differed.

Summary

The structure of the British government and the Conservative agenda under Thatcher influenced both the choice of reform strategies and the pace of the NHS reforms. Managed competition fit with the Conservative government's aim to reduce or, in the case of the NHS, at least contain welfare spending. The Conservative government, in the runup to an election, pushed through a review of the NHS that won approval of Parliament in 1990; yet, the implementation of the reforms proceeded slowly. Choosing competition over regulation, the British government placed the onus on providers and purchasers to derive more value from NHS appropriations.

The VHA chose a managed care approach, which mirrored U.S. health industry trends; managed competition models had been set aside with the

Table 6.6: Byproducts of the NHS and VHA Reforms

	Strategy/Area	NHS	VHA
P	Power shifts		↑↑ To PC from Specialists
		↑↑ To HA	↑↑↑↑ To Network
		↑↑ To NHS Executive	↑↑↑↑ To Headquarters
P	Strategic national planning	↓↓ Impact of HAs	↓↓↓ Impact of Networks
P	Incrementalism	↑↑ "New NHS" in 1998	?
P	Perverse incentives from performance contracts	? Not apparent	↑↑ Performance contracts/bonuses
P	Quality management	↑↑	↓↓↓
D	Change in mission	↑	↑↑
D	Rationing	↑↑	↑
D	Access	↓↓ Long term care; mental health; waiting lists grew	↓↓↓ Acute care; long term care; mental health; substance abuse waiting lists appear to remain problematic
D	Patient satisfaction	=?	↓↓
ME	Management support of Medical Education and Training	↓	↓↓
R	Management support of Research	↓	↓↓
HR	Human Resources	↓↓ Staff morale; staff shortages	↓↓↓ Staff morale; staff losses
HR	Communications	↓↓	↓↓↓↓
HR	Organizational culture change	↑↑ Manager dominated; cost consciousness	↑↑ Manager dominated; cost consciousness
HR	Creative energies	↑↑ Some Trusts; GP fundholders	↑ Some Networks

Key:

P = policy;   D = delivery;   ME = medical education & training;
R = research;   HR = human resources

↑ = slight use/increase   ↑↑ = moderate use/increase
↑↑↑ = great use/increase   ↑↑↑↑ = extreme use/increase
↓ = slight use/decrease   ↓↓ = moderate use/decrease
↓↓↓ = great use/decrease   ↓↓↓↓ = extreme use/decrease
? = uncertain   = = unchanged

Arrows (↑) indicate the relative degree of reliance on or the direction of change a particular strategy elicited. The number of arrows assigned is an approximation based on the synthesis of the quantitative and qualitative data gathered and reviewed.

Clinton administration's failed attempt for national reform. The evidence suggests that the pace of the VHA reforms was in response to the political context. Clinton faced an upcoming election in 1996. Rapid congressional approval of the VHA 1995 reforms was needed and was obtained before campaign issues flourished in 1996. The comparably fast pace of the VHA reforms fit with the relatively brief window of support of the Republican Congress as again, in 1999, the political focus would be on the upcoming presidential election.

The evidence suggests that the differences in the U.S. and British governmental structures and political agendas help explain the distinctions in the NHS and VHA reform strategies. The British Government had been successful in containing costs in the NHS, but wanted to diffuse the angry public and professional sentiments toward funding and waiting lists. A reform strategy that had competition as its base resonated with the Thatcher government, which aimed to increase the effectiveness of NHS expenditures (Glennerster 1993, 66-67). The VHA wanted and needed rapid results; the use of performance contracts and measures helped achieve those aims.

Conclusions

The NHS and VHA reforms demonstrate the ability of large public systems to take on significant reforms. The magnitude of these changes is unparalleled in the history of the NHS and VHA. The convergence of various conditions provided both the NHS and the VHA the necessary windows for reform. Their individual approaches to reform reflect not only the past practices and culture of the NHS and VHA, but their respective institutional and political contexts.

While some changes following the reforms cannot be unraveled with certainty from environmental influences and simultaneous changes in the health industry, particularly the changes in health service utilization, other changes are directly attributable to the reforms. These include the reorganization of Health Authorities and VISNs; creation of the NHS internal market; introduction of VHA performance contracts; devolution of power; and change in the role of GPs. The following conclusions highlight the distinctions, as well as areas of convergence, in NHS and VHA reforms.

1. The VHA had more notable changes in health service delivery than the NHS.

Differences in health service delivery in the NHS and VHA following the reforms can be described in inputs and outputs. The NHS had steady or slightly increased inputs (as measured by expenditures) and maintained approximately the same, or slightly increased, outputs (as measured by the number of patients, admissions, outpatient attendance, and day cases). By contrast, the VHA decreased inputs (flat budget appropriation, decreased cost per patient, staff cuts) and increased outputs (numbers of unique patients, number of clinics, outpatient visits). The VHA expanded primary care and enhanced the importance of the role of the primary-care providers. The expansion of primary care in the VHA shifted power and status from specialists to primary care providers and is similar to the effects of the NHS reforms.

Significant Findings

Reform Windows and Strategies
- The timing and duration of the reform windows influenced the reform strategy and effects.
- Differences between NHS and VHA goals and strategies appear congruent with their respective reliance on market versus deregulation models of public governance.
- Managed competition had little impact on the health service delivery as measured.
- The VHA's use of performance contracts promoted change.

Mission Impacts
- GP fundholding was successful in improving care for patients; however, it fostered "two tiers" of service.
- The expansion of primary care increased the continuity of care for veterans.
- Access decreased for costly patients (NHS and VHA) and increased for inexpensive patients (VHA).
- The reforms failed to improve waiting lists.
- The shift in primary versus specialty mix reflects pre-reform baselines.
- The reforms in both systems increased reliance on primary care providers.
- Market-inspired reforms focused on short-term goals at the expense of long-term missions.
- Reform damaged staff morale.

2. The NHS GP fundholding was the main success of the reforms.

The NHS, through its introduction of GP fundholding, rearranged power structures, and the status and function of GPs, which improved services for the patients of fundholders. However, GP fundholding appears to have contributed to two tiers of service in the NHS. Fundholding, which increased the power of GP gatekeepers in order to contain costs and improve services, brought General Practitioners back into the forefront of care in the UK. The success of GP fundholding, as well as some impacts of fundholding, which generated two tiers of service, were underestimated by policy makers.

3. Neither the NHS nor VHA was successful in reducing waiting lists. Similarly, access to chronic costly care, such as long-term care and mental health, decreased.

The failure to reduce the number of patients on NHS waiting lists and the wait for outpatient appointments in the VHA suggests the need for other policy measures, which may include the need for additional resources or the use of different incentives.

The evidence suggests that following the reforms some patients were made better off, but some were made worse off. Several strategies fostered changes that appear to have diminished access for the mentally ill and those with long term care needs.

Although these changes may have been logical consequences of policy aims to reduce costs, there is an irony in that the NHS and VHA, which started as government interventions for market failures, have, in their incremental metamorphoses, adopted reform strategies that, as the evidence suggests, appear to be creating "public system failures" in terms of access for these vulnerable populations.

4. The NHS and VHA reforms posed challenges to the commitment to medical education and training, and research.

The balance among health service delivery, medical education and training, and research missions was altered following the reforms in both the NHS and VHA.

Pressure for short-term change and cost containment caused these systems to emphasize health service delivery. In the process, the regard for medical education and training and research—missions associated with long-term benefits—diminished.

The confluence of reform pressures with external factors in medical education and training confounded the implementation of reform in both systems. External events, simultaneous to the reforms, impacted medical education and training in the NHS ("New Deal," physician shortages, and

redesign of medical education) and the VHA (pressures for increased resident supervision, growth of primary care training, and decrease in specialty
training). Both the NHS and VHA relied on the use of in locum physicians
and foreign medical graduate physicians to augment clinical delivery where
resident/trainee time decreased. Following the reforms, pressure for short-
term results increased pressure on physicians for clinical service in both the
NHS and VHA.

5. The workforce was impacted by the reforms.
Poor communications, marginalization of professionals from the policy
process, and the downsizing of staff resulted in staff dissatisfaction and
damaged morale.

The NHS and VHA had different responses to staffing following the
reforms: the NHS increased the number of Consultants and continues to
struggle with a national nursing shortage; the VHA staff reductions were
larger, and the VHA decreased the number of physicians and nurses
following the reforms.

Staff adjustments following reform in the NHS and VHA reflect pre-
reform supply and the agendas for cost reduction. The accommodation of
professionals by health system reform may be a function of supply and
demand of professionals, as well as a reflection of the established political-
cultural contexts and accords between professionals and the health setting.

Lessons Learned

Several lessons emerge from these case studies that are instructive to organizations and agencies considering large-scale change or reform.

Lesson 1: Assess whether there is a window of opportunity
Various environmental factors, which include socio-economic and political conditions, and pressure from the public or interests groups, often prompt
the need for organizational transformation. These factors help build a window
for change. Windows vary in duration and may be a function of the political
cycle or the support of interest groups and constituencies. The conditions for
and duration of the windows for reform differed in the NHS and VHA.

The NHS reforms were precipitated by growing public and professional
unrest over chronic low funding levels of the NHS. Constrained resources
compounded long waiting lists and problems with access to health service
delivery. By the late 1980s, the pressures from professionals and the public
reached a critical level. In 1988, Prime Minister Thatcher announced a

review of the NHS and won Parliamentary approval of the reforms before the runup to the 1990 election. The resulting policy paper, *Working for Patients*, which outlined the NHS reforms, was approved by Parliament in 1990, with formal implementation of the reforms in April 1991. However, despite the push for rapid approval, implementation of the NHS reforms was slow compared to the VHA reforms. Yet, the long tenure of the Conservative Party in the UK, compared to U.S. political cycles, provided the continuity to establish the reforms and gain experience with the internal market and GP fundholding.

The antecedent for the VHA reforms was the 1993-94 U.S. attempt at national health reform. The VHA had participated in the national reform deliberations and, following those efforts, recognized the need to demonstrate improved clinical efficiency.

The VHA reforms were outlined in *Vision for Change* and approved by Congress in September 1995, with formal implementation commencing in October 1995. Compared with the NHS, the VHA's reforms were fast-paced. They were timed for approval before the 1996 election campaign took off and were implemented quickly between election cycles.

Lesson 2: Establish and clearly communicate goals and strategies

Transformation of large systems is best accomplished by setting goals and communicating those objectives both within the organization and to interest groups. Goals, which are best linked to the agency's mission, allow measures for performance and evaluation. Specific goals and strategies may be controversial within the organization as well as with interest groups.

The NHS reforms created an internal market in the NHS that split purchasers from providers of service and introduced competition among providers. The reforms emphasized patient choice, devolved responsibility to providers, and sought better value for money. Yet, the key policy document *Working for Patients* (UK Secretaries of State 1989), was remarkable in its lack of detail. By comparison with the VHA, the NHS set few specific targets or measurable goals. While there was pressure for change, there was more focus on process—namely, establishing the internal market—than on outcomes. The reforms were met with mixed reactions: resistance among providers, NHS employees, and the public, and support within the NHS and government.

The VHA, drawing on work of prior advisory groups and greatly influenced by the managed-care movement and reinventing government, established a list of targets around cost reduction and clinical efficiency. These objectives were tied to performance evaluation of VHA executives. While the goals were clearly communicated to the VISN and medical center executives, communication varied across other levels of staff and was often lacking to interest groups.

Lesson 3: Evaluate and modify the organizational design as needed

Large-scale change may necessitate organizational redesign. The agency's structure should facilitate reform, and consideration should be given to the function, size, and organizational placement of various managerial and advisory units within the organization. The distance between the agency "center" and "field" is important to ensure sound communication and exchange of information. As too much change can create chaos, thoughtfully planned and executed redesign is key. Such redesign should consider the reform objectives as well as the organizational culture and the existing productive linkages.

The NHS reforms focused on process, and the early NHS reform incentives promised increased freedom for Trusts and financial rewards for Trusts and GP fundholders. Over time, the NHS streamlined its administrative structures, but the main share of the administrative reorganization came later in the reform process compared with the VHA reforms. It was not until 1995, several years into the reforms, that 100 Health Authorities were established from the merger of the over 235 District and Family Health Services Authorities. This redesign was to improve administrative effectiveness, and Health Authorities were given enhanced responsibility for population-based planning. While Health Authorities have been key in shepherding change, they have been viewed by some as centers of command and control and remain closely linked to the central government.

As a key component of the reforms, the VHA reorganized four large regions into 22 Veteran Integrated Service Networks and devolved authority for health service planning to these newly formed Networks. Given the operational authority of the Networks, VHA medical centers became less autonomous following the reforms.

Central control and new structures were key to the implementation of VHA's reforms. The VHA built its reform strategies on establishment of the 22 VISNs. Recruitment of staff and getting the Networks operational was the priority in the early days of the reforms. As part of its strategies, the VHA developed a management framework to integrate strategic planning and operations with new performance targets and the VHA budget process. The use of performance measures and contracts introduced a new level of central control despite the organizational flattening. The new Network structures created a new form of competition in the VHA, which was compounded by scarce resources due to VHA's constrained funding levels and the adoption of VERA, a new resource allocation model.

The brief window that the VHA had for reform appears to have encouraged the VHA's reliance on central control and the use of performance contracts and measures to achieve change. Performance contracts fostered rapid implementation of reform strategies and focused on results, which significantly altered health service delivery.

Lesson 4: Anticipate byproducts and unexpected consequences

Policy interventions and organizational change can have unintended effects. In addition, reform can accomplish an implicit agenda that is not explicitly expressed or described in formal policy documents. The purpose of an implicit agenda can be a response to the institutional or political context, to appease interest groups, or to produce effects that are too controversial to formalize as part of the formal policy. The described unexpected consequences and byproducts of the NHS and VHA reforms are the perceived effects that were unintended or not explicitly described in the NHS and VHA reform policies and strategies.

The NHS and VHA reforms precipitated several similar byproducts that were greater in magnitude and/or more problematic than anticipated: power shifts, changes in national planning, impacts on staff morale, communications problems, and changes in organizational culture. For both the NHS and VHA, reform strategies that reduced access to services caused dissatisfaction among patients, interest groups, and providers. Despite the differences in the NHS and VHA institutional contexts, the convergence in the nature of unexpected consequences appears to reflect similar responses to the reforms in terms of organizational and managerial behaviors as well as staff reactions.

Lesson 5: Engage and empower staff in the process

The manner in which reform is introduced, particularly regarding staff involvement and communication, affects the response of staff to the reform process. Leaders should be knowledgeable and sensitive to the process of change as well as the desired objectives. Employees who are empowered and engaged in the change are more involved in the reform process.

The reforms generated anxiety for NHS and VHA staff. Fears over privatization or demise of each health system, change in roles and status, staff cuts, changes in medical education and training, and research impacted the workforce in both systems.

Communication in both the NHS and VHA suffered as a result of the reform, and employees were marginalized. Following the reforms, there were staff reductions, morale problems, and strained communications in both systems. The reductions in staff were more pronounced in the VHA. However, the NHS's bottom-up market approach to reform, given its political, cultural, and institutional contexts, generated less tension among staff than the VHA's top-down deregulation strategies, which were associated with fast-paced change in a more strained environment.

Lesson 6: Involve interest groups

Involve interest groups and the pertinent community members in reform discussions and debates around workable strategies. While interest-group participation may be perceived as slowing the change process or, more commonly, be restricted due to concerns that these groups may derail or undermine change, exclusion of interest groups limits the effectiveness of the reforms in the long run. Cooperative partnerships that permit participation in change, an emphasis on communication, and avoidance of perverse incentives minimize dissatisfaction and tension among staff as well as interest groups.

Both the NHS and VHA limited the involvement of interest groups, professionals, affiliates, and the public from the reforms. Over time, the NHS and VHA reforms generated distinct interest-group reactions that had political implications. The NHS reforms, although controversial, aimed to contain costs and reduce public criticism and were followed by comparatively less change in health service delivery. In the end, NHS affiliates were more successful than their VHA counterparts in gaining a place on Health Authority Boards.

The VHA reforms aimed at and accomplished reducing costs and increasing the number of veterans cared for. However, several VHA reform strategies produced unpopular change from the perspective of interest groups. Pressure from the more influential interest groups resulted in reversal and/or change in some reform policy, most notably the recent recentralization of the Spinal Cord Injury and Transplant Programs, as well as the recentralization of authority for changes in mental health programs.

Lesson 7: Evaluate the reforms

Evaluation of reform moves beyond descriptive accounts of policy intent and attempts to assess the impacts and effects, as they can best be unraveled. Implementation of policy completes the policy process and often determines the nature of reform strategies. Comprehensive evaluation can provide information on the intended effects as well as unexpected byproducts of reform. Yet, the urgency for change and the associated costs, both in time and resources, frequently discourage evaluation.

Both the NHS and VHA needed to demonstrate success through their reform interventions. However, political and institutional agendas in the NHS and VHA suppressed evaluation. In addition, both systems have data constraints related to availability and reliability. Interest in and concerns about the impacts of the reforms prompted numerous reviews by other government agencies (VHA), academic policy analysis and evaluation (NHS), as well as comments from the media.

Implications for the Future

What lessons can the NHS and VHA share with each other as well as with other health systems entertaining reform? What could each system have done differently to improve the effectiveness of the reforms and take full advantage of the window for change?

Both the NHS and VHA experiences point to the need to preserve the large picture through national planning and coordination of health services and other agency missions, which include education and training of the future workforce and research. Agency goals and adequate controls are needed to balance long-term objectives with the immediate pressures for change. The experience of both health systems demonstrates the importance of a sound quality management structure and reliable data.

Several common areas emerge for the NHS and VHA to address in the future: (1) continued improvement of inpatient and outpatient care; (2) integration of information across health service measures and evidenced-based medicine; (3) assurance of health service access for vulnerable and costly patient populations; (4) evaluation of the future directions for partnering with interest groups, employees, and the public; (5) assessment of the long-term commitment to medical education and training and to research in light of the urgency for short-term results; and (6) development of strategies to promote public health in coordination with the community. Future change in the NHS and VHA depends on the balance among the perceived need for change, managerial effectiveness, and political forces. Moreover, future reform initiatives will benefit by reflecting on the lessons learned from these reform efforts.

The findings of this work prompt further study on various aspects of the NHS and VHA reforms and health reform in public systems. Areas for future inquiry include: (1) the role of the windows for reform and their influence on reform strategies and impacts; (2) the relationships among policy implementation, managerial performance, and performance evaluation; (3) the influence of an individual leader on health system change; (4) the effects of the reforms at the NHS hospital and VHA medical center levels; (5) the factors that shaped the individual responses of Health Authorities and Networks to the reforms; (6) the impact of reform strategies on vulnerable patient populations in market versus deregulation models of public administration; (7) the impact of reform strategies on staff morale in market versus deregulation models of public administration; and (8) the long-term impacts of reform strategies on affiliations, medical education and training, and research missions.

Finally, this research is intended to encourage cross-national studies on health reform in other public systems. The reforms, which introduced market mechanisms and managed care strategies into these public systems, precipitated their own caveats. While the reforms transformed the NHS and VHA, improved services for fundholder patients (NHS), and reduced patient costs (VHA), the introduction of market-inspired strategies, the preoccupation with costs, and budget constraints challenged the commitment of these public systems to underserved populations. This finding reiterates the need to evaluate the effects of market-based strategies in regards to the effects on equity (Saltman 1994). The perverse incentives created by the use of performance measures and contracts (VHA), coupled with the lack of comprehensive assessment of expected as well as unexpected reform consequences, posed risks to the success of these expensive policy experiments. In order to minimize untoward consequences, the success of future health reform interventions resides in recruiting the proper number and mix of leaders, setting productive incentives, and assuring the organizational supervision to promote desired outcomes.

The NHS and VHA are large, comparatively well-organized and sophisticated health systems, both in terms of the scope and complexity of their missions. The NHS and VHA reforms demonstrate the ability of large public systems to undertake significant reform interventions. The magnitude of these changes are unparalleled in the history of the NHS and the VHA, with the exception, perhaps, of when, in 1946, the VA was reorganized into the Department of Medicine and Surgery and began its affiliations with U.S. medical schools. Their reform interventions reflect not only the past practices and organizational cultures of the NHS and VHA, but their respective institutional and political contexts and how each system responded to a window for reform. The impacts of the recent reform interventions on their missions of health service delivery, medical education and training, and research, as well as on the workforce, offer insight for future interventions and are instructive to other systems.

The lessons from this research have implications for other settings as national health systems face similar challenges and assess the public-private mix of funding and provision of health services. Increased demand, emerging and costly technologies, and concern for the health needs of the poor and underserved will continue to challenge policy making. Carefully designed policy interventions that promote accountability, ensure access to appropriate clinical services, and balance short-term agendas with long-term goals will strengthen the future effectiveness of public healthcare systems as they respond to windows for change.

Endnotes

1. This report is based on the research done in the course of the doctoral dissertation: *Health Reform in Public Systems: Recent Reforms in the UK's National Health Service and the U.S. Veterans Health Administration*, Marilyn A. DeLuca, Robert F. Wagner School of Public Service, New York University, January 2000.

2. Although the NHS is primarily supported by general taxes, since 1948 there has been an increasing reliance on NHS contributions, patient charges, and other income. In 1995, 82 percent of NHS funding was derived from general taxes, 12 percent from NHS contributions, 2 percent from charges for items such as dentures and eyeglasses, 3 percent from capital refunds, and 1 percent from miscellaneous sources (UK NHS Health Service Confederation 1998, 76). Through contracts with the private sector, a percentage of capital costs are derived through the Private Finance Initiative (PFI).

The VHA is funded from congressional appropriations of general tax revenues. Small amounts of funds are from means-tested co-payments for treatment of veterans' non-service-connected conditions and, since 1986, third party insurance collections. As of 1998, VHA medical centers were permitted to retain the third party insurance collections rather than return them to the U.S. Treasury.

3. Before 1996, with the exception of three categories of high-priority service-connected veterans, veterans could only be treated as VHA outpatients if they had been inpatients or were in another high-priority discretionary eligibility category.

Bibliography

Aaron, H., and W. B. Schwartz. *The Painful Prescription: Rationing Hospital Care*. The Brookings Institute, Washington, D.C., 1984.

Appleby, J., P. Smith, W. Ranade, V. Little, and R. Robinson. "Monitoring Managed Competition." In *Evaluation of the NHS Reforms*, ed. R. Robinson and J. Le Grand. King's Fund Institute, London, 1994, pp. 24-49.

Bunce, V. *Do New Leaders Make a Difference? Executive Succession and Public Policy Under Capitalism and Socialism*. Princeton University Press, Princeton, New Jersey, 1981.

Campbell, J. *How Policies Change: The Japanese Government and The Aging Society*. Princeton University Press, Princeton, New Jersey, 1992.

Cohen, J. "Jump Start Needed for Long Standing AAMC-VA Partnerships." *NAVAPAL Newsbrief*, Spring 1999, p. 4.

DeLuca, M. *Health Reform in Public Systems: Recent Reforms in the UK's National Health Service and the US Veterans Health Administration*. Doctoral Dissertation, Robert F. Wagner School of Public Administration, New York University, January 2000.

Dobson, F. "Modernizing Britain's National Health Service." *Health Affairs* (18) 3, 1999, pp. 40-41.

Enthoven, A. *Reflections on the Management of the National Health Service*. Nuffield Provincial Hospital Trust, Occasional Paper 5, London, 1985.

Glennerster, H. "The UK Health Reforms." In *The Changing Roles of Government and Markets in the Health Care System*, JDC/Brookdale Institute, Jerusalem, 1993.

Goodin, R. "The Importance of Winning Big." *Legislative Studies Quarterly* (2) 1977, pp. 399-407.

Health Affairs (HA). "Managed Care Performance: Is Quality of Care Better or Worse?" (16) 5, September/October 1997.

Health Affairs (HA). "Media & Managed Care" (17) 1, January/February 1998.

Hunter, D. "Pain But No Gain?" *European Health Reform* (5) May 1997, pp. 14-15.

Ikegami, N. "Japanese Health Care: Low Cost Through Regulated Fees." *Health Affairs* (10) 3, Fall, 1991, pp. 87-109.

Immergut, E. M. *Health Politics: Interests and Institutions in Western Europe*. Cambridge University Press, Cambridge, 1992.

Jacobs, A. "Seeing the Difference: Market Health Reform in Europe." *Journal of Health Politics, Policy and Law* (23) 1, February 1998, pp. 1-33.

Jacobs, L. *The Health of Nations: Public Opinion and Making of American and British Health Policy*. Cornell University Press, Ithaca, New York, 1993.

Journal of Health Politics, Policy and Law (JHPPL). Special Issue: "The Managed Care Backlash" (24) 5, October 1999.

Keeler, John T. S., "Opening the Window for Reform: Mandates, Crises, and Extraordinary Policy-Making." *Comparative Political Studies,* Special Issue (25) 4, "The Politics of Reform in Comparative Perspective," January 1993.

Kingdon, J. W. Agendas, *Alternatives and Public Policies.* Little, Brown, Boston, Massachusetts, 1984.

Klein, R. "Can We Restrict The Health Care Menu?" *Health Policy* (27) 1994, pp. 103-112.

_____. "Big Bang Health Care Reform: Does It Work? The Case of Britain's 1991 National Health Service Reforms." *The Milbank Quarterly* (73) 2, 1995, pp. 299-336.

Le Grand, J. "Evaluating the NHS Reforms." In *Evaluating the NHS Reforms,* ed. R. Robinson and J. Le Grand. King's Fund Institute, London, 1994, pp. 243-260.

_____. "Competition, Cooperation or Control? Tales from the British National Health Service." *Health Affairs* (18) 3, 1999, pp. 27-39.

Le Grand, J., N. Mays, and J. Dixon. "The Reforms: Success or Failure or Neither?" In *Learning from the NHS Internal Market,* ed. J. Le Grand, N. Mays, and J. Mulligan, King's Fund Institute, London, 1998, pp. 117-143.

Light, D. "Managed Care: False and Real Solutions." *The Lancet* (344) October 29, 1994, pp. 1197-1199.

_____. "Homo Economicus: Escaping the Traps of Managed Competition." *European Journal of Public Health,* (5) 30, September 1995, pp. 145-154.

_____. "From Managed Competition to Managed Cooperation: Theory and Lessons From the British Experience." *Milbank Quarterly* (75) 3, 1997, 297-341.

_____. *Effective Commissioning: Lessons from Purchasing in American Managed Care.* Office of Health Care Economics, London, 1998.

March, J. and J. Olsen. *Rediscovering Institutions: The Organizational Basis of Politics.* Free Press, New York, 1989.

Maynard, A. "Performance Incentives in General Practices." In *Health Education in General Practice,* ed. G.Teeling-Smith, Office of Health Economics, London, 1986, pp. 44-46.

Maynard, A. and K. Bloor. "Introducing A Market to The United Kingdom's National Health Service." *The New England Journal of Medicine,* (334) February 29, 1996, pp. 604-608.

Mechanic, D. "The Americanization of the British National Health Service." *Health Affairs,* (14) 2, 1995, pp. 51-67.

Mulligan, J. "Health Authority Purchasing." In *Learning from the NHS Internal Market*, ed. J. Le Grand, N. Mays, and J. Mulligan, King's Fund Institute, London, 1998, pp. 20-42.

Osborne, D., and T. Graelber. *Reinventing Government*. Addison-Wesley, Reading, Massachusetts, 1992.

Peters, B. Guy. "Models of Governance for the 1990s." In *The State of Public Management*, ed. D. Kettl, and H. Milward. The Johns Hopkins University Press, Baltimore, 1996, pp. 15-44.

Pressman, J. and A. Wildavsky. *Implementation*. 3rd edition, University of California Press, Berkeley, California, 1984.

Redmayne, S., P. Day, and R. Klein. *Reshaping the NHS: Strategies, Priorities and Resource Allocation*. NAHAT and Nuffield Provincial Hospitals Trusts, 1995.

Robinson, R. and J. Le Grand, ed. *Evaluating the NHS Reforms*. King's Fund Institute, London, 1994.

Salter, B. "Change in the British National Health Service: Policy Paradox and the Rationing Issue." *International Journal of Health Services* (24) 1, 1994, pp. 45-72.

Saltman, R. "A Conceptual Overview of Recent Health Reforms." *European Journal of Public Health* (4) 1994, pp. 287-293.

Scharpf, F. "Policy Failure and Institutional Reform: Why Should Form Follow Function?" *The Study of Public Policy* (108), 1986, pp.179-189.

Sullivan, A. "There Will Always Be an England." *The New York Times Magazine*, February 21, 1999, pp. 39-54.

Thompson, F., and N. Riccucci. "Reinventing Government." *Annual Review of Political Science* (1) 1998, pp. 231-257.

United Kingdom. Department of Health. *The New NHS*. HMSO, London, 1997.

United Kingdom. Department of Health. *A First Class Service-Quality in the New NHS*. Department of Health, London, 1998.

United Kingdom. Independent Inquiry, 1998.

United Kingdom. National Health Service (NHS) Confederation. *1998/99 NHS Handbook*, 13th ed., ed. P. Merry. JMH Publishing, Kent, 1998.

United Kingdom. Office of Health Economics (OHE). *Compendium of Health Statistics*, 9th ed., OHE, London, 1995.

United Kingdom. Secretaries of State for Health Wales, Northern Ireland and Scotland. *Working For Patients: The Health Service Caring For the 1990s*. Cm555, HMSO, London, 1989.

U.S. Congress. "Veterans Eligibility Reform Act of 1996." *Public Law* 104-262, Washington, D.C., 1996.

U.S. Department of Veterans Affairs. *Vision for Change*. Department of Veterans Affairs, Washington, D.C., March 17, 1995.

U.S. Department of Veterans Administration. Office of the Inspector General. *Quality Management in the Department of Veterans Affairs Veterans Health Administration.* Office of Healthcare Inspections, Report 8HI-A28-072, Washington, D.C., February 17, 1998.

U.S. Department of Veterans Administration. Office of the Inspector General. *Evaluation of Quality Management Structure and Resources in the Department of Veterans Affairs Veterans Health Administration.* Office of Healthcare Inspections, Report 9HI-A28-042, Washington, D.C., February 18, 1999.

U.S. General Accounting Office. *VA Community Clinics: Networks' Efforts to Improve Veterans' Access to Primary Care Vary.* GAO, Washington, D.C., June 1998.

U.S. General Accounting Office. *Major Management Challenges and Program Risks: Department of Veterans Affairs.* GAO/OCG-99-15, GAO, Washington, D.C., January 1999.

U.S. National Performance Review. *From Red Tape to Results: Creating a Government That Works Better & Costs Less.* GPO, Washington, D.C., 1993.

U.S. Senate. Minority Staff of the Committee on Veterans' Affairs. *Staff Report on Quality Management in the Veterans Health Administration, Department of Veterans Affairs.* Minority Committee on Veterans' Affairs, Washington, D.C., December 19, 1997.

U.S. Veteran Service Organizations (VSOs). *The Independent Budget: Fiscal Year 2000.* AMVETS, Disabled American Veterans, Paralyzed Veterans of America, and Veterans of Foreign Wars of the United States, Washington, D.C., 1999.

Whitehead, M. "Is It Fair? Evaluating the Equity Implications of the NHS Reforms." In *Evaluating the NHS Reforms*, ed. R. Robinson, and J. Le Grand. King's Fund Institute, London, 1994, pp. 208-242.

Appendix I:
Study Framework

The study's framework draws on the role of political institutions and governmental structures in the health policy process (Immergut 1992; Klein 1995; Jacobs 1993; Campbell 1992). The framework posits that socioeconomic, political, and societal factors, as well as pressure groups, can influence health reform policy and open a window for reform. Occasionally, the convergence of socioeconomic and political conditions and events opens a window for "extraordinary" political redirection and policy reform (Keeler 1993; Kingdon 1984; Goodin 1977; Bunce 1981). The window for reform allows the usual constraints that hamper governments to be put aside (Kingdon 1984). In short, the conceptual framework proposes: (1) reform interventions are permitted by salient political conditions (Keeler 1993; Kingdon 1984; Goodin 1977; Bunce 1981); (2) reform policies and their implementation strategies reflect institutional and political contexts (Pressman and Wildavsky 1984; March and Olsen 1989; Scharpf 1986; Immergut 1992) and are products of stated as well as unstated reform intents, which are derived from and shaped by the institutional context of policy formation through implementation; and (3) reforms can affect health care delivery, medical education and research, and human resources (Figure 6.9).

Furthermore, while it may appear that there is growing convergence in health policy, particularly around market models, significant divergence exists in the content and aims of health reform strategies (Jacobs 1998). This divergence reflects the influence of the institutional setting, the design of political institutions, and the different ideological orientations of the ruling party, as well as the influence of the pre-reform health system (Ibid.).

Figure 6.9: Casual Model to Assess Health Reform

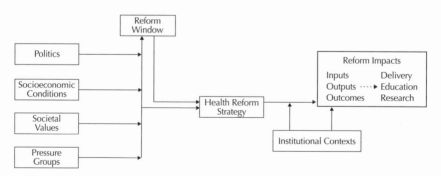

Appendix II:
Study Methods

A multiple (two) case study design was used to examine the NHS and VHA reforms. The unit of analysis for the research was the health system, specifically the NHS and VHA health systems. The research employed a mixed-methods design, the triangulation of qualitative and quantitative data and multiple sources to enhance construct validity and reliability. The comparative logic of the study design included before/after within case (NHS) (VHA) comparisons, and between case (NHS & VHA) comparisons to assess areas of convergence and divergence. The majority of the data were derived through document analyses from secondary data sources and included archival records, published articles and studies, agency documents and databases, survey and audit reports, and media articles. Primary data collection included 44 in-depth interviews with policy makers, staff, providers, and academics employed by, or knowledgeable in, the NHS and VHA. In addition, other data gathering and fact finding included preliminary interviews; numerous contacts via phone, electronic mail, and letter correspondences; and participant-observer experiences (VHA).

[Participant-observer experiences, which occurred during the time that the researcher was an employee of the VHA from 1971 through 1996, include the years just prior to as well as during the early phase of the implementation of the VHA reforms. Experiences included daily contact with staff, managers, and executive level officials in two urban affiliated VA medical centers in the Northeast, as well as in a Network office. Other "typical" employee activities included participation in meetings and conferences. There was frequent contact with officials in Headquarters in Washington, D.C., and occasional contact with staff and managers from VHA sites across the U.S. The participant-observer experience helped identify relevant areas and data for the VHA case. The researcher did not have the same opportunity to observe the NHS, which is a limitation of the study. However, the research attempted to augment data for the NHS by review of the extensive literature on the NHS, as well as through comparably numerous preliminary interviews and ongoing informal and electronic contacts with those knowledgeable in the NHS and the reforms.]

The quantitative data examined included annual data on expenditures, inpatient and outpatient utilization, bed numbers, waiting times, performance measures, and staffing data. These data span the five years (NHS: 1986-1990; VHA: 1991-1995) prior to the formal implementation of the reforms and the respective seven-year (NHS: 1991-1997) and three-year periods (VHA: 1996-1998) following the start of formal implementation.

The post-reform periods of seven (NHS) and three years (VHA) reflect the years of available post-reform data. For each system, the corresponding fiscal year calendar was used, which begins on April 1 for the NHS and on October 1 for the VHA. The NHS analysis stopped with the end of fiscal year 1997 (March 1998). The election of the new Labour government in May 1997 began a phase of new policies that included implementation of the "new NHS" (UK DOH 1997). These changes impact various aspects of the 1991 reforms, affect purchaser-provider arrangements and fundholding, and introduced Primary Care Group commissioning (Ibid.). Given these events, the inclusion of NHS data after fiscal year 1997 would have confounded analyses of the effects of the 1991 reforms.

Table 6.7: Quantitative Study Data by Calendar Year

	1986	1987	1988	1989	1990	1991	1992
NHS	1	2	3	4	5	X^r=6	7
VHA						1	2

	1993	1994	1995	1996	1997	1998
NHS	8	9	10	11	12	
VHA	3	4	5	X^r=6	7	8

X^r= formal date for implementation of reform

About the Contributors

Mark A. Abramson is executive director of The PricewaterhouseCoopers Endowment for The Business of Government, a position he has held since July 1998. Prior to the Endowment, he was chairman of Leadership Inc. From 1983 to 1994, Mr. Abramson served as the first president of the Council for Excellence in Government. Previously, Mr. Abramson served as a senior program evaluator in the Office of the Assistant Secretary for Planning and Evaluation, U.S. Department of Health and Human Services.

He is a Fellow of the National Academy of Public Administration. In 1995, he served as president of the National Capital Area Chapter of the American Society for Public Administration. Mr. Abramson has taught at George Mason University and the Federal Executive Institute in Charlottesville, Virginia.

Mr. Abramson recently edited *Memos to the President: Management Advice from the Nation's Top Public Administrators* and *Toward a 21st Century Public Service: Reports from Four Forums*. He is also the co-editor (with Joseph S. Wholey and Christopher Bellavita) of *Performance and Credibility: Developing Excellence in Public and Nonprofit Organizations*, and the author of *The Federal Funding of Social Knowledge Production and Application*.

He received his Bachelor of Arts degree from Florida State University. He received a Master of Arts degree in history from New York University and a Master of Arts degree in political science from the Maxwell School of Citizenship and Public Affairs, Syracuse University.

Carolyn L. Clark-Daniels is retired from Iowa State University. She has received grants related to disaster management from The PricewaterhouseCoopers Endowment for The Business of Government, National Science Foundation, and the Gerald R. Ford Foundation. Solely and jointly, she has presented 12 convention papers on Presidential decision making, FEMA, and disaster management. She is the author or coauthor of 16 articles and two research reports in the areas of public administration, gerontology, decision making, and welfare policy in such journals as *Social Science Quarterly, The Gerontologist, The Journal of Criminal Justice,* and *The Journal of Elder Abuse and Neglect.* She has also worked as an auditor for the U.S. Army Corps of Engineers and the U.S. Department of Health, Education, and Welfare (now the Department of Health and Human Services). Her doctorate is from the University of Alabama.

R. Steven Daniels is Professor and Chair of the Department of Public Policy and Administration at California State University, Bakersfield. Dr. Daniels has received grants related to disaster management from The PricewaterhouseCoopers Endowment for The Business of Government, the Gerald R. Ford Foundation, and the University of Alabama at Birmingham Graduate School, and presented 12 convention papers on presidential decision making, FEMA, and disaster management. He is the author or coauthor of 14 refereed publications and book chapters in the areas of decision making, aging, legislative behavior, and public policy in such journals as *The American Political Science Review, The Gerontologist, Social Science Quarterly, The Journal of Criminal Justice,* and *The Policy Studies Review.* His doctorate is from the University of Oregon.

Marilyn A. DeLuca is a consultant in health policy and health systems management. Her interests include international health and comparative health system analysis.

Dr. DeLuca has substantial managerial and clinical experience in public healthcare systems, most notably in the Veterans Health Administration, where she held several leadership positions. Dr. DeLuca served as Chief Operations Officer of the VHA NY/NJ Network, a health system with over 170,000 veteran patients; 13,000 employees; and an operating budget of $1 billion. She also served as Special Assistant to the Director at the Bronx VHA (1985-1996) and New York VA Medical Centers (1984-1985) as well as in various clinical and leadership roles in critical care (1971-1984).

Dr. DeLuca holds a master's in public administration (NYU 1995) and a master's in nursing (NYU 1976) as well as a bachelor of science in nursing (Hunter College CUNY 1971). Dr. DeLuca recently completed a Ph.D. in public administration with a concentration in comparative health systems at New York University, Robert F. Wagner Graduate School of Public Service. Her dissertation is entitled: *Health Reform in Public Systems: Recent Reforms in the UK's National Health Service and the US Veterans Health Administration.*

Dr. DeLuca has had various teaching positions at the graduate and undergraduate levels. Her publications include chapters in two texts, one on critical care and the second on primary-care nursing. Dr. DeLuca was principal investigator on research projects, which include a study on organizational climate and professional satisfaction, and one on congestive heart failure and length of stay. She has served on numerous local and national VHA committees as well as committees in the New York City healthcare community.

Dr. DeLuca is a long-standing member of Sigma Theta Tau, the national nursing honor society. She has held her American Nurse Association Certification in nursing administration since 1984 and was listed in Who's Who in American Nursing. She is the recipient of numerous awards for program management and innovative leadership.

Kimberly A. Harokopus produced this work while serving as a Visiting Scholar in the Political Science Department of Boston College. Prior to that position, Dr. Harokopus was a research fellow of the National Security Program at the John F. Kennedy School of Government, Harvard University. There she conducted Department of Defense-sponsored research on the globalization of defense technologies, technology transfer, and the impact of industry concentration and price competition factors on U.S. military readiness.

Dr. Harokopus is a former officer in the U.S. Air Force. She served as a speechwriter and executive officer to the Vice Commander of Electronic Systems Center, Hanscom Air Force Base. She was also a lead negotiator for the Center's Strategic Systems office, and the Engineering Manager for the Anti-Radiation Missile Decoy Program.

Currently, Dr. Harokopus is CEO of Cambridge Communication Systems, Inc., an information technology firm that provides emerging technology analysis, systems engineering, and network design and implementation. Dr. Harokopus earned a B.S. in Electrical Engineering from the University of Pennsylvania, an A.L.M. in Government from Harvard University, and a Ph.D. in Political Science from Boston College.

W. Henry Lambright is Professor of Political Science and Public Administration and Director of the Center for Environmental Policy and Administration at the Maxwell School of Citizenship and Public Affairs at Syracuse University. He teaches courses at the Maxwell School on Technology and Politics; Energy, Environment, and Resources Policy; and Bureaucracy and Politics.

Dr. Lambright served as a guest scholar at The Brookings Institution, and as the director of the Science and Technology Policy Center at the Syracuse Research Corporation. He served as an adjunct professor in the

Graduate Program of Environmental Science in the College of Environmental Science and Forestry at the State University of New York. He has testified before Congress on many topics, including the environment, science and technology, and government management.

A long-standing NASA-watcher, he has worked for NASA as a special assistant in its Office of University Affairs and has been a member of its History Advisory Committee. Dr. Lambright has performed research for NASA, the Department of Energy, the Department of Defense, and the State Department. Recently, he chaired a symposium on "NASA in the 21st Century." A book will be published from this symposium.

Dr. Lambright is the author or editor of six additional books, including *Powering Apollo: James E. Webb of NASA*; *Technology and U.S. Competitiveness: An Institutional Focus*; and *Presidential Management of Science and Technology: The Johnson Presidency*. In addition, he has written more than 250 articles, papers, and reports.

His doctorate is from Columbia University, where he also received a master's degree. Dr. Lambright received his undergraduate degree from Johns Hopkins University.

Paul R. Lawrence is a partner in the Public Sector Practice of PricewaterhouseCoopers. He leads the Banking, Finance and International portion of the practice, focusing on how government organizations can apply private sector financial practices to operate more efficiently. His clients include the U.S. Department of Treasury, the Department of Defense, and the Department of Housing and Urban Development.

He is also the co-chairman of The PricewaterhouseCoopers Endowment for The Business of Government, which seeks to advance knowledge on how to improve public sector effectiveness. He is the host of the weekly radio show *The Business of Government Hour*.

Mr. Lawrence has written extensively on technology and government. He has testified before Congress and several state legislatures. He serves on the board of Junior Achievement and is a member of the Advisory Committee to the Virginia Assembly's Joint Committee on Technology and Science. He was selected by *Federal Computer Week* as one of the top 100 public service business leaders in 2000.

Mr. Lawrence earned his M.A. and Ph.D. in economics from Virginia Tech and his undergraduate degree in economics from the University of Massachusetts, Amherst. He is the author of *Unsportsmanlike Conduct: The NCAA and the Business of College Football* (Praeger, 1987).

Gary J. Young is a senior researcher at the Management Decision and Research Center, a research and consulting component within the Veterans Affairs Health Services Research and Development Service. He is also an Associate Professor of Health Services at the Boston University School of Public Health and Co-Director of the School of Public Health's Program on Health Policy and Management. Dr. Young previously worked as a senior associate for a national health care management and policy consulting firm and as an analyst for the Agency for Health Care Policy and Research, U.S. Department of Health and Human Services.

His research and publications focus on organizational, managerial, and legal issues associated with the delivery of health care services. He recently completed a project for the Robert Wood Johnson Foundation that examined the community impact of nonprofit hospital conversions and a project for the Agency for Health Care Policy and Research that examined from an antitrust perspective the pricing patterns of nonprofit hospitals. He is currently conducting a project for the National Science Foundation to identify strategies for managing organizational change efforts in health care organizations. His published work has appeared in such journals as *Health Services Research, Inquiry, Health Affairs, Medical Care, Journal of Health Politics, Policy and Law*, and *Journal of Management*. Dr. Young also has served on various advisory groups focusing on health policy issues. He currently serves as a member of a National Academy of Social Insurance study panel on restructuring the Medicare program.

Dr. Young has received a number of awards for his research from such organizations as the Academy of Management and the American College of Healthcare Executives. In 1998, he received the John D. Thompson Prize for Young Investigators from the Association of University Programs in Health Administration (AUPHA).

Dr. Young earned a Ph.D. in management and a law degree from the State University of New York.

About The PricewaterhouseCoopers Endowment for The Business of Government

Through grants for research, The PricewaterhouseCoopers Endowment for The Business of Government stimulates research and facilitates discussion of new approaches to improving the effectiveness of government at the federal, state, local, and international levels.

Research grants of $15,000 are awarded competitively to outstanding scholars in academic and nonprofit institutions across the United States. Each grantee is expected to produce a 30- to 40-page research report in one of the areas presented on pages 226-228. Grant reports will be published and disseminated by The Endowment. All the chapters presented in this book were originally prepared as grant reports to The Endowment.

Founded in 1998 by PricewaterhouseCoopers, The Endowment is one of the ways that PricewaterhouseCoopers seeks to advance knowledge on how to improve public sector effectiveness. The PricewaterhouseCoopers Endowment focuses on the future of the operations and management of the public sector.

Who is Eligible?
Individuals working in:
- Universities
- Nonprofit organizations

Description of Grant

Individuals receiving grants will be responsible for producing a 30- to 40-page research report in one of the areas presented on pages 226-228. The research paper should be completed within a six-month period from the start of the project. Grantees select the start and end dates of the research project.

Size of Grant

$15,000 for each research paper

Who Receives the Grant

Individuals will receive the grant, not the institution in which they are located.

Application Process

Interested individuals should submit:
- A three-page description of the proposed research
- A résumé, including list of publications

Application Deadlines

There are three funding cycles annually, with deadlines of:
- The last day of February
- The last day of June
- The last day of October

Applications must be postmarked or received online by the above dates.

Submitting Applications

Hard copy:

Mark A. Abramson
Executive Director
The PricewaterhouseCoopers Endowment for The Business of Government
1616 North Fort Myer Drive
Arlington, VA 22209

Online:

endowment.pwcglobal.com/apply

Program Areas

E-Government

The Endowment is seeking proposals that examine the implementation of e-government in the following areas: (1) Government to Business (G2B); (2) Government to Citizen (G2C); (3) Government to Employee (G2E); and (4) Government to Government (G2G). The Endowment is especially interested in innovative approaches to providing information so citizens can make their own choices, complete service transactions electronically, hold government more accountable for results, and offer feedback.

Examples of previous grants in this area:
- The Auction Model: How the Public Sector Can Leverage the Power of E-Commerce Through Dynamic Pricing *by David Wyld*
- Commerce Comes to Government on the Desktop: E-Commerce Applications in the Public Sector *by Genie N. L. Stowers*
- The Use of the Internet in Government Service Delivery *by Steven Cohen and William B. Eimicke*

Financial Management

The Endowment is seeking proposals that examine specific financial management issues, such as cost accounting and management, financial and resource analysis, financial risk management and modeling, internal controls, operational and systems risk management, financial auditing, contract management, reconciliation, and overpayment recovery. The Endowment is especially interested in full costs and budgeting approaches for support services and capital assets, retirement, and other employee benefits, and other nondirect costs associated with delivering program services.

Examples of previous grants in this area:
- Audited Financial Statements: Getting and Sustaining "Clean" Opinions *by Douglas A. Brook*
- Credit Scoring and Loan Scoring: Tools for Improved Management of Federal Credit Programs *by Thomas H. Stanton*
- Using Activity-Based Costing to Manage More Effectively *by Michael H. Granof, David E. Platt, and Igor Vaysman*

Human Capital

The Endowment is seeking proposals that examine human capital issues related to public service. Human capital consists of the knowledge, skills, abilities, attitudes, and experience required to accomplish an organization's mission. It also includes an organization's ability to recruit and retain employees, as well as to undertake workforce planning and analysis.

Examples of previous grants in this area:
- Leaders Growing Leaders: Preparing the Next Generation of Public Service Executives *by Ray Blunt*
- Reflections on Mobility: Case Studies of Six Federal Executives *by Michael D. Serlin*
- Winning the Best and Brightest: Increasing the Attraction of Public Service *by Carol Chetkovich*

Managing for Results

The Endowment is seeking proposals that examine how organizations align their processes—such as budgeting, workforce, and business processes—around their strategic goals. This area also focuses on how organizations use performance and results information to make policy, management, and resource allocation decisions. The Endowment is especially interested in how different organizations work collaboratively to achieve common outcomes. The Endowment is also interested in case studies of the use of balanced scorecards, including the measurement of customer service.

Examples of previous grants in this area:
- The Challenge of Developing Cross-Agency Measures: A Case Study of the Office of National Drug Control Policy *by Patrick Murphy and John Carnevale*
- Managing for Results: The Use of Computer Statistical (CompSTAT) Systems *by Paul O'Connell*
- Using Evaluation to Support Performance Management: A Guide for Federal Executives *by Kathryn E. Newcomer and Mary Ann Scheirer*

New Ways to Manage

The Endowment is seeking proposals that examine specific instances of new ways of delivering programs and services to the public, including contracting out, competition, outsourcing, privatization, and public-private partnerships. The Endowment is also interested in innovations in the way public organizations are managed.

Examples of previous grants in this area:
* Entrepreneurial Government: Bureaucrats as Businesspeople *by Anne Laurent*
* San Diego County's Innovation Program: Using Competition and a Whole Lot More to Improve Public Services *by William B. Eimicke*
* The Challenge of Innovating in Government *by Sandford Borins*

Transforming Organizations

The Endowment is seeking proposals that examine how specific public sector organizations have been transformed with new values, changed cultures, and enhanced performance. This area also includes studies of outstanding public sector leaders.

Examples of previous grants in this area:
* Transforming Government: The Renewal and Revitalization of the Federal Emergency Management Agency *by R. Steven Daniels and Carolyn L. Clark-Daniels*
* Transforming Government: The Revitalization of the Veterans Health Administration *by Gary J. Young*
* Transforming Government: Dan Goldin and the Remaking of NASA *by W. Henry Lambright*

For more information about The Endowment

Visit our website at: endowment.pwcglobal.com
Send an e-mail to: endowment@us.pwcglobal.com
Call: (703) 741-1077

About PricewaterhouseCoopers

The Management Consulting Services practice of PricewaterhouseCoopers helps clients maximize their business performance by integrating strategic change, performance improvement, and technology solutions. Through a worldwide network of skills and resources, consultants manage complex projects with global capabilities and local knowledge, from strategy through implementation. PricewaterhouseCoopers (www.pwcglobal.com) is the world's largest professional services organization. Drawing on the knowledge and skills of more than 150,000 people in 150 countries, we help our clients solve complex business problems and measurably enhance their ability to build value, manage risk, and improve performance in an Internet-enabled world. PricewaterhouseCoopers refers to the member firms of the worldwide PricewaterhouseCoopers organization.